Study Guide

for use with

FINANCIAL ACCOUNTING

Study Guide

for use with

FINANCIAL ACCOUNTING

FOURTH EDITION

Walter B. Meigs
University of Southern California

Robert F. Meigs
San Diego State University

McGraw-Hill Book Company

New York   St. Louis   San Francisco   Auckland   Bogotá   Hamburg   Johannesburg
London   Madrid   Mexico   Montreal   New Delhi   Panama   Paris   São Paulo
Singapore   Sydney   Tokyo   Toronto

Study Guide for use with
FINANCIAL ACCOUNTING

3 4 5 6 7 8 9 0 WEBWEB 8 9 8 7 6 5 4

ISBN 0-07-041536-6

This book was set in Century Schoolbook by Intergraphic Technology, Inc.
The editors were Donald G. Mason and Edwin Hanson;
the production supervisor was Phil Galea.
The cover was designed by Jo Jones.
The cover photograph was taken by Martin Bough.
Webcrafters, Inc., was printer and binder.

CONTENTS

TO THE STUDENT

This self-study guide is designed for your use as a student taking your first course in accounting at either the undergraduate or the graduate level. It is prepared to accompany *Financial Accounting*, fourth edition, by Meigs and Meigs. However, it can be used effectively with other introductory accounting texts. The key purposes of this study guide are:

1 To help you in *mastering the material* as you initially study each chapter.

2 To *summarize the essential points* in each chapter and to *test your knowledge* with a series of objective questions and exercises, thus making it possible for you to *review the material quickly* from time to time, particularly before examinations.

3 To make the study of accounting *more enjoyable and less tedious* for you. This is accomplished by presenting an informal and concise summary of each chapter, followed by three groups of objective questions and some short exercises. The answers to these questions and exercises are provided at the back of the study guide *in order to give you immediate feedback and point out areas that need additional attention.*

The manner in which each student uses this study guide may differ. However, we recommend the following approach:

1 Study the chapter in your textbook.

2 Read the *Highlights of the Chapter* section of the study guide. If you encounter any statements that you do not understand, refer to the textbook for a more detailed discussion of the topic.

3 Work the questions and exercises in the *Test Yourself* section of the study guide, and compare your answers and solutions with those provided in the back of the guide. This will show you how well you really understand the material contained in the related chapter of your textbook. Again, if you find something you do not understand, refer to your text for a thorough discussion of the subject.

4 Work the problems assigned as homework in your text.

Once you have mastered the material in this manner, rereading the *Highlights of the Chapter* section of the study guide will assist you in quickly reviewing the material before examinations.

Walter B. Meigs
Robert F. Meigs

Study Guide

for use with

FINANCIAL ACCOUNTING

1

ACCOUNTING: THE LANGUAGE OF BUSINESS

HIGHLIGHTS OF THE CHAPTER

1 The basic purpose of accounting is to provide financial information about a business enterprise or any other economic entity. This information is needed internally by managers and also by outsiders such as bankers, other creditors, investors, and certain government agencies. In short, anyone who must make *decisions* regarding a business enterprise has need of *accounting information*.

2 Most businesses enter into so many different transactions every year that a complete list of these transactions would be too long to be useful to decision makers. An accounting system creates *useful* information by (a) *recording* business events as they occur, (b) *classifying* these events into related groups, and (c) *summarizing* this information into accounting reports designed to meet the information needs of decision makers.

3 The major types of accounting reports include (a) financial statements, (b) tax returns, (c) specialized reports to management, and (d) reports to governmental regulatory agencies. In this accounting course, we shall emphasize the information contained in financial statements.

4 Financial statements are useful to management and also are the primary source of accounting information to persons outside the business enterprise. These statements show the financial position of the business at a given date and also the operating results which caused it to arrive at this position.

5 The accounting concepts, measurement techniques, and standards of presentation used in the preparation of financial statements are called *generally accepted accounting principles*. Developing accounting information in conformity with generally accepted accounting principles is often termed *financial accounting*. Developing accounting information to fill the specialized needs of management, on the other hand, is called *managerial accounting*.

6 *Bookkeeping* refers to the mechanical aspects of recording and classifying transactions, and is but a small part of the field of accounting. *Accounting* includes the design of the financial information system, preparation of financial statements, development of forecasts, cost studies, tax consulting, and the *analysis* and *interpretation* of accounting information to assist decision makers in making *informed* decisions.

7 Careers in accounting may be divided into three broad areas: (a) the public accounting profession, (b) private accounting, and (c) governmental accounting.

8 Public accounting is practiced by *certified public accountants*, called CPAs. CPAs are granted a license to practice by the state, and perform professional accounting services for clients for a fee. These services include:

a *Auditing* An audit is an investigation of a company's accounting system to determine that the financial statements *present fairly* its financial positions and operating results. All large corporations and many small companies are audited annually by a CPA firm.

b *Tax services* Taxes often play an important role in financial decisions. CPA firms offer "tax planning" services to minimize the impact of taxes on their clients, and also assist in the preparation of their clients' income tax returns.

c *Management advisory services* CPA firms may become familiar with their clients' problems and be able to recommend corrective action. This service is actually *management consulting*.

9 *Private accounting* refers to the work of accountants employed directly by private industry. The functions of accountants in private industry include:

a *Design of accounting systems* Although most business concerns follow the same basic accounting principles, each firm will require its own individually tailored accounting system.

b *Cost accounting* This is the specialized field of determining the cost of manufacturing a product or performing a specific process.

c *Financial forecasting* A financial *forecast (budget) is a plan* of financial operations for the future. The forecast helps management to set goals, and then to measure actual performance relative to these goals.

d *Tax accounting* Tax specialists play as important a role in private accounting as they do in public accounting.

e *Internal auditing* Internal auditors are responsible for seeing that the objectives of a company are being carried out efficiently in all departments. Unlike CPAs, internal auditors are *not* responsible for determining the fairness of annual financial statements.

10 *Governmental accounting* includes many specialized areas such as monitoring regulated industries, auditing tax returns, and preparing budgets for governmental agencies. Two important governmental agencies using accounting information are:

a *Internal Revenue Service* The IRS processes the federal income tax returns filed by individuals and corporations.

b *Securities and Exchange Commission* The SEC reviews and approves the financial disclosure by corporations which offer their securities for sale to the public.

11 In the United States, four groups which have been influential in improving accounting principles and practices are the *American Institute of Certified Public Accountants* (AICPA), the *Securities and Exchange Commission* (SEC), the *American Accounting Association* (AAA), and the *Financial Accounting Standards Board* (FASB). The FASB conducts research and issues Statements of Financial Accounting Standards which represent authoritative expressions of generally accepted accounting principles.

12 Two primary objectives of most business concerns are to make a profit and remain solvent. Being *solvent* means having the cash to pay debts on time. The accounting system is the means by which profitability and solvency are measured.

13 Steps taken to ensure the reliability of accounting information and to safeguard the resources of a business against waste, fraud, or inefficient use are called the system of *internal control*.

14 Accounting information is gathered for specific business entities. A business *entity* is any economic unit which enters into business transactions. The business entity is regarded as separate from its owners; the entity owns its own property and has its own debts.

15 The three most common forms of business entities are single proprietorships, partnerships, and corporations. Accounting principles and concepts apply to all three forms of organization.

a A single proprietorship is a business owned by one individual.

b A partnership is a business owned by two or more people who have agreed to act as partners.

c A corporation is a business granted a charter by the state and owned by *stockholders*. Ownership is evidenced by shares of capital stock which may be sold by one investor to another. The stockholders elect a *board of directors* to oversee the operation of the business; the directors, in turn, appoint officers and managers of the business.

16 A corporation is legally an entity separate from its owners. Thus, the stockholders' liability for the losses incurred by an unsuccessful corporation is limited to the amount they have invested in the business. Nearly all large businesses and many small ones are organized as corporations.

17 The two most widely used financial statements are the *balance sheet* and the *income*

statement. A balance sheet shows the financial position of a business at a particular date. It consists of a list of the company's assets, liabilities, and owners' equity. (The income statement will be discussed in Chapter 3.)

18 Assets are economic resources owned by a business, such as land, buildings, and cash. Assets are valued on a balance sheet at their *cost*, rather than at current market prices, because cost is more factual and can be more *objectively determined* than current market value. Another reason for valuing assets at cost is that a business is assumed to be a *going concern* that will keep and use such assets as land and buildings rather than sell them.

19 The validity of the *cost principle* is weakened by inflation. Inflation has caused many accountants to recommend valuing assets at appraised value or replacement cost rather than at original (historical) cost. In Great Britain, for example, current values are used in accounting for assets. The problem of asset valuation is complex and will be given much attention in later chapters.

20 Liabilities are debts. Either borrowing money or buying on credit will create a liability. Liabilities represent the claims of *creditors* to the resources of the business. Examples of liabilities are accounts payable and notes payable.

21 Owners' equity represents the owners' investment in the business; it is equal to total assets minus liabilities. Owners' equity in a corporation is called *stockholders' equity*. The equity of the owners is a residual amount. It is the claim to all resources (assets) of the business *after* the claims of the creditors have been satisfied. If a loss occurs, it is the owners' equity rather than the creditors' claims which must absorb the loss. Thus, creditors view the owners' equity as a "buffer" which protects the safety of their claims to the resources of the business.

22 Increases in stockholders' equity result from (a) the owners investing cash or other assets in the business in exchange for capital stock and (b) profitable operation of the business. Stockholders' equity is decreased by (a) the payment of *dividends* to stockholders and (b) unprofitable operation of the business.

23 In the balance sheet of a corporation, stockholders' equity is presented in two parts: capital stock and retained earnings. *Capital stock* represents the owners' equity resulting from the owners investing assets in the business. *Retained earnings* represents the increase in owners' equity resulting from profitable operation of the business. The term retained earnings describes only those earnings which were *not* paid out as dividends to stockholders.

24 The "accounting equation" is *Assets = Liabilities + Owners' Equity*. The listing of assets shows us what things the business owns; the listing of liabilities and owners' equity tells us who supplied these resources to the business and how much each group supplied.

25 You should become familiar with the effects of various transactions upon a balance sheet.

a Purchasing an asset for cash is merely trading one kind of asset for another. Total assets will not change.

b Purchasing an asset on credit will cause total assets to increase because additional resources are being acquired, and none is being given up. However, total liabilities will increase by the same amount.

c Paying a liability with cash will cause both total assets and total liabilities to decrease.

TEST YOURSELF ON THIS INTRODUCTORY CHAPTER

True or False

For each of the following statements, circle the T or the F to indicate whether the statement is true or false.

 T F **1** The basic purpose of accounting is to provide financial information to economic decision makers.

 T F **2** Bookkeeping is only a small part of the field of accounting and probably the simplest part.

 T F **3** The most useful financial statement would be a detailed list of every business transaction in which the business enterprise has been involved.

 T F **4** Financial statements are confidential documents made available only to the top management of a business enterprise.

 T F **5** The chief accounting officer of a corporation is usually called the controller.

T *F* 6 A forecast for a business enterprise is always prepared by the CPA firm conducting the annual audit.

T F 7 The Financial Accounting Standards Board is an authoritative source of generally accepted accounting principles in the United States.

T F 8 A business may be profitable, but not solvent.

T F 9 A business may be solvent, but not profitable.

T *F* 10 One characteristic of a corporation is that its owners are personally liable for any losses incurred by the business.

T *F* 11 Assets are valued on the balance sheet at current liquidation values to show how much cash would be realized if the business went broke.

T *F* 12 The cost principle of asset valuation is no longer widely used in the U.S.

T F 13 Losses from unprofitable operations cause the owners' equity in a business enterprise to decrease.

T *F* 14 The purchase of a building for cash will cause total assets to increase.

T *F* 15 The payment of a liability will not affect total assets, but will cause total liabilities to decrease.

T F 16 In the balance sheet of a single proprietorship, any increase in capital earned through profitable operations and retained in the business is added to the capital originally invested, and a single figure is shown for the owners' capital.

T F 17 State laws require corporations to show capital stock and retained earnings separately in the balance sheet.

Completion Statements

Fill in the necessary words or amounts to complete the following statements:

1 Two major financial statements are the _balance sheet_ and the _income statement_

2 The three basic steps in the accounting process are (a) _recording_ transactions, (b) _classifying_ these events into groups, and (c) _recording_ the information in accounting reports.

3 The accounting concepts, measurement techniques, and standards of presentation used in the preparation of financial statements are called _generally accepted accounting principles_.

4 An investigation of the accounting system of a business to determine the fairness of the firm's financial statements is called an _audit_.

5 The governmental agency which reviews and approves the financial disclosure by companies which offer their securities to the public is the_____ _____ _____ _____.

6 *Statements of Financial Accounting Standards* are authoritative expressions of generally accepted accounting principles issued by the_____ _____ _____ _____.

7 Two primary objectives of most business concerns are (a) making a _profit_ and (b) remaining _solvent_.

8 The steps taken to ensure the reliability of the accounting information and to safeguard the assets of the firm against waste, fraud, or inefficient use make up the system of _internal_ _control_.

9 The three common forms of business organizations are (a)_____, (b)_____, and (c)_____.

10 The heading of a balance sheet should include (a)_____, (b)_____, and (c)_____.

11 Two reasons supporting the cost principle of asset valuation are the "_____" assumption and the _____ principle. Some accountants, however, suggest that assets should be valued at appraisal value or _____cost rather than at _____cost.

12 Since the claims of _____ have priority over those of the _____ of a business, the owners' equity is called a _____ claim.

13 The accounting equation states that _____ = _____ + _____.

14 Land advertised for sale at $90,000 was purchased for $80,000 cash by a development company. For property tax purposes, the property was assessed by the county at $25,000. The development firm intended to sell the property in parcels for a total of $150,000. The land would appear on the balance sheet of the development company among the _____ at a value of $ _____ .

15 On December 15, Shadow Mountain Golf Course had a contractor install a $90,000 sprinkler system. Since no payment to the contractor was required until the following month, the transaction was not recorded in December and was not reflected in any way in the December 31 balance sheet. Indicate for each of the following elements of the balance sheet whether the amounts were overstated, understated, or correct. Total assets _____ , total liabilities _____ , owners' equity _____ .

16 The owners' equity in a business comes from two sources: (a) _____ and (b) _____ .

17 A transaction which causes total liabilities to increase but which has no effect on owners' equity must cause total assets to _____ .

18 Retained earnings represent the total earnings (profits) of a business which have not been paid out as _____ to the _____ .

Multiple Choice

Choose the best answer for each of the following questions and enter the identifying letter in the space provided.

____ **1** Which of the following best describes the nature of an asset?
a Something with a ready market value.
b An economic resource, which will provide some future benefits, owned by a business.
c Tangible property (something with physical form) owned by a business.
d The amount of the owners' investment in a business.

____ **2** The principal reason for annual audit of a business corporation by a firm of certified public accountants (CPAs) is:
a To obtain an independent expert opinion on the fairness and dependability of the financial statements prepared by the company and distributed to stockholders, bankers, and other outsiders.
b To detect fraud on the part of company personnel.
c To assist the accounting department of the company in handling the heavy year-end work of preparing financial statements.
d To relieve management of the responsibility for financial reporting to stockholders and other outsiders.

____ **3** The primary objective of the internal auditor is to:
a Conduct an annual audit of a company's accounting system to determine that the financial statements present fairly its financial position and operating results.
b Observe the business transactions of the firm to be sure the annual tax returns are accurately prepared.
c Aid management by investigating and reporting on accounting, financial, and other operations of the company.
d Render a professional opinion as to the fairness and accuracy of the budget.

____ **4** Which of the following equations *cannot* be derived from the basic accounting equation (Assets = liabilities + owners' equity)?
a Assets — Liabilities = Owners' Equity.
b Liabilities = Assets — Owners' Equity.
c Owners' Equity = Liabilities — Assets.
d Assets — Owners' Equity = Liabilities.

____ **5** The balance sheet item, Retained Earnings:
a Appears in the stockholders' equity section for a corporation in which earnings have exceeded dividends.
b Is always equal to the amount of cash owned.
c Appears on the balance sheet of a single proprietorship if the earnings of the business have exceeded the withdrawals by the proprietor.
d Appears among the assets of any form of business organization in which earnings have exceeded amounts distributed to owners.

____ **6** Magic Forest Land Development Company sold a parcel of land at a profit. This will cause:
a A decrease in assets and liabilities.
b An increase in assets and owners' equity.
c An increase in assets and liabilities.

d A decrease in liabilities and owners' equity.

_____7 Lake Arrowhead Boat Shop bought a $700 electric hoist to lift engines out of boats. The boat shop paid $200 in cash for the hoist and signed a note to pay the balance in 60 days. This transaction will cause:

a The boat shop's assets to increase by $700 and liabilities to increase by $500.

b Assets to increase by $500 and owners' equity to decrease.

c No change in total assets, but a $500 increase in liabilities and a similar decrease in owners' equity.

d No change in owners' equity, but a $500 increase in both assets and liabilities.

Exercises

1 In the space provided below, prepare a balance sheet for the Titan Corporation at December 31, 19___, from the following alphabetical list of accounts:

Accounts payable.	$ 28,000
Accounts receivable.	37,000
Automobiles.	8,000
Buildings.	60,000
Capital stock.	100,000
Cash	14,000
Income taxes payable.	12,000
Land	35,000
Office equipment	16,000
Retained earnings.	30,000

TITAN CORPORATION
Balance Sheet
December 31, 19___

Assets		Liabilities & Stockholders' Equity	
	$	Liabilities:	
			$
	$		$

2 Use the following information to complete the balance sheet of the Unitrex Corporation on December 31, 19___.

a The corporation was organized on January 1, 19___, and has operated for the full year 19___.

b Earnings have amounted to $100,000, and dividends of $20,000 have been paid to stockholders.

c Cash and Accounts Receivable together amount to three times as much as Accounts Payable.

UNITREX CORPORATION
Balance Sheet
December 31, 19___

Assets		Liabilities & Stockholders' Equity	
Cash	$ 42,000	Liabilities:	
Accounts receivable.		Notes payable.	$
Land	90,000	Accounts payable.	
Building	260,000	Income taxes payable	40,000
Office equipment	56,000	Total liabilities	$112,000
		Stockholders' equity:	
		Capital stock . . . . $	
		Retained earnings.	
Total assets	_____	Total liabilities & stockholders' equity	$592,000
	$		

3 The Billiard Den was organized by Robert Neal on July 1 of the current year. In the space below, indicate the effect of each of the following transactions on the various balance sheet items of the Billiard Den. Indicate the new balance for every item after the July 3 transaction and each subsequent transaction. The effects of the July 1 transaction are already filled in to provide you with an example.

July 1 Issued capital stock to Robert Neal in exchange for $20,000 cash invested in the business.

3 Purchased an existing pool hall at a price of $21,000 for the land and $30,000 for the building. Neal paid the former owner $10,000 in cash and issued a short-term note payable for the balance of the purchase price.

10 Purchase 10 pool tables for $1,000 each, paying $6,000 cash and agreeing to pay the balance due in 30 days.

14 Sold one pool table to a friend for $1,000. The friend paid $500 cash to the Billiard Den and promised to pay the balance within 30 days.

20 Paid $2,000 of the amount owed on the pool tables.

24 Collected $200 from the friend who had bought the pool table.

30 Purchased one used pool table from another pool hall, paying $600 cash.

	Assets					=	Liabilities		+	Owners' Equity
	Cash	Accounts Receivable	Land	Building	Pool Tables		Notes Payable	Accounts Payable		Capital Stock
July 1	+$20,000									+$20,000
3										
Balances										
10										
Balances										
14										
Balances										
20										
Balances										
24										
Balances										
30										
Balances										

2

RECORDING CHANGES IN FINANCIAL POSITION

HIGHLIGHTS OF THE CHAPTER

1 Many businesses engage in hundreds or even thousands of business transactions every day. Obviously, it would be too costly and time-consuming to prepare a new balance sheet after each transaction. Instead, the effects of these transactions are stored in the *ledger* until the end of a month or year, when new financial statements are prepared.

2 A *ledger account* is maintained for every item on the balance sheet. Thus, we have a ledger account for each type of asset (such as Cash), for each type of liability (such as Accounts Payable), and for each element of owners' equity (such as Capital Stock).

3 Each ledger account occupies a separate page in a loose-leaf book called a *ledger*. The ledger is a permanent, important, and basic accounting record. For example, the first page in a ledger might be the ledger account entitled *Cash*. It would show increases and decreases in cash, resulting from the many transactions in which cash is received or paid.

4 A balance sheet is usually prepared at the end of each month by listing the cumulative balances of accounts contained in the ledger.

5 A ledger page is divided into two sections by a vertical line drawn down the center of the page. The left half of the page is called the *debit* side; the right half of the page is the *credit* side.

6 An amount recorded on the left side of a ledger page is called a *debit entry*; an amount recorded on the right side is called a *credit entry*.

7 Asset accounts normally have debit balances; that is, the amounts entered on the debit (or left) side are larger than the amounts entered on the credit (or right) side. For example, Cash is an asset account and has a debit balance.

8 Liability accounts and owners' equity accounts normally have credit balances because the amounts entered on the credit (right-hand) side of such accounts are greater than the amounts entered on the debit (left-hand) side.

9 For all *asset* accounts, increases are recorded by debits, and decreases are recorded by credits.

10 For all *liability* accounts and *owners' equity* accounts, increases are recorded by credits, and decreases are recorded by debits.

11 The double-entry system of accounting (which is almost universally used) requires that *equal debits and credits* be recorded for *every* transaction.

12 Most ledger accounts are actually designed in a *running balance* form. This means there is a third column, on the extreme right side of the account, which shows the *balance* (the amount by which the debits exceed the credits, or vice versa) of the account.

13 Since every transaction results in recording equal dollar amounts of debits and credits (double entry), it follows that the total of the debit entries in the ledger must equal the total of the credit entries. It also follows that the total of the debit balance accounts must equal the total of the credit balance accounts. When this equality of debits and credits exists, we say the ledger is *in balance*.

Otherwise, one or more errors must have been made in recording transactions.

14 Accounts are arranged in the ledger in the same sequence as they appear on the balance sheet: asset accounts first, then liabilities, and finally owners' equity. Each account has a number, but many numbers are skipped, so that later a new account may be inserted in the ledger if the business acquires a new type of asset, liability, or owners' equity.

15 A very small business could record transactions directly in the ledger as they occurred. However, this procedure would be inefficient and it would be difficult to locate errors because you could not locate all the parts of one transaction. Therefore, virtually every business also maintains a *journal*, or *book of original entry*. A journal is a chronological record listing the transactions in the order they occur.

16 The journal shows all information about one transaction in one place. It shows (a) the date of the transaction, (b) the account(s) debited, (c) the account(s) credited, and (d) a written explanation of the transaction.

17 After a transaction has first been recorded in the journal, each debit and credit is later transferred to the proper ledger accounts. This transfer is called *posting*.

18 At month-end, when all entries in the journal have been posted to the ledger, the debit or credit balance of each account is computed (unless running balance form ledger accounts are maintained). These balances are listed in a *trial balance*. The trial balance is a two-column schedule listing the names and balances of all accounts in the order they appear in the ledger. Debit balances are listed in the left-hand column of the trial balance, and credit balances are listed in the right-hand column. Since the total of the debit balances should equal the total of the credit balances, the totals of the two columns of the trial balance *should be equal*, if the ledger is in balance.

19 The trial balance proves that an equal number of debits and credits were posted to the ledger, and also that the arithmetic in determining the account balances was correct. However, it does not prove that all transactions were correctly recorded in the journal. For example, the trial balance would not disclose the omission of an entire transaction (both the debit and credit parts) from the journal. Also if the *right amount*

of debits or credits was entered in the ledger but the entry was made to the *wrong account*, the trial balance would not reveal the error.

20 The trial balance is not a formal financial statement, but merely a preliminary step to preparing financial statements.

21 The balance sheet is prepared from the trial balance.

22 Businesses using computers maintain accounting records on magnetic tape instead of loose-leaf notebooks (ledgers), but the accounting principles of analyzing and recording transactions and preparing financial statements *are the same* as for a manual system. An understanding of accounting concepts is more easily acquired by studying a manual system.

TEST YOURSELF ON RECORDING CHANGES IN FINANCIAL POSITION

True or False

For each of the following statements, circle the T or the F to indicate whether the statement is true or false.

 1 In a prosperous and solvent business the accounts with credit balances will normally exceed in total dollar amount the accounts with debit balances.

 2 The term *debit* may signify either an increase or a decrease; the same is true of the term *credit*.

 3 All transactions are recorded in the journal and in ledger accounts by equal amounts of debits and credits.

 4 A business transaction is always recorded in the ledger by entries to two or more different ledger accounts.

 5 An entry on the left side of a ledger account is called a debit entry, and an entry on the right side is called a credit entry, regardless of whether the account represents an asset, a liability, or owners' equity.

 6 Accounts representing items which appear on the left-hand side of the balance sheet usually have credit balances.

 7 Decreases in a ledger account are recorded by debits and increases are recorded by credits, regardless of whether the account represents an asset, a liability, or owners' equity.

T F **8** The balance of a T account is entered in small pencil figures opposite the last entry on the side having the larger column total.

T F **9** A trial balance with equal debit and credit totals proves that all transactions have been correctly journalized and posted to the proper ledger accounts.

T F **10** The sequence of the account titles in a trial balance depends upon the size of the account balances.

T F **11** A journal entry may include debits to more than one account and credits to more than one account, but the total of the debits must always equal the total of the credits.

T F **12** One advantage of using a journal and a ledger rather than recording transactions directly in the ledger accounts is that the journal provides all information about a particular transaction in one place.

T F **13** The purchase of a typewriter on account would be recorded as a debit to Accounts Payable and a credit to Office Equipment.

T F **14** Of the following eleven accounts, six normally have debit balances and five have credit balances: Accounts Receivable, Accounts Payable, Buildings, Capital Stock, Cash, Land, Machinery, Mortgage Payable, Notes Payable, Notes Receivable, Retained Earnings.

T F **15** A transposition error means a posting of a journal entry to the wrong ledger account.

T F **16** The footings, or memoranda totals of the entries in a ledger account, do not relate to a specific transaction, but are merely a step in determining the balance of the account.

T F **17** If a business transaction is recorded correctly, it cannot possibly upset the equality of debits and credits in the ledger.

T F **18** More knowledge of accounting is required to post amounts from the journal to the ledger than is required to record transactions in journal entry form.

T F **19** In a journal entry recording the purchase of a desk for $275.80, both the debit and credit were recorded and posted as $257.80. This *transposition error* would *not* be disclosed by the preparation of a trial balance.

T F **20** The double-entry accounting system means that transactions are recorded both in the journal and in the ledger.

Completion Statements

Fill in the necessary words to complete the following statements:

1 In accounting, the term *debit* refers to the _____ side of a _____ _____, while the term *credit* refers to the _____ side.

2 The unit of organization for a journal is the _____ and the unit of organization for the ledger is the_____ _____.

3 A T account is a simplified model of a formal ledger account and consists of only three elements: (a) an account _____, (b) a _____ _____ , and (c) a _____ _____.

4 Increases in assets are recorded by_____ _____ and decreases in assets are recorded by credits; increases in accounts appearing on the right side of a balance sheet are recorded by_____ , while decreases in those accounts are recorded by_____.

5 Asset accounts appear on the_____ side of the balance sheet and normally have _____ balances. Liability and owners' equity accounts appear on the _____ side of a balance sheet and normally have_____balances.

6 When a company borrows from a bank, two accounts immediately affected are_____ and_____ _____ . The journal entry to record the transaction requires a _____ to the first account and a _____ to the second one.

7 If you charge a sweater at a clothing store where you have an account, the store will

_____ your account for the amount of your purchase.

8 A journal entry shows (a) the_____ _____ of the transaction, (b) the_____ _____ to be_____ , (c) the _____ to be_____ , and also (d) an _____ of the transaction.

9 When making a journal entry the_____ _____column just to the left of the debit column remains blank. When the debits and credits are later_____ to the ledger, the _____ of the ledger accounts are listed in this column to provide a convenient _____ _____ with the ledger.

10 A_____ _____ is prepared from the ledger accounts at the end of the month (or other accounting period) in order to prove that the total of accounts with_____ _____ is equal to the total of accounts with _____ _____.

11 The journal may also be called the_____ _____ _____ _____

12 With respect to (a) posting, (b) journalizing, (c) preparation of a balance sheet, (d) preparation of a trial balance, and (e) occurrence of a business transaction, the normal sequence of these events is denoted by the following list of letters _____ _____.

Multiple Choice

Choose the best answer for each of the following questions and enter the identifying letter in the space provided.

____ 1 Mohawk Company completed a transaction which caused both its total assets and its total liabilities to increase by $6,000. The transaction could have been:
a Purchase of a fork lift by paying $4,000 cash and issuing a note payable for $6,000.
b Purchase of a drill press by a payment of $2,000 in cash and issuance of a $4,000 note payable.

c Sale of land costing $6,000 for $6,000 in cash.
d None of the above.

____ 2 Red Hill Vineyards completes a transaction which causes an asset account to decrease. Which of the following related effects may also occur?
a An increase of an equal amount in a liability account.
b An increase of an equal amount in owners' equity.
c An increase of an equal amount in another asset account.
d None of the above.

____ 3 The term *posting* means:
a Entering transactions in a book of original entry.
b Transferring debit and credit amounts from the journal to the ledger.
c Proving the equality of debits and credits in the ledger.
d Determining the balances of individual ledger accounts.

____ 4 If a computer is acquired by paying $10,000 in cash and signing a note payable for $40,000:
a Total assets are increased and total owners' equity is increased.
b Total liabilities are increased and total owners' equity is decreased.
c Total assets are decreased and total liabilities are increased.
d Total assets are increased and total liabilities are increased.

____ 5 Which of the following errors would *not* be disclosed by the trial balance?
a The collection of a $520 account receivable was journalized as a $520 debit to Cash and a $502 credit to Accounts Receivable.
b The collection of a $200 account receivable was journalized as a $200 debit to Cash and a $200 debit to Accounts Receivable.
c The collection of a $1,000 account receivable was journalized correctly, but the debit was posted to the Land account instead of Cash.
d None of the above.

____ 6 The accountant of the Midas Company made an error in posting from the journal to the ledger accounts. He posted a debit to Office Equipment as a debit to Accounts Receivable. The procedure which is most likely to disclose this error is:
a Refooting all the accounts in the ledger.
b Sending month-end bills to all customers.

c Taking a trial balance.

d Comparing the written explanation of the journal entry with the accounts mentioned in the journal.

_____ 7 If a trial balance is out of balance, a possible cause is:

a A transaction calling for a debit to an asset account and a credit to a liability account was entered in the journal as a debit to a liability account and a credit to an asset account.

b A transaction was entirely omitted from the records.

c An error was made in determining the balance of the Cash account.

d The balances of the Cash account and the Accounts Receivable account were switched in the preparation of the trial balance.

_____ 8 Peckham Investment Company entered into a transaction which did not change total assets, total liabilities, or total owners' equity. The transaction could have been:

a The sale of land for cash at a price equal to the cost of the land.

b An investment of cash in the business by stockholders.

c The settlement of a liability by paying the creditor some asset other than cash.

d None of the above.

Exercises

1 Show the change in total assets, total liabilities, and total owners' equity that will be caused by posting each amount in the following journal entries. In the *effect of transaction* row, show the total change in assets, liabilities, and owners' equity that has occurred after all parts of the transaction have been posted. *Hint:* The effect of each transaction should be that the total change on the left side of the balance sheet (change in assets) should equal the change on the right side (change in liabilities + change in owners' equity). Explanations have been omitted from journal entries to conserve space.

Journal Entry	Dr	Cr	Assets	=	Lia-bilities	+	Owners' Equity
Example:							
Office Equipment	600		+ 600		−		−
Cash		150	− 150		−		−
Accounts Payable		450	−		+ 450		−
Effect of Transaction			+ 450	=	+ 450	+	−
a Accounts Receivable	230						
Cash		230					
Effect of transaction				=		+	
b Cash	5,000						
Capital Stock		5,000					
Effect of transaction				=		+	
c Cash	800						
Notes Payable		800					
Effect of transaction				=		+	
d Accounts Payable	350						
Cash		350					
Effect of transaction				=		+	
e Land	8,000						
Cash		2,000					
Notes Payable		6,000					
Effect of transaction				=		+	

2 Enter the following transactions of Riviera Corporation in the T accounts provided, and then prepare a trial balance at September 30, 19___.

(1) Issued capital stock of $70,000 par value for $70,000 cash.

(2) Borrowed $12,000 cash from a bank and signed a note payable for that amount.

(3) Purchased land and building for $90,000, paying $40,000 in cash and issuing a $50,000 note payable. The land was estimated to represent one-third of the total purchase price.

(4) Purchased office equipment on credit at a cost of $6,000.

(5) Added a balcony to the building at a cost of $5,000; agreed to pay contractor in full in 30 days.

(6) Returned part of the office equipment to the supplier and received full credit of $600.

(7) Made a partial payment of $3,000 on the amount owed for office equipment.

Cash		Notes Payable	
70,000	40,000		50,000
12,000	3,000		12,000
600			

Land		Accounts Payable	
30,000		3,000	6,000
		600	5,000

Building		Capital Stock	
60,000			70,000
5,000			

Office Equipment	
6,000	600

RIVIERA CORPORATION
Trial Balance
September 30, 19___

	Debit	Credit
Cash	$ 39,600	$
Land	30,000	
Building	65,000	
Office equipment	5,400	
Notes payable		50,000
Accounts payable		14,000
Capital stock		70,000
	$	$

3

MEASURING BUSINESS INCOME

HIGHLIGHTS OF THE CHAPTER

1 Two things can cause a change in the owners' equity in a business concern: (a) a change in the owners' investment (stockholders putting assets in or taking assets out of the business) and (b) profits or losses resulting from operation of the business.

2 The change in owners' equity resulting from profits or losses is very important to every business. Profits increase owners' equity. These profits may be either distributed to the stockholders as dividends, or retained in the business to help finance expansion and growth. Losses, however, reduce owners' equity and make the business and its owners economically worse off.

3 The increase in owners' equity resulting from operating profitably is presented in the balance sheet in the *Retained Earnings* account. Distributing profits to stockholders as *dividends* causes a decrease in total assets and owners' equity. This decrease in owners' equity decreases the Retained Earnings account. Thus, retained earnings represent only the profits *retained in the business*. Many large companies started with small investments but were able to grow by operating profitably and reinvesting their profits in the business.

4 *Net income* is the term accountants use for the *increase in owners' equity resulting from profitable operation* of the business; *net loss* means the *decrease in owners' equity resulting from unprofitable operations*.

5 Net income (or loss) is measured by deducting the *expenses* of a given period from the *revenue* earned in that period. Thus, *revenue minus expenses equals net income*.

6 *Revenue is the price of goods sold and services rendered during a given period*. Revenue comes into existence when the goods are sold or the service is rendered, even though cash is not collected until some later date. If a customer buys our product on credit in July and pays us in August, we should recognize the revenue from the sale in July. In August we are merely converting one asset (an account receivable) into another asset (cash).

7 Revenue causes both assets (accounts receivable or cash) and owners' equity to increase. Sometimes revenue is defined as the inflow of cash and receivables from sales of goods and services during a period.

8 *Expenses are the cost of goods and services used up in the process of obtaining revenue*. Expenses are recorded when the good or service is used up, even though cash payment is not made until later. If we use electricity in January but do not pay the electric company until February, we should recognize the expense from using the good (electricity) in January. In February, we are merely paying a liability owed to the electric company.

9 To measure net income, we first show all revenue earned during the period and then deduct all expenses incurred in producing that revenue. This policy of offsetting revenue with the related expenses is called the *matching principle*.

10 Not all cash payments are expenses; for instance, cash used to buy a building is an exchange of assets, not an expense. *Expenses cause owners' equity to decrease.*

11 A *dividend* is a distribution of assets by a corporation to its stockholders. This causes owners' equity to change but has *nothing to do with net income*. This kind of change in equity is a *change in the owners' investment* in the business. Dividends are disinvestments; they are *not expenses* of the business.

12 To be meaningful, net income must be measured *for some time period* (such as a month or year). To determine the net income of a time period, we must first measure the revenue and expenses of *that same time period*. The span of time for which net income is determined is called the *accounting period*.

13 Many transactions affect two or more accounting periods. A building, for instance, is an asset which is used up over 20 or 30 years. The cost of the building should be recognized as expense as it is used up, but that period of time is not precisely determinable in advance.

14 The rules of debit and credit for revenue and expenses are based on the changes caused in owners' equity. Revenue increases owners' equity; therefore revenue is recorded by a credit. Expenses decrease owners' equity; therefore expenses are recorded by debits.

15 Every transaction which affects a revenue or an expense account also affects a balance sheet account. For example, credits to revenue are usually offset by debits to asset accounts; debits to expense are offset by credits to asset or liability accounts.

16 A separate ledger account is maintained for each major category of revenue and expense. Revenue accounts have credit balances; examples are Fees Earned, Commissions Earned, and Sales. Expense accounts have debit balances; examples are Telephone Expense, Office Salaries, and Insurance Expense.

17 The sequence of accounts in the ledger is as follows: (a) assets, (b) liabilities, (c) owners' equity, (d) revenue, and (e) expenses. This sequence is called *financial statement order*, because the three groups of balance sheet accounts (assets, liabilities, owners' equity) come before the income statement accounts (revenue and expenses).

18 Buildings, office equipment, and other *plant assets* have limited useful lives over which the asset is used up. A portion of the cost of the asset becomes expense (price of goods used up) during each year of its use. This process of allocating the cost of a plant asset over its useful life is called *depreciation*. For example, if we acquire a $100,000 building with an estimated life of 25 years and no salvage value, the depreciation expense each year will be $1/_{25}$ of $100,000, or $4,000. To ignore depreciation would cause expenses to be understated and therefore net income to be overstated.

19 Depreciation differs from most expenses in that no immediate or near-term cash outlay is required. The cash outlay was made *in advance* when the plant asset was acquired.

20 The journal entry to record depreciation is made at the end of the period by a debit to *Depreciation Expense* and a credit to *Accumulated Depreciation*. The Accumulated Depreciation account, with a credit balance, appears on the balance sheet as a deduction from the related asset account. The net amount (asset cost minus accumulated depreciation) represents the undepreciated cost (benefits remaining) of the asset. Undepreciated cost is also called *book value* or *carrying value*.

21 No one sends us a bill to show us how much of our building was "used up" in a specific accounting period. The entry to record depreciation expense is based on our understanding of what constitutes "expenses." Entries to record expenses and revenue that are not evidenced by transactions in the current period are called *adjusting entries*.

22 After the adjusting entries, such as recognizing depreciation expense, are made, an *adjusted trial balance* is prepared to prove that the ledger is still in balance.

23 The *income statement* is a formal financial statement which lists the revenue, deducts the expenses, and shows the net income of a business for a specified period of time (the accounting period).

24 The income statement is of great interest to managers, investors, and other groups, but it has certain limitations. It is not entirely accurate, because many transactions overlap accounting periods and their effect on each period is merely an estimate. Also the economic significance of some events (such as the discovery of an oil well) cannot be objectively measured and reflected in the income statement.

25 The *statement of retained earnings* covers the same time period as the income statement. It shows the beginning balance of retained earnings, the net income or loss for the period, a deduction for any dividends, and the ending balance of retained earnings.

26 The *report form* of balance sheet contains the same information as the *account form* previously illustrated. However, in the report form the assets are listed and totaled in the upper half of the page. The liabilities and stockholders' equity constitute a separate section in the lower half of the page.

27 The stockholders' equity section of the balance sheet shows two items: Capital Stock, representing the amounts invested by stockholders, and Retained Earnings, representing the accumulated net earnings since the date of incorporation minus all dividends distributed to stockholders.

28 The income statement and statement of retained earnings may be viewed as "links" between two successive balance sheets. The statement of retained earnings summarizes the factors (net income and dividends) which have caused the amount of retained earnings to change between the two balance sheet dates. The income statement explains in greater detail the change in retained earnings resulting from profitable (or unprofitable) operation of the business.

29 *Closing the accounts* means transferring the balances of the revenue and expense accounts at the end of each accounting period into an account used to measure net income, called the *Income Summary* account. If revenue (credit balances) exceeds expenses (debit balances), the Income Summary account will have a credit balance representing net income for the period. If the expenses exceed the revenue, the Income Summary account will have a debit balance, representing a net loss. In either case, the Income Summary account is then closed by transferring its balance to the Retained Earnings account. Transferring a credit balance from the Income Summary account (representing net income) causes the Retained Earnings account to increase; transferring a debit balance (net loss) into Retained Earnings causes that account to decrease.

30 The Dividends account is closed by transferring its debit balance to the Retained Earnings account. It does not go through the Income Summary account because dividends are not an expense.

31 The principal purpose of closing the revenue and expense accounts is to reduce their balances to zero at the end of the period so that they are ready to measure the revenue and expenses of the next period.

32 Four journal entries are generally used to close the accounts: (a) close revenue accounts into the Income Summary, (b) close expense accounts into the Income Summary, (c) close the Income Summary account into the Retained Earnings account, and (d) close the Dividends account into Retained Earnings. These journal entries are called *closing entries*.

33 After closing the accounts, an *after-closing trial balance* is prepared to prove that the ledger is still in balance. The after-closing trial balance will contain only balance sheet accounts since all others will have zero balances.

34 The accounting procedures covered thus far may be summarized in eight steps: (a) journalize transactions, (b) post to ledger accounts, (c) prepare a trial balance, (d) make end-of-period adjustments, (e) prepare an adjusted trial balance, (f) prepare financial statements, (g) journalize and post closing entries, and (h) prepare an after-closing trial balance.

35 We have defined revenue as the price of goods and services delivered or rendered to customers during a period and we have defined expenses as the price of goods and services used during a period, regardless of when cash payment is made. These definitions of revenue and expenses result in *accrual basis* accounting. An alternative to accrual basis accounting is *cash basis* accounting. Under cash basis accounting, revenue is not recorded until received in cash; expenses are recognized in the period in which cash payment is made. The cash basis does not give a fair measure of profitability. For instance, the cash basis ignores revenue earned but not yet received and expenses incurred but not yet paid. We shall therefore use only the *accrual basis* to determine net income.

TEST YOURSELF ON MEASURING BUSINESS INCOME

True or False

For each of the following statements, circle the T or the F to indicate whether the statement is true or false.

T F **1** If a real estate firm using the accrual basis of accounting sells a client's building in May but the commission is not collected until July, the revenue is earned in May and should be included in the May income statement.

T F **2** Expenses cause a decrease in owners' equity and are recorded by debits.

T F **3** If cash receipts are $10,000 greater than total expenses for a given period, the business will earn a net income of $10,000 or more.

T F **4** The journal entry to recognize a revenue or an expense must always affect an asset or liability account as well.

T F **5** Under accrual basis accounting, revenue is recognized when cash is received, and expenses are recognized when cash is paid.

T F **6** An expense may be recognized and recorded even though no cash outlay has been made.

T F **7** Buying a building for cash is just exchanging one asset for another and will not result in an expense even in future periods.

T F **8** Revenue increases owners' equity and is recorded by a credit.

T F **9** Revenue accounts are closed at the end of the period by debiting the revenue accounts and transferring their balances by crediting the Income Summary account.

T F **10** If a business is operating profitably, the entry to close the Income Summary account will consist of a debit to Income Summary and a credit to Retained Earnings.

T F **11** If expenses are larger than revenue, the Income Summary account will have a debit balance.

T F **12** The Dividends account is closed at the end of the period by transferring its balance to the Income Summary account.

T F **13** The entry to recognize depreciation is an example of an adjusting entry.

T F **14** An increase in an expense account is the equivalent of a decrease in owners' equity.

T F **15** An adjusted trial balance contains only balance sheet accounts.

T F **16** In a well-established business which had been audited annually by a CPA, it would be reasonable to expect the Depreciation Expense account and the Accumulated Depreciation account to have equal balances.

T F **17** Retained earnings represent an amount of cash available to pay dividends.

T F **18** The Retained Earnings account is closed at the end of each period, and begins the next period with a zero balance.

Completion Statements

Fill in the necessary words or amounts to complete the following statements:

1 Owners' equity may be changed by either _____ and _____ or a change in the owners' _____ .

2 The Income Summary account is used to bring together the _____ and _____ accounts.

3 The process of allocating the _____ of a plant asset to expense as that asset is used up is called _____ .

4 Performance Products Company began business on July 7. The company made the following total cash sales: July, $18,000; August, $26,000. Sales on 30-day credit were July, $31,000; August, $42,000. All the July credit sales were collected in August, and all accounts receivable originating in August were collected in September. The total revenue for July was $ _____ and total revenue for August was $ _____ . Total cash receipts in August were $ _____ .

5 The principal distinction between expenses and dividends to stockholders is that expenses are incurred for the purpose of _____ . A similarity between the two is that both expenses and dividends cause a _____ in _____ .

6 A credit balance in the Income Summary account indicates a ___NET___ ___Income___ for the period. This will cause owners' equity to ___increase___ .

7 If expenses exceed revenue, the Income Summary account will be closed into the ___Retained Earnings___ account by an entry which ___Credits___ the Income Summary account.

8 Assets, liabilities, and owners' equity are the only accounts that will have balances after the ___Closing Entries___ have all been posted.

9 A dividend is declared by the board of directors of Sonic Corporation on July 1, and is payable on August 10 to stockholders of record on July 31. The journal entry on July 1 would consist of a debit to ___Dividends___ and a credit to ___Dividends Payable___. The entry on August 10 would consist of a debit to ___Dividends Payable___ and a credit to ___Cash___ .

Multiple Choice

Choose the best answer for each of the following questions and enter the identifying letter in the space provided.

___c___ **1** On April 1, Hudson Company received and paid a $700 bill for advertising done in March. In addition to this bill, the company paid $6,100 during April for expenses incurred in that month. On May 2, Hudson Company paid a $4,600 payroll to employees for work done in April. Based on these facts, total expenses for the month of April were:

a $ 6,100
b $ 6,800
c $10,700
d $11,400

___a___ **2** If a journal entry recognizes revenue, the other part of the entry might:

a Increase an asset account.
b Increase a liability account.
c Decrease an asset account.
d Increase the Retained Earnings account.

___b___ **3** The principal difference between depreciation and most types of expense is that depreciation:

a Is deductible only in years in which a profit is earned.
b Does not require an immediate or near-term cash outlay.
c Can be avoided if management creates a cash fund for use in replacing worn-out assets.
d Is subject to more precise measurement.

___c___ **4** Of the following accounts, which one would *not* appear in an after-closing trial balance?

a Accumulated Depreciation.
b Accounts Receivable.
c Depreciation Expense.
d Retained Earnings.

___d___ **5** If a journal entry recognizes an expense, the other part of the entry might:

a Increase an asset account.
b Decrease the Retained Earnings account.
c Decrease a liability account.
d Increase a liability account.

___c___ **6** The statement of retained earnings:

a Shows the revenue and expenses of a business for a given time period.
b Indicates whether the cash position of the corporation will permit the payment of dividends.
c Provides a link between the income statement and the balance sheet.
d Has no relationship with the balance sheet.

___a___ **7** Dividends on capital stock:

a Are recorded by a debit to Dividends, and this account is later closed into Retained Earnings.
b Are shown on the income statement among general administrative expenses.
c Are recorded in the accounts by a debit to Dividends Payable and a credit to Retained Earnings.
d Are recorded by a debit to Income Summary and a credit to Dividends Paid.

___b___ **8** Gulfside, Inc., had net income of $92,000 during the current year and paid dividends of $48,000. If the balance of the Retained Earnings account at the end of the year was $250,000, the beginning balance was:

a $294,000
b $206,000
c $390,000
d $110,000

Exercises

1 Using the adjusted trial balance below,

prepare (a) an income statement, (b) a statement of retained earnings, and (c) a balance sheet in *report form* for Mission Auto Repair, Inc., for the month ended May 31, 19 .

MISSION AUTO REPAIR, INC.
Adjusted Trial Balance
May 31, 19 ____

	Debit	Credit
Cash	$ 18,600	
Notes receivable	4,000	
Accounts receivable	42,000	
Garage equipment	33,600	
Accumulated depreciation:		
garage equipment		$ 9,100
Notes payable		8,200
Accounts payable		10,300
Capital stock		30,000
Retained earnings		40,000
Dividends	8,000	
Repair revenue		24,000
Rent expense	2,000	
Wages expense	11,350	
Advertising expense	1,400	
Utilities expense	300	
Depreciation expense:		
garage equipment	350	
	$121,600	$121,600

a

MISSION AUTO REPAIR, INC.
Income Statement
For the Month Ended May 31, 19 ____

Repair Revenue		24,000
Rent Exp	2000	
Wages Expense	11350	
Util expense	300	
Depre Exp	350	
adv exp	1400	
Net Income		8600

b

MISSION AUTO REPAIR, INC.
Statement of Retained Earnings
For the Month Ended May 31, 19 ____

Retained Earning	100000	40,000
Net Income		8600
Sub	100000	48,600
Dividends		118000
Ret Earning		206000

+ 40000
50000

c

MISSION AUTO REPAIR, INC.
Balance Sheet
May 31, 19 ____

Assets		
Cash	18600	
N/ec	4000	
Accts receivable	42000	
Equip	33600	
Less Df		9100
Liabilities & Stockholders' Equity		
		9100
		8200
		10,300
		30,000
		40,600
	89100	89100

for a gain

Income Summary   Dr   Cr
                              X
Net Income Retained earning   X

for a loss   Dr   Cr
Income Summary   X
     Retained ea   X

2 Indicate the effect of the following errors on each of the accounting elements described in the column headings below. Use the following symbols:

O = Overstated
U = Understated
NE = NO effect

Error	Total Revenue	Total Expenses	Net Income	Total Assets	Total Liabilities	Total Owners' Equity
Example: Rendered services to a customer and received immediate payment in cash but made no record of transaction.	U	NE	U	U	NE	U
1 Payment for repairs erroneously debited to Building account.	O	NE				
2 Recorded collection of an account receivable by debiting Cash and crediting a revenue account.	O	NE	O	O	NE	O
3 Failed to record depreciation for the current period.	NE	U	O	O	NE	O
4 Recorded declaration of a dividend to be paid in a later month by debiting Dividends and crediting Retained Earnings.	NE	NE	NE	NE	U	O
5 Recorded the purchase of office equipment for cash as a debit to Office Equipment and a credit to Depreciation Expense.	NE	U	O	O	NE	NE
6 Recorded cash payment for advertising by debiting Repairs Expense and crediting Cash.	NE	NE	NE	NE	NE	NE

4
COMPLETION OF THE ACCOUNTING CYCLE

HIGHLIGHTS OF THE CHAPTER

1 For the purpose of measuring income, the life of a business is divided into accounting periods of *equal length*. This helps us to compare revenue and expenses of the current period with those of prior periods and determine whether operating results are improving or declining.

2 Many business transactions are begun in one accounting period and completed in a later period. A precise cutoff of transactions at the end of each accounting period is essential to the preparation of reliable financial statements.

3 *Adjusting entries* are made at the end of the accounting period to apportion transactions between periods. We want to be sure that the income statement contains all revenue earned and all expenses incurred in the period covered, but does not contain any revenue or expense applicable to the following period. Similarly, the balance sheet must contain all the assets owned and all liabilities owed on the last day of the period.

4 Every adjusting entry affects both a balance sheet account and an income statement account. Two purposes are accomplished by adjusting entries: (a) the proper amount of revenue and expense is apportioned to the current accounting period and (b) the proper amount of related asset or liability is established for the balance sheet.

5 Four types of transactions requiring adjusting entries are recorded costs, recorded revenue, unrecorded expenses, and unrecorded revenue. *Recorded costs* consist of costs which have been recorded in one period but which will benefit more than one accounting period. A fire insurance policy, for example, may cost $3,600 and run for three years. In this case, $1/36$ of the policy is used up in each month and should be recognized as an expense of that month. A recorded-cost adjusting entry at the end of each month would transfer to expense the portion of the total cost that had been used up in the period. In journal entry form, we would debit Insurance Expense $100 and credit Unexpired Insurance $100. Depreciation is another recorded-cost adjusting entry.

6 *Recorded-revenue* adjusting entries are necessary when revenue has been received (and therefore recorded) before it has been earned. An example is a fee received in advance for services we are to render in the future. When we are paid in advance, a liability exists either to render the service or to refund the customer's money. As we render the service (or deliver the goods), we are earning the revenue and reducing our liability. At the end of the period, an adjusting entry would be made debiting (reducing) the liability and crediting a revenue account for the portion of the advance payments we have earned during the period.

7 *Unrecorded-expenses* adjusting entries are necessary when an expense has been incurred, but payment will not have to be made until a future period. For example, if employees will not be paid until February 2 for work they did in January, the cost of this work should be recognized as expense

in January. Also, at the end of January, a liability exists to pay the employees. The unrecorded-expense adjusting entry at the end of January would debit Wages Expense (to recognize the expense in January) and credit Wages Payable (to record the liability to make a future payment).

8 Revenue which has been earned but not yet recorded must be brought on the books by an *unrecorded-revenue* adjusting entry. For example, at the end of a period, services may have been rendered but no accounting entry made and no bill sent to the customer. The necessary adjusting entry would debit an account receivable and credit a revenue account.

9 Because so much detailed work is necessary at the end of the period in adjusting and closing the books and preparing financial statements, it is easy to make errors. One way to simplify this work and avoid errors in the permanent accounting records is to use a *work sheet*.

10 A work sheet is a large columnar sheet of paper, prepared in pencil, and organizing all accounting data required at the end of the period. An error made on the work sheet is easily corrected; furthermore, the work sheet is self-balancing so that many types of errors are automatically brought to light. The work sheet is a working tool of accountants which helps them prepare reliable financial statements at the end of the period. It also serves as a guide to making the necessary adjusting and closing entries in the accounting records. The work sheet, as the name suggests, is not a financial statement nor part of the permanent accounting records. It is the source from which financial statements are prepared, and from which adjusting and closing entries are made in the journal.

11 To prepare a work sheet, carry out the following steps:
a Enter ledger account balances in the Trial Balance columns.
b Enter all necessary adjusting entries in columns 3 and 4, the Adjustments columns.
c Combine the trial balance amounts with the related adjustments and enter the adjusted balances in the Adjusted Trial Balance columns.
d Extend the amounts in the Adjusted Trial Balance columns horizontally across the work sheet into one of the four remaining columns. Revenue and expense accounts go

to the Income Statement columns. Asset, liability, and owners' equity accounts go to the Balance Sheet columns.
e Total the Income Statement columns and enter the net income or loss as the balancing figure. This net income or loss is also entered in the Balance Sheet columns, since net income or loss becomes a part of owners' equity. Total both pairs of columns.

12 Financial statements are easily prepared from the work sheet as the data needed are already classified in the last four columns.

13 Adjusting entries are entered in the journal by taking data directly from the Adjustments columns of the work sheet. Preparation of closing entries from the work sheet may be summarized as follows:
a Close the revenue accounts by debiting each account listed in the credit column of the Income Statement columns, and credit Income Summary.
b Close the expense accounts by crediting each account in the debit column of the Income Statement columns, and debit Income Summary.
c To close the Income Summary account, transfer the balancing figure of the Income Statement columns of the work sheet (also the balance of the Income Summary account) to the Retained Earnings account.
d Close the Dividends account by debiting the Retained Earnings account and crediting the Dividends account.

14 When a work sheet is used, the sequence of procedures making up the accounting cycle may be summarized in six steps:
a Record all transactions daily in the journal.
b Post journal entries to ledger accounts.
c Prepare the work sheet.
d Prepare financial statements from the work sheet.
e Enter adjusting and closing entries in the journal using the work sheet as a source. Post these entries to ledger accounts.
f Prepare an after-closing trial balance.

15 Most companies prepare *monthly* financial statements from work sheets, but close the books only once a year. Monthly and quarterly financial statements are called *interim statements*.

16 *Reversing entries* are an optional bookkeeping procedure in which certain year-end adjusting entries are reversed on the first day of the next accounting period. The reversing

entry is exactly the opposite of the related adjusting entry: it contains the same account titles and the same dollar amounts as the adjusting entry, but the debits and credits are the reverse of those in the adjusting entry. The purpose of reversing entries is to permit accounting personnel to record routine transactions in a standard manner, without referring to the amounts of revenue or expense accrued at year-end.

17 Reversing entries may be used for those adjusting entries which (a) accrue a liability for an expense or (b) accrue a receivable for revenue. Adjusting entries that apportion a recorded cost between accounting periods (such as the adjusting entry to record depreciation) are not reversed.

TEST YOURSELF ON COMPLETION OF THE ACCOUNTING CYCLE

True or False

For each of the following statements, circle the T or the F to indicate whether the statement is true or false.

T (F) 1 If all transactions were originally recorded in conformity with generally accepted accounting principles, there would be no need for adjusting entries at the end of the period.

(T) F 2 Adjusting entries contribute to accurate financial reporting by allocating revenues to the period in which they were earned and expenses to the period in which they were incurred.

(T) F 3 Every adjusting entry must change both an income statement account and a balance sheet account.

T (F) 4 An account called Unearned Commissions Revenue is a revenue account.

T (F) 5 The adjusting entry to allocate the cost of a three-year fire insurance policy to expense will cause total assets to increase.

(T) F 6 The adjusting entry to recognize that commission revenue not previously recorded (or billed to a customer) has now been earned will cause total assets to increase.

T (F) 7 The adjusting entry to recognize an expense which has not yet been recorded and will not be paid until some future period will cause total assets to decrease.

T (F) 8 The adjusting entry to recognize that a fee received in advance from a customer has now been earned will cause total liabilities to increase.

(T) F 9 If employees have worked eight days in a period for which they will not be paid until the first payday next period and if no adjusting entry is made at the end of this period, total liabilities will be understated and both net income and owners' equity will be overstated.

(T) F 10 The original cost of a building minus the accumulated depreciation is called the *book value*, or *carrying value*.

(T) F 11 The balance of the Accumulated Depreciation account will appear in the Balance Sheet credit column of a work sheet.

T (F) 12 The balances of any unearned revenue accounts will appear in the Income Statement credit column of the work sheet.

T (F) (13) The Balance Sheet credit column of the work sheet usually contains only liability accounts and owners' equity accounts.

(T) F 14 Net income will appear on the work sheet as a balancing figure in the Income Statement debit column and the Balance Sheet credit column.

T F 15 Sullivan's Car Wash borrowed $10,000 from its bank on June 1, signing a six-month 9% interest-bearing note for that amount. The proper adjusting entry at June 30 will be a $75 debit to an expense account and a $75 credit to a liability account.

(T) F 16 A separate trial balance is unnecessary when a work sheet is used.

T (F) 17 The total of the Balance Sheet columns of the work sheet will usually be the same as the totals appearing on a formal balance sheet.

T (F) 18 The Adjustments columns of the work sheet for Martin's Cabinet Shop contained only two adjustments: one to allocate a portion of the three-year fire insurance policy to expense, and the other to record the earnings of a revenue which had been received in advance. The totals of the Adjusted Trial Balance columns would be larger than the totals of the Trial Balance columns.

T F 19 The adjusting entries to accrue fees earned and salaries expense through year-end may both be reversed on the first day of the next accounting period.

Completion Statements

Fill in the necessary words or amounts to complete the following statements:

1 The four types of transactions requiring adjusting entries are _Recorded cost_ _Recorded reve_ , _UNRECORDED_ _Revenue_ , and _"_ _Expenses_ transactions.

2 An adjusting entry at November 30 concerning the cost of an insurance policy serves two purposes: (a) it _distrib_ the proper amount of _ins exp_ to November operations, and (b) it reduces the _ass_ account entitled _Unexpired Exp_ so that the correct amount will appear on the November 30 balance sheet.

3 Adjusting entries always recognize either a _Revenue_ or an _EXPENSE_ .

4 The adjusting entry to record receiving some of the benefits in the current period from an expenditure made in an earlier period consists of a _debit_ to an _expense_ account and a _Credit_ to an _ASSET_ account.

5 If a customer pays in advance for services to be rendered, the entry to record the receipt of the payment consists of a _debit_ to an _Asset_ account and a _CREDIT_ to a _liability_ account.

6 If an expense has been accumulating from day to day (such as wages) without being recorded, the proper adjusting entry would _debit_ an _expense_ account and _credit_ a _liability_ account.

7 If an expenditure will yield benefits to a business only during the period in which it is made, the entry for the expenditure consists of a _debit_ to an _asset exp_ account and a _credit_ to an _liability_ account and/or a _cash_ account.

8 If an expenditure will yield benefits to the business over several periods, the entry for the expenditure consists of a _debit_ to an _asset_ account and a credit to an _liability_ account and/or a _asset_ account.

9 In the work sheet prepared by a business operating at a loss, the Income Statement _debit_ column will exceed the _credit_ column and the excess of the _amount_ over the _credit_ will be entered in the _credit_ column in order to bring the two Income Statement columns into balance.

10 The South Bay Management Company agreed to manage an apartment building beginning May 15, 19___, for 1 year at a management fee of $400 per month. The first $400 payment is received June 15, 19___. The adjusting entry at May 31, 19___, should consist of a debit to _Mgt FEES Receivable 200_ and a credit to _Earned Mgt Fees_ . When the first payment is received on June 15, the collection should be recorded by an entry debiting _Cash_ for $400, and crediting _Fees Receivable_ for $_200_ and _Earned mgt fees_ for $_200_ .

11 On December 31, Year 4, the accountant of Morrow Company made an adjusting entry to accrue salaries expense through year-end. The appropriate reversing entry should consist of a debit to _Salaries payable_ and a credit to _Salary exp_ and should be dated _Janway , 1_ .

Multiple Choice

Choose the best answer for each of the following

questions and enter the identifying letter in the space provided.

1 An adjusting entry should never consist of:
a A debit to an asset and a credit to revenue.
b A debit to an asset and a credit to a liability.
c A debit to expense and a credit to a liability.
d A debit to a liability and a credit to revenue.

2 Assets would be overstated if a necessary adjusting entry were omitted for:
a Expired insurance.
b Accrued salaries.
c Accrued interest earned.
d Revenue collected in advance during the period.

3 The preparation of a work sheet:
a Constitutes creation of a formal financial statement.
b Eliminates the need for entering adjusting entries in the journal.
c Provides the information needed for journalizing adjusting and closing entries.
d Serves no purposes unless the books are to be closed.

4 The entry recording the liability to employees for work done during the period for which they have not yet been paid is an example of which type of adjusting entry?
a Recorded costs.
b Recorded revenue.
c Unrecorded expenses.
d Unrecorded revenue.

5 Both the accounts for Depreciation Expense and Accumulated Depreciation:
a Are closed at the end of the period.
b Appear in the Trial Balance columns of the work sheet.
c Appear in the Adjusted Trial Balance columns of the work sheet.
d Appear in the after-closing trial balance.

6 Failure to make an adjusting entry to recognize accrued interest receivable would cause:
a An understatement of assets, net income, and owners' equity.

b An understatement of liabilities and an overstatement of net income and owners' equity.
c An overstatement of assets, net income, and owners' equity.
d No effect on assets, liabilities, net income, and owners' equity.

7 Which of the following adjusting entries will result in a decrease in assets and owners' equity?
a The entry to record the earned portion of rent received in advance.
b The entry to record accrued wages payable.
c The entry to record a revenue earned but not yet received.
d None of the above.

8 A balance sheet account was debited in the amount of $1,240 for office supplies purchased during the first year of operations. At year-end, the office supplies on hand were counted and determined to represent a cost of $360. The appropriate adjusting entry would:
a Have no effect on net income.
b Consist of a debit to expense of $360 and a credit to the balance sheet account.
c Decrease assets of $1,240.
d Increase expenses $880.

9 Which of the following amounts appears in both the Income Statement credit column and the Balance Sheet debit column of a work sheet?
a Net income.
b Net loss.
c Accumulated depreciation.
d Dividends.

10 When a work sheet is used, the normal sequence of accounting procedures would call for:
a Journalizing the adjusting entries before preparing the work sheet.
b Posting adjusting entries to the ledger after preparing an after-closing trial balance.
c Preparing a work sheet before journalizing adjusting and closing entries.
d Journalizing closing entries before preparing an adjusted trial balance.

Exercise

1 Use the following adjustments to complete the work sheet below for the month ended June 30, 19___ .

a Unexpired insurance at June 30 amounted to $300.

b Office supplies on hand were determined by count to amount to $250.

c The office equipment is being depreciated on the basis of a 10-year life with no salvage value. Record one month's depreciation.

d Accrued interest on notes payable at June 30 amounted to $50.

e Commissions still unearned at June 30 amounted to $700.

f Accrued salaries payable at June 30 were $200.

	Trial Balance Debit	Credit	Adjustments Debit	Credit	Adjusted Trial Balance Debit	Credit	Income Statement Debit	Credit	Balance Sheet Debit	Credit
Cash	5,100				5,100				5,100	
Accounts receivable	17,300				17,300				17,300	
Unexpired insurance	360			a 60	300				300	
Office supplies	900			b 650	250				250	
Office equipment	4,800				4,800				4,800	
Accumulated depreciation: office equipment		560		c 40		600				600
Notes payable		8,000				8,000				8,000
Accounts payable		1,800				1,800				1,800
Unearned commissions		1,500	800			700				700
Capital stock		9,000				9,000				9,000
Retained earnings, June 1, 19___		7,000				7,000				7,000
Dividends	2,000				2,000				2,000	
Commissions earned		16,000	e 800	800		16,800		16,800		
Rent expense	2,400				2,400		2,400			
Salaries expense	11,000		200		11,200		11,200			
	43,860	43,860			45,150	45,960				
Insurance expense			a 60		60		60			
Office supplies expense			b 650		650		650			
Depreciation expense: office equipment			c 40		40		40			
Interest expense			d 50		50		50			
Interest payable				d 50		50				50
Salaries payable				200		200				200
Net income							44,150	2,400		2,400
									29,750	29,750

2 On the journal page below, prepare adjusting and closing entries using the information contained in the work sheet prepared in Exercise 1.

General Journal

19___		Adjusting Entries		
		a		
June	30	Ins Exp	60	
		Unexpired Ins		60
		b		
	30	Office Supplies Exp	650	
		Office Supplies		650
		c		
	30	Depreciation Exp	40	
		Accum Dep		40
		d		
	30	Interest Exp	50	
		Interest Payable		50
		e		
	30	Unearned Comm	800	
		Earned Comm		800
		f		
	30	Salary Exp	200	
		Salaries Payable		200
		Closing Entries		
	30	Commission Earned	16800	
		Income Summary		16800
		Income Summary	14460	
		Salary expense		11200
		Rent expense		2400
		Ins Exp		60
		Off Supplies Exp		650
		Dep Exp		40
		Int. Exp		50
		Income Summary	2400	
		Retained Earn		2400
		Retained Earnings	2000	
		Dividends		2000

5

ACCOUNTING FOR PURCHASES AND SALES OF MERCHANDISE

HIGHLIGHTS OF THE CHAPTER

1 A merchandising company is one whose principal activity is buying and selling merchandise. It uses the same accounting concepts and methods as the service-type business we studied in Chapters 1 to 4. The merchandising company, however, requires some other accounts and techniques to control and record the purchase and sale of merchandise.

2 The principal source of revenue for a merchandising company is from the sale of goods. To succeed, it must sell its goods at prices higher than the prices paid in acquiring those goods from manufacturers or other suppliers. The selling price of goods in a retail store must cover both (a) the cost of the goods to the store and (b) the operating expenses, such as rent and advertising, and still leave a reasonable profit (net income).

3 The *revenue* of a merchandising company comes from *selling goods to customers*. A sale of merchandise is recorded by debiting Cash or Accounts Receivable and crediting a revenue account called *Sales*.

4 The customers of the merchandising company concern may occasionally find that the goods they bought are unsatisfactory, and return them to the store. This is called a *sales return*. Sales returns are recorded by debiting *Sales Returns and Allowances* and crediting either the customer's account or Cash.

5 The seller may offer a *cash discount* to encourage customers to pay invoices early. Thus, credit terms of *2/10, n/30* would mean the customers may take a deduction of 2% of their invoices if they pay within 10 days. Otherwise, they have 30 days to pay the full amount of the invoices. A cash discount is called a *sales discount* by the seller and a *purchase discount* by the buyer.

6 The seller records a sales discount by debiting an account called Sales Discounts and crediting Accounts Receivable. In the income statement, both the Sales Discounts and the Sales Returns and Allowances accounts are deducted from Sales to show a *net sales* figure.

7 In a multiple-step income statement (see Highlight 29), the *cost of goods sold* is deducted from the net sales figure to determine the amount of *gross profit*. Gross profit is the *excess* of the sales price of goods sold over the seller's cost for those goods. Gross profit often is expressed as a *percentage of net sales* which is called the *gross profit rate*.

8 An *inventory* of merchandise consists of the stock of goods on hand and *available for sale* to customers. There are two alternative approaches to determine the amount of inventory and the cost of goods sold: (a) the *perpetual inventory method* and (b) the *periodic inventory method*.

9 For articles of high unit value, such as automobiles, the *perpetual inventory method* is appropriate. Under this method, the *Inventory* account is debited when merchandise is purchased. As each unit is sold, its cost is transferred from the Inventory account to an account called *Cost of Goods Sold*. Thus we have a perpetual or running

record of the cost of goods sold during the period and the cost of goods on hand. In this chapter we will concentrate on the *periodic inventory method*, which is very widely used.

10 Under the *periodic inventory system*, the cost of merchandise acquired is debited to an account entitled *Purchases*, instead of being debited to Inventory. As units are sold, *no entry is made to record the cost of the goods sold*: Thus, the accounting records do not show from day to day the cost of the goods on hand (inventory) or the cost of goods sold during the period. Instead, the value of the inventory is determined *at the end of each accounting period* by taking a *physical count* of the merchandise in stock.

11 The *cost of goods sold* is computed by the following steps:

a Add the goods on hand at the beginning of the period (the ending inventory from last period plus any additional goods acquired during the period (purchases) to get the *cost of goods available for sale*.

b From the cost of goods available for sale, subtract the goods which were not sold (namely, the inventory on hand at the end of the current period) to get the *cost of goods sold* during the period.

12 The cost of goods sold section of the income statement of a merchandising company using the *periodic inventory method* would appear as follows for the month of May:

Cost of goods sold:	
Inventory (Apr. 30)	$ 5,100
Purchases	6,300
Cost of goods available for sale	$11,400
Less: Inventory (May 31)	5,400
Cost of goods sold	$ 6,000

13 Several other factors may have to be considered in computing the cost of goods sold. For example, when merchandise purchased is found to be unsatisfactory and returned to the supplier, the return is recorded by debiting Accounts Payable and crediting *Purchase Returns and Allowances*. Purchase Returns and Allowances must then be *deducted* from Purchases in the cost of goods sold section of the income statement because the cost of goods that were returned to the supplier should not be included in the cost of goods available for sale.

14 If merchandise is paid for within the discount period, the buyer may take advantage of the cash discount. For example, if $1,000 of merchandise is purchased on terms of 2/10, n/30, the buyer may take a 2% purchase discount ($20) if payment is made within 10 days. The buyer records a purchase discount by debiting Accounts Payable and crediting Purchase Discounts. Since a purchase discount reduces the cost of purchased merchandise, the Purchase Discounts account is deducted from Purchases in arriving at the cost of goods available for sale.

15 The freight charges on goods acquired during the period are a legitimate part of the cost of goods available for sale. Freight charges on *inbound* shipments of merchandise are recorded by debiting an account called *Transportation-in*. Transportation-in must then be added to Purchases to determine the total cost of goods acquired during the period. *Note*: Do not confuse Transportation-in with the freight expense on *outbound* shipments. Freight on outbound shipments is a selling expense, not part of the cost of goods being acquired.

16 Look at an expanded cost of goods sold section, including Purchase Returns and Allowances, Purchase Discounts, and Transportation-in, in your textbook (page 170).

17 Note that the income statement illustrated in your text includes a deduction for *income taxes expense*. A corporation is a legal entity subject to corporate income taxes. Income taxes are based upon the corporation's before-tax earnings and are recorded by an adjusting entry at the end of each period. This adjusting entry consists of a debit to Income Taxes Expense and a credit to Income Taxes Payable.

18 In a work sheet for a merchandising business, the ending inventory does not appear in the trial balance. It is written on a line below the trial balance and the adjustments. The amount of the ending inventory is placed in the Income Statement credit column and in the Balance Sheet debit column. This treatment results in reporting the ending inventory in the income statement (cost of goods sold section) and in the balance sheet among the assets.

19 Closing entries for a merchandising business include entries to (a) eliminate the beginning inventory, (b) record the ending inventory,

and (c) close the accounts relating to the sales and purchases of merchandise.

20 The beginning inventory is cleared out of the Inventory account by a debit to Income Summary and a credit to Inventory. The ending inventory is brought on the books by a debit to Inventory and a credit to Income Summary.

21 Purchases, Transportation-in, Sales Returns and Allowances, and Sales Discounts have *debit* balances and are closed in the same entry that closes the *expense* accounts. Purchase Returns and Allowances, and Purchase Discounts have *credit* balances and are closed with the *revenue* accounts.

22 Standard *classifications* are used on financial statements to make them easier to read and more informative. Standard classifications help the banker and investor in making comparisons between companies.

23 On the balance sheet, assets are usually classified into three groups: current assets, plant and equipment, and other assets. *Current assets* consist of cash and items capable of being *converted into cash* within a short period without interfering with normal business operations. Examples are marketable securities, receivables, inventories, and prepaid expenses.

24 Liabilities are divided between current and long-term. Those debts which must be paid within one year or the *operating cycle* (whichever is longer) are called *current liabilities*. Those maturing at more distant dates are long-term. Accounts payable and accrued wages payable are examples of current liabilities.

25 The operating cycle is the period of time a business usually takes to perform its function of buying (or making) inventory, selling that inventory, and collecting the accounts receivable generated by those sales. This may be described as the period of time a business takes to convert cash into inventory, into accounts receivable, and then back into cash, as illustrated by the following diagram of the operating cycle.

(buy inventory) (sell inventory) (collect receivables)

Cash→Inventory→Accounts Receivable→Cash

26 Current assets and liabilities are used to measure a firm's *solvency*, or debt-paying ability.

One measure of solvency is the *current ratio*. The current ratio is computed by dividing the total of current assets by total current liabilities. A current ratio of about 2 to 1 is generally considered indicative of reasonable debt-paying ability.

27 Another measure of solvency is the amount of *working capital*. Working capital is the *excess* of current assets over current liabilities (current assets *minus* current liabilities).

28 In the income statement, operating expenses are classified as either *selling expenses* or *administrative expenses*. The amount of detail appearing in an income statement depends upon whether the statement is prepared in a multiple-step or a single-step format.

29 In a *multiple-step* income statement, costs and expenses are deducted from revenue in a series of steps. First, the cost of goods sold is deducted to arrive at gross profit. Next, operating expenses are deducted to determine the Income from Operations. Finally, income taxes are deducted to determine net income. A multiple-step income statement is illustrated on page 170 of your text. In a *single-step* income statement, all costs and expenses are deducted from total revenue in one single step. An illustration appears on page 182 of your text.

30 A system of internal control consists of all steps taken to (a) safeguard assets against waste, fraud, or inefficient use; (b) ensure reliability in accounting data; (c) promote compliance with company policies; and (d) evaluate the level of performance in all divisions of the business. In short, a system of internal control consists of all measures taken by management to provide assurance that everything goes according to plan.

31 Internal controls may be classified into two categories:

a *Accounting controls*   These are the internal controls which have a direct bearing upon the reliability of the financial statements. Accounting controls include the measures concerned with safeguarding assets, authorizing and approving transactions, and the reliability of accounting data. An example of an accounting control is the requirement that a person whose duties include handling cash shall not be responsible for maintaining accounting records.

b *Administrative controls*   These are internal controls that apply primarily to operational efficiency and compliance with company policies but have *no* direct bearing upon the reliability of the financial statements. Examples of administrative controls include rules that no employees be required to work more than a specified number of consecutive hours and policies regarding refunds and exchanges of merchandise by customers.

32 The Foreign Corrupt Practices Act of 1977 requires large corporations to maintain a system of internal control which provides assurance that transactions are executed only with the knowledge and authorization of management. Also, the act requires periodic comparisons of accounting records for assets with assets actually on hand. The purpose of these requirements is to prevent the creation of secret "slush funds" or other misuses of corporate assets. Thus, a strong system of internal control is not required by federal law.

33 No "standard" system of internal control can be designed to fit all businesses; each system must be "tailor-made" to fit the needs of the organization. However, there are several basic concepts of internal control which apply to most businesses. These include:

a *A logical organization plan* This should clearly indicate the departments or persons responsible for such functions as purchasing, receiving incoming shipments, maintaining accounting records, handling cash, and approving customers' credit. A separate person (or department) should be responsible for each function. Lines of responsibility and authority can be shown by an *organization chart*.

b *Adequate subdivision of duties* No one person should handle all aspects of a transaction from beginning to end. When several people are involved in each transaction, the work of one employee tends to serve as a check upon the work of another. Each transaction should go through four steps: it should be *authorized, approved, executed*, and *recorded*. Internal control is strengthened when each of these steps is handled by a different employee (or department).

c *Use of serially numbered documents* Most business documents, such as invoices, checks, and sales tickets, are serially numbered by the printer. The serial numbers help keep track of all documents. Without serial numbers on the documents, no one would know how many had been written or whether some had been lost or concealed.

d *Personnel with competence and integrity* No system of internal control will work unless the people assigned to operate it are competent.

e *Preparation of financial forecasts* Internal control is strengthened by the use of financial forecasts because errors or irregularities which cause actual results to differ from planned results will be identified and investigated.

f *An internal audit staff* Internal auditors have as their objective improving the operational efficiency of the business. They continuously study and evaluate both accounting and administrative controls and make recommendations to management for improving the system. All large businesses have an internal audit staff.

34 Strong internal control is more difficult to achieve in a small business than in a large one, because with only a few employees it is not possible to have extensive subdivision of duties. Even the smallest businesses, however, should follow such control procedures as using serially numbered documents and separating the responsibility for maintaining accounting records from responsibility for handling cash. Active participation by the owner in the key control procedures also strengthens internal control in a small business.

35 Although strong internal control is highly effective in protecting assets and increasing the reliability of accounting data, no system of internal control is foolproof. *Collusion* between two or more employees can defeat the system. Carelessness or misunderstandings can cause breakdowns in the system. Also, a system of internal control should not be so elaborate that its cost exceeds the value of the protection gained.

36 While strong internal control calls for the division of duties between departments, it is necessary for these departments to know what the other departments are doing so that they may work efficiently together. Carefully designed business documents are used to coordinate the efforts of the departments and ensure that all transactions are properly authorized, approved, and recorded.

37 *A purchase order* should always be prepared by the purchasing department whenever

goods are ordered. One copy of the purchase order is sent to the supplier; this is the supplier's authorization to send the goods. Carbon copies of the purchase order go to the receiving department and the accounting department.

38 The seller of the goods prepares an *invoice* when a purchase order is received. The invoice describes the quantities and prices of goods which will be sent to the buyer. From the viewpoint of the seller an invoice is a *sales invoice*; from the buyer's viewpoint it is a *purchase invoice*. The seller mails the invoice to the buyer at the same time the goods are shipped. At the time the invoice is issued the seller of the goods will record the sale.

39 The goods will arrive at the receiving department of the buyer. The receiving department will inspect the goods as to quality, condition, and quantities received. A *receiving report* is then prepared and sent to the accounting department.

40 The accounting department will then verify the invoice to see if payment should be made. Verifying an invoice consists of three basic steps:

a Comparing the invoice with the purchase order to see that the goods were actually ordered at the terms stated on the invoice.

b Comparing the receiving report with the purchase order and invoice to see that all the goods were received in satisfactory condition.

c Verifying the arithmetic extensions and footings of the invoice.

41 If any discrepancy exists between the amount the buyer is willing to pay and the amount of the invoice, the buyer will send a *debit* or *credit memorandum* to the seller. This is notice to the seller that the buyer is debiting (reducing) or crediting (increasing) the *account payable on the buyer's books*. The seller will respond with a debit or credit memorandum to show that the corresponding *account receivable on the selling company's books* is being debited (increased) or credited (decreased).

42 Most companies follow a policy of taking all available purchase discounts. The buyer may record purchases involving a purchase discount by using either (a) the gross price method or (b) the net price method.

43 Under the *gross price method*, the buyer records an account payable at the full invoice price and records payment within the discount period by debiting Accounts Payable and crediting Cash and Purchase Discounts. This method was discussed in Highlight **14**.

44 Under the alternative *net price method*, the buyer records the account payable at the invoice price *minus the discount*, which is called the *net price*. Payment within the discount period is then recorded merely by debiting Accounts Payable and crediting Cash for the amount paid. However, when the buyer fails to pay within the discount period, he or she will have to pay an amount *greater* than the balance of the account payable. When this occurs, the buyer should debit Accounts Payable for net price, debit *Purchase Discounts Lost* for the amount of the discount not taken, and credit Cash for the amount of the payment.

45 The gross price method results in recording purchase discounts *taken*, which is deducted from Purchases in the income statement, just like Purchase Returns and Allowances. If the net price method is used, Purchase Discounts Lost shows the discounts *not taken* and appears in the income statement as an operating expense. The net price method has the advantage of directing management's attention to the company's failure to follow the policy of taking all purchase discounts.

TEST YOURSELF ON ACCOUNTING FOR PURCHASES AND SALES OF MERCHANDISE

True or False

For each of the following statements, circle the T or the F to indicate whether the statement is true or false.

T F **1** Gross profit is the profit the business would have made if all the goods available for sale had been sold during the period.

T F **2** When a cash sale is made by a merchandising business, the transaction is described by a debit to Cash and a credit to Sales, whether or not the sales price exceeded the cost of the goods sold.

T (F) **3** The purchase of either merchandise or office equipment by a merchandising concern would be recorded as a debit to Purchases and a credit to either Cash or Accounts Payable.

(T) F **4** The perpetual inventory method will reflect from day to day the cost of goods sold so far during the period and the current balance of goods on hand.

(T) F **5** The perpetual inventory system is appropriate for businesses handling high unit-cost goods, such as automobiles or fur coats, but is less practical for stores handling a large quantity of low-priced items.

T (F) **6** When the periodic inventory method is used, the Inventory account is debited when merchandise is purchased and credited when goods are sold.

(T) F **7** The Transportation-in account contains the freight charges paid on inbound shipments of merchandise and is added to the Purchases account as a step toward finding the cost of goods available for sale.

(T) F **8** When a periodic inventory system is in use, the cost of goods sold section contains two amounts for Inventory: a beginning inventory which is added in arriving at the cost of goods available for sale, and an ending inventory which is subtracted to determine the cost of goods sold.

(T) F **9** At the end of the period, the beginning inventory is eliminated by debiting Income Summary and crediting Inventory.

(T) F **10** The beginning inventory figure on this period's income statement was the ending inventory figure on last period's income statement.

(T) F **11** The entry to place the ending inventory on the books consists of a debit to Inventory and a credit to Accounts Payable.

(T) F **12** In the work sheet the ending inventory amount will appear in the Income Statement credit column and the Balance Sheet debit column but will not appear in the Trial Balance columns.

T (F) **13** Income taxes expense appears only in a multiple-step income statement.

T (F) **14** Sound internal control would call for the same employee to keep all the accounting records and handle all cash transactions so that responsibility for cash shortages could be attached to one person.

T (F) **15** When internal control is weak, the financial statements are always in error.

T (F) **16** Subdivision of duties to achieve strong internal control means that many employees should be authorized to make purchases or payment for purchases.

T (F) **17** In a strong system of internal control, losses from fraud or embezzlement are impossible.

(T) F **18** Collusion between two or more employees can cause a breakdown in internal control.

(T) F **19** It is easier to achieve strong internal control in a large business than in a small one.

T F **20** Comparing the purchase invoice to the purchase order provides assurance that all goods ordered have been received in satisfactory condition.

T (F) **21** The invoice is prepared by the buyer of the goods and a copy is sent to the seller.

(T) F **22** Comparing the purchase order to the receiving report will show that all the goods ordered actually arrived and that all goods that arrived were actually ordered.

T (F) **23** The employee who authorized the purchase of merchandise should inspect the merchandise on arrival and prepare a receiving report.

T (F) **24** 2/10, n/30 means that a customer is entitled to a 10% discount if the invoice is paid within two days, or the whole amount may be paid within 30 days.

T (F) **25** The operating cycle of a business is the period of time between payroll dates.

(T F) **26** Prepaid expenses are part of a firm's *True* working capital.

(T) F **27** When the net price method is used to record purchases of merchandise, the buyer's accounting records will show the amount of purchase discounts lost, rather than the amount of purchase discounts taken.

(T) F **28** When a customer pays an amount which includes sales tax, part of the total receipts represent a liability account rather than revenue.

Completion Statements

Fill in the necessary words to complete the following statements:

1 The Inventory account is debited when goods are acquired and credited when they are sold according to the _perpetual_ inventory method. Inventory is determined by a _physical count_ when the _periodic_ inventory method is used.

2 The excess of sales revenue over the cost of goods sold is called _net gross profit_ .

3 Under the periodic inventory system, the journal entry to eliminate beginning inventory involves a _credit_ to the Inventory account and a _debit_ to the _Income Summary_ account. The entry to enter ending inventory involves a debit to the _Inventory_ account and a credit to the _Income Summary_ account.

4 There are two ways to account for state sales taxes: either (a) credit a _liability_ account for the amount of the tax at the time of sale or (b) wait until the end of the period and transfer the total tax owed out of the _Sales_ account and into an account called _Sales Tax Payable_ .

5 In a classified balance sheet, the three groups of assets are: (a) _current assets_, (b) _plant and equipment_, and (c) _other_ .

6 The amount by which current assets exceed current liabilities is called _working capital_ . Current assets divided by current liabilities is called the _current ratio_ . These two computations are made to measure the _solvency_ of a business enterprise.

7 Internal controls which have no direct bearing upon the reliability of the financial statements are called _management_ controls, and internal controls which relate to safeguarding assets and promoting the reliability of accounting data are called _accting_ controls.

8 Factors contributing to strong internal control include adequate _div't_ of duties, a logical _organization_

plan, use of _____ _____ documents, and an _____ _____ staff.

9 Comparison of the _purchase order_ with the _receiving report_ shows whether the same quantity and quality of goods were received as had been ordered.

10 The seller of goods prepares a _sales_ invoice and mails one copy to the buyer. The buyer refers to this document as a _purchase_ invoice, and compares it with the _receiving report_ to see that the seller is providing the same goods at the same terms the buyer has agreed to pay.

11 When the buyer returns some damaged merdise to the seller, he will also send the seller a _debit_ memorandum . If the seller accepts the return goods as partial settlement of the buyer's account, he will send a _credit_ memorandum to the buyer.

12 Jade Company uses the net price method to record the purchase of merchandise with an invoice price of $5,000, at terms of 2/10, n/30. If payment is not made until *after* the discount period, the issuance of the check should be recorded by a debit to Accounts Payable for $ _4900_ , a _debit_ to _discounts lost_ for $ _100_ , and a credit to Cash for $ _5000_ .

Multiple Choice

Choose the best answer for each of the following questions and enter the identifying letter in the space provided.

___ 1 Which of the following list of accounts is used to compute the cost of goods sold?
a Purchases, Inventory, and Sales Returns and Allowances.
b Gross Profit, Purchase Returns and Allowances, and Transportation-in.
c Inventory, Net Sales, and Purchases.
d None of the above.

___ 2 By adding the purchases during the period to the beginning inventory and deducting the ending inventory, we obtain an amount called the:
a Cost of goods available for sale.
b Cost of goods sold.
c Gross profit on sales.
d Operating expenses.

___ **3** The ending inventory of Bar Marine was $42,000. If the beginning inventory had been $50,000 and the cost of goods available for sale during the period totaled $104,000, the cost of goods sold must have been:

a $196,000

b $112,000

c $ 62,000

d None of the above

___ **4** The beginning inventory is removed from the books by a closing entry which:

a Debits Inventory and credits Income Summary.

b Debits Income Summary and credits Inventory.

c Debits Inventory and credits Cost of Goods Sold.

d Debits Cost of Goods Sold and credits Inventory.

___ **5** The net sales of Austin Saddlery were $200,000 for the current month. If the cost of goods available for sale was $180,000 and the gross profit rate was 35%, the ending inventory must have been:

a $70,000

b $130,000

c $50,000

d $63,000

___ **6** Gourmet Groceries purchased canned goods at an invoice price of $1,000 and terms of 2/10, n/30. Half of the goods were mislabeled and therefore were returned immediately to the supplier. If Gourmet Groceries pays the invoice within the discount period, the amount paid will be:

a $1,000

b $980

c $480

d $490

___ **7** The Toy Castle, a retail toy store, had current assets of $72,000 and a current ratio of 2 to 1. The amount of working capital must have been:

a $144,000

b $108,000

c $72,000

d $36,000

___ **8** Internal control over purchases is strengthened when the functions of ordering and receiving merchandise are performed:

a By two separate departments.

b By the accounting department.

c By a department which has no responsibilities other than purchasing and receiving merchandise.

d By serially numbered employees.

___ **9** If the seller ships goods to a customer but charges more than the customer had expected to pay, the discrepancy should come to light when:

a The purchase order is compared with the purchase invoice.

b The receiving report is compared with the purchase invoice.

c The receiving report is compared with the purchase order.

d The purchase invoice is compared with the sales invoice.

___ **10** The company receiving a shipment of goods might send a credit memorandum to the supplier if:

a Some of the goods were damaged.

b The purchase invoice was understated.

c The shipment was late.

d The purchase invoice was overstated.

___ **11** The principal advantage of using the net price method in recording purchases is that:

a The goods cost less.

b The accounting records will draw attention to the failure to take available discounts.

c The buyer's accounting records will agree with those of the seller.

d It is not necessary to pay within the discount period in order to take advantage of the discount.

Exercises

1 Insert the missing figures in the following income statement. Gross profit is 40% of net sales and net income is 10% of net sales.

Sales			$ *161,000*
Sales returns & allowances		$ 4,500	
Sales discounts		1,500	*6000*
Net sales			$ *155,000*
Cost of goods sold:			
Inventory, Jan. 1			$ 22,000
Purchases		$ 98,500	
Transportation-in		3,600	
Delivered cost of purchases		$ *102,100*	
Purchase returns & allowances	$3,100		
Purchase discounts	2,000	*5,100*	
Net purchases			*97,000*
Cost of goods available for sale			$ *119,000*
Inventory, Dec. 31			26,000
Cost of goods sold			*93,000*
Gross profit on sales			$ 62,000
Operating expenses			*46,500*
Net income			$ *15,500*

2 Fill in the missing amounts, discounts, or credit terms to complete the following schedule of the Gitane Company's purchases:

Invoice Number	Invoice Date	List Price	Trade Discount	Purchase Price	Credit Terms	Date Paid	Amount Paid
2071	July 17	$1,000	40%	$ *600*	2/10, n/30	Aug. 16	$ *600*
42	July 24	500	*20%*	400	*2/10* n/30	Aug. 3	392
4286	Aug. 5	*1600*	25%	1,200	5/20, n/60	Aug. 25	*1140*
0093	Aug. 12	640	None	*640*	10 eom	Sept. 10	*640*
1249	Aug. 23	2,000	50%	*1000*	2/10, n/30	Sept. 2	*980*
8163	Sept. 3	240	25%	*180*	*10 eom*	Oct. 10	180

$$LP - (P(D\omega)) = 1200$$

$$LP - .25(LP) = 1200$$

$$.75 LP = 1200$$

6

ACCOUNTING SYSTEMS: MANUAL AND EDP

HIGHLIGHTS OF THE CHAPTER

1 In the preceding chapters we have used the general journal entry as a tool for analyzing the effects of various financial transactions upon business entities. Although the general journal entry is an effective analytical tool, it is not the fastest way to record a large number of transactions. Every general journal entry requires writing at least two account titles and an explanation of the transaction, as well as posting at least two amounts to the ledger. Since many businesses engage in thousands of individual transactions every day, it is often necessary to streamline the recording process to save time and labor.

2 A *manual data processing system* is a means of providing increased speed and economy in the accounting process without using costly business machines or computers. This type of system *groups transactions* into like classes and uses a *special journal* for each class. This permits division of labor and specialization because each special journal can be maintained by a different employee. Time is also saved because special journals are designed to handle transactions with much less writing and posting than is necessary in the general journal.

3 About 80 or 90% of all transactions fall into four types. These four types and the corresponding special journals are shown at the top of the next column.

Type of Transaction	Name of Special Journal
Sales of merchandise *on credit*	Sales journal
Purchase of merchandise *on credit*	Purchases journal
Receipts of cash	Cash receipts journal
Payments of cash	Cash payments journal

Any transaction not falling into one of the above four types will be recorded in the *general journal*.

4 The *sales journal* is used to record all transactions which are a debit to Accounts Receivable and a credit to Sales (sales on credit). Columns are provided for the date, customer's name, invoice number, and amount of sale. At the end of the month the amount column is totaled and the *total* posted as a debit to Accounts Receivable and a credit to Sales. Detailed postings are made throughout the month to accounts of individual customers in the *accounts receivable subsidiary ledger*.

5 In prior chapters we have assumed that all sales on credit to customers were posted as debits to a single account called Accounts Receivable. Now, with our revised assumption of large volume (perhaps hundreds of customers), we divide the ledger into three separate ledgers: (a) an *accounts receivable subsidiary ledger* with a page for each customer, (b) an *accounts payable subsidiary*

ledger with a page for each creditor, and (c) a *general ledger* containing all accounts except those with individual customers and creditors.

6   When the accounts with individual customers are placed in a separate ledger, a single account with the title of Accounts Receivable continues to be maintained in the general ledger. This *controlling account* represents the *sum* of all the customers' accounts in the subsidiary ledger. A controlling account called Accounts Payable is also maintained in the general ledger representing all the accounts with creditors which form the accounts payable subsidiary ledger. The general ledger still is in balance since all the individual receivable and payable accounts are represented by these two controlling accounts.

7   The *purchases journal* is used to record all purchases of merchandise *on credit*. At the end of the month the journal is totaled and the total is posted to the general ledger as a debit to Purchases and a credit to Accounts Payable. During the month individual postings are made on a current basis to accounts with individual creditors in the *accounts payable subsidiary ledger*.

8   The *cash receipts journal* is used to record *all transactions involving the receipt of cash*. Separate columns are established for cash and for other accounts frequently debited or credited in this type of transaction, such as Sales Discounts and Accounts Receivable. Debit and credit columns are provided for Other Accounts; we write in the name of any other account affected in these columns, and at the end of the month we make an individual posting to that account in the general ledger. The totals of the columns for Cash, Sales Discounts, Accounts Receivable, and Sales are posted to the general ledger at the end of the month.

9   The *cash payments journal* is used to record all transactions involving a cash payment. Separate columns are established for Cash and for accounts such as Purchase Discounts, Accounts Payable, and Purchases, which are frequently affected by a cash payment. Debit and credit columns are also provided for Other Accounts so that any account title required may be written in. The posting of the cash payments journal parallels that described for the cash receipts journal in paragraph 8 above.

10   Most transactions will be recorded in the four special journals we have described. Any transactions which do not affect cash or the purchase or sale of merchandise on credit will be entered in the general journal. Double posting will be required if a general journal entry affects accounts receivable or accounts payable. For example, when a customer returns merchandise for credit to his or her account, we post the credit to the accounts receivable controlling account in the general ledger and also to the individual customer's account in the accounts receivable subsidiary ledger.

11   Accounts with customers and creditors in the subsidiary ledgers are usually of the three-column, running balance type. The right-hand column shows the new balance after each debit or credit entry. Many companies also prefer this form of account for the general ledger.

12   *Posting references* provide a cross reference between ledgers and journals. We use the following symbols: *S*, sales journal; *P*, purchases journal; *CR*, cash receipts journal; *CP*, cash payments journal; and *J*, general journal. The symbol is combined with a number, so that in looking at any debit or credit entry in any ledger, we can identify the journal from which it came and the page number of that journal. (For example, *S7* as a posting reference in the accounts receivable subsidiary ledger would tell us that the debit to a customer's account came from page 7 of the sales journal.)

13   To prove that all ledgers are in balance at the end of the period, a trial balance of the general ledger is prepared, and in addition a list of the balances in each subsidiary ledger is prepared to prove that the total agrees with the related controlling account.

14   Many variations in special journals are possible. For example, a special column can be added for any account which is frequently debited or credited. An additional special journal can be created for any type of transaction which *occurs frequently*, such as sales returns by credit customers of a retail store.

15   Some businesses keep a file of invoices and post directly from these to the ledger accounts rather than copying data from invoices into a sales journal or a purchases journal. This system is called *direct posting from invoices*. At the end of the month the

file of invoices is totaled and a general journal entry is used to post the total to the controlling account in the general ledger.

16 Although a manual system of processing accounting data, strictly defined, would call for handwritten records, such machines as cash registers, multicopy forms, desk calculators, and other machines are used in many small businesses.

17 Computers can perform routine tasks, such as posting, arithmetic computations, and the preparation of schedules, with incredible speed and accuracy. The basic concepts of data processing, however, are the same in EDP systems as in manual systems.

18 Although EDP equipment is highly reliable, errors may still occur in computer output. Errors in input data, failure to record transactions, fraudulent human intervention, improper programming, and operator errors may all lead to errors in computer output.

19 A strong system of internal control is necessary to ensure the reliability of computer output. These internal controls should include *input controls* and *program controls*.
 a *Input controls* are the precautions taken to ensure that input data entered into the computer are correct. Two common input controls are the use of *control totals* and a *verifier key punch*.
 b *Program controls* (or processing controls) are error-detecting routines built into the computer program. An *item count* and a *limit* (or *reasonableness*) *test* are examples of program controls.

TEST YOURSELF ON DATA PROCESSING SYSTEMS

True or False

For each of the following statements, circle the T or the F to indicate whether the statement is true or false.

T F 1 Sale on credit of old office equipment no longer needed in the business would be recorded in the sales journal.

T F 2 The total of the Accounts Payable column in the cash payments journal is posted at the end of the month as a debit to Accounts Payable and a credit to Cash.

T F 3 The purchase of office supplies on credit is recorded in the purchases journal.

T F 4 Purchases of merchandise on credit are recorded in the purchases journal.

T F 5 The Accounts Receivable column in the cash receipts journal is intended for credit entries.

T F 6 When customers are permitted to return merchandise for credit to their accounts, the transactions are usually recorded in the general journal.

T F 7 The sale of merchandise for cash is recorded in the sales journal.

T F 8 The total of the Other Accounts column in the debit section of the cash receipts journal is not posted to the ledger.

T F 9 If a trial balance of the general ledger is in balance, this proves that each controlling account is in agreement with the related subsidiary ledger.

T F 10 A subsidiary ledger for accounts receivable is usually arranged in alphabetical order of customers' names.

T F 11 *Double posting* of a general journal entry crediting Accounts Receivable means posting the credit to the controlling account in the general ledger and to a customer's account in the subsidiary ledger.

T F 12 When special journals, controlling accounts, and subsidiary ledgers are used, no posting to any ledger is performed until the end of the month.

T F 13 The basic concepts of data processing are similar in both EDP systems and manual systems.

T F 14 The use of EDP equipment virtually eliminates the need to maintain a strong system of internal control.

T F 15 Computer output will always be correct unless the computer malfunctions.

T F 16 One input control is to have the computer add up the dollar total of items being processed and compare this sum with a predetermined control total.

T F 17 A *limit test* is a program control which will detect if any of the input data are missing.

T F 18 Computers are used to post accounts receivable and prepare payrolls but not to maintain journals and ledgers and prepare financial statements.

T F 19 A *limit test* and an *item count* would both be appropriate program controls in the preparation of weekly paychecks by computer.

Completion Statements

Fill in the necessary words to complete the following statements:

1 Special journals have the advantage of saving much time in journalizing and _____ .

2 When merchandise is purchased on credit, the transaction is recorded in the _____ _____ journal. If a portion of the merchandise is returned for credit to the supplier, the return is recorded in the _____ journal and the _____ side of the entry is double-posted.

3 The column total of the sales journal is posted at the end of the month as a _____ to _____ _____ and as a _____ to _____ .

4 Some companies do not use a sales journal but instead post directly from the _____ _____ to the customers' accounts in the accounts receivable ledger. When this is done, the _____ are totaled and an entry is made in the _____ journal debiting the Accounts Receivable _____ _____ account and crediting Sales.

5 Measures taken to assure the reliability of data entered into a computer system are termed _____ controls. Error detecting routines written into the computer program are called _____ controls.

6 The symbol (X) placed below a column total in the cash receipts journal or cash payments journal means the column total should _____ _____ _____ .

7 A business will usually benefit by establishing a special journal for any type of transaction that _____ _____ .

8 The amount of an employee's salary was accidentally keypunched as $8,000 instead of $800. A verifier key punch is not used. A computer preparing paychecks should detect this error because the total payroll will not agree with the _____ _____ _____ , and a _____ _____ should prevent an $8,000 item from being processed.

Multiple Choice

Choose the best answer for each of the following questions and enter the identifying letter in the space provided.

_____ 1 The total of a single-column purchases journal is posted at the end of the month:

a As a debit to Accounts Payable and a credit to Purchases.
b To the Purchases account, Cash account, and Sales account.
c To the Purchases account only.
d As a debit to Purchases and a credit to Accounts Payable.

_____ 2 The Rex Company records all transactions in a two-column general journal but is considering the installation of special journals. The number of sales on credit during January was 325 and the number of sales for cash was 275. Therefore:

a The use of a sales journal in January would have saved 324 postings to the Sales account.
b The use of a cash receipts journal would have reduced the number of postings to the Cash account but would not have affected the number of postings to the Sales account.
c The total number of transactions recorded in the sales journal (if one had been used in January) would have been 600, but only two postings would have been necessary from that journal.
d If special journals were installed, the entry to close the Sales and Purchases accounts at the end of the period would be made in the sales journal and the purchases journal, respectively.

_____ 3 The purchases journal is a book of original entry used to record:

a Purchase of any asset on credit.
b Purchase of merchandise for cash or on credit.
c Purchase of merchandise on credit only.
d Purchases and purchase returns and allowances.

_____ 4 A major advantage of controlling accounts is that their use makes it possible:

a To reduce the number of accounts in the general ledger.
b To determine on a daily basis the total amount due from customers and total amount owing to creditors.
c To reduce the number of entries in subsidiary ledgers.
d To increase the number of columns in special journals.

_____ 5 When a general journal and four special journals are in use, the entries in the Cash account will come:

a From all of the books of original entry.
b From the four special journals.
c From only two of the four special journals.
d Principally at month-end from adjusting and closing entries.

_____ 6 The cash receipts journal is used:

a For transactions involving a debit to Cash and debits or credits to other balance sheet accounts.
b For all transactions involving the receipt of cash, regardless of the number of other accounts involved.
c For transactions involving not more than two accounts.
d For transactions involving the receipt of cash but not affecting subsidiary ledgers.

_____ 7 Which of the following is *not* an advantage that can be achieved by an EDP system?

a Operating data can be made available to managers faster than with a manual system.
b The accuracy of EDP equipment eliminates the need for internal control.
c Sales transactions can be recorded instantaneously in the accounting records as the sales clerk rings up the sale on an electronic cash register.
d The need for manual labor to perform the posting function can virtually be eliminated.

_____ 8 Posting of accounts receivable with individual customers is done by computer. Credit sales totaling $19,742 were made to 809 customers. A key-punch operator made a keypunching error and recorded a $35 sale to Roger Jones at $53. Two controls which could detect this error are:

a An item count and a limit test.
b A limit test and a control total.
c A control total and a verifier key punch.
d A verifier key punch and an item count.

Exercises

1 For each of the following transactions, indicate the journal which should be used by placing the appropriate symbol in the space provided.

S = sales journal, *P* = purchase journal, *CR* = cash receipts journal, *CP* = cash payments journal, *J* = general journal

a	Sold merchandise on credit . . . .
b	Purchased merchandise for cash . . . .
c	Purchased truck for cash for use in business . . . . .
d	Collected account receivable and allowed a cash discount . . . .
e	Recorded depreciation for the period . . . .
f	Made entry to close the expense accounts at end of period . . . .
g	Accepted note receivable from customer in settlement of account receivable . . . .
h	Paid employee salaries . . . .
i	Made entry to accrue salaries at end of year . . . . .
j	Sold merchandise for cash . . . .
k	Purchased merchandise on credit . . . .
l	Returned merchandise to supplier for credit . . . .
m	Purchased office equipment on credit . . . .
n	Allowed customer to return merchandise for credit . . . .

2 For each of the following general ledger accounts indicate the source of debit and credit postings by entering a symbol representing the proper journal. Use the same code as in Exercise 1.

		Debit	Credit
a	Purchases		
b	Purchase Returns and Allowances		
c	Purchase Discounts		
d	Sales		
e	Sales Returns and Allowances		
f	Sales Discounts		
	Accounts Payable		
h	Accounts Receivable		
i	Cash		
j	Depreciation Expense		

7
CASH AND MARKETABLE SECURITIES

HIGHLIGHTS OF THE CHAPTER

1 The term *cash* includes currency, coin, checks, money orders, and money on deposit with banks. Items which a bank will *not* accept for deposit, such as postage stamps and postdated checks, are *not* included in cash. Cash is a current asset and the most liquid of all assets. A company may have numerous bank accounts plus cash on hand, but these will be lumped together to show a single figure for cash in the balance sheet.

2 Management's job with respect to cash includes (a) preventing loss from fraud or theft; (b) accounting for cash receipts, cash payments, and cash balances; and (c) always having enough cash to make necessary payments, but not excessive cash deposits which produce no revenue. To meet these objectives, management needs a strong system of internal control.

3 Cash offers the greatest temptation to theft, and this makes the problem of internal control especially important. Basic rules to achieve strong internal control over cash include:

a Separating the handling of cash from the maintenance of accounting records.

b Establishing specific and separate routines to be followed in handling cash receipts, making cash payments, and recording cash transactions.

c Depositing all cash receipts in the bank daily and making all payments by check.

d Requiring that every expenditure be verified and approved before payment is made.

e Separating the function of signing checks from the functions of approving expenditures and recording cash transactions.

4 *Cash receipts* may be received over the counter from customers or through the mail. All cash received over the counter should be promptly recorded on a cash register in plain view of the customer. Prenumbered sales tickets should be prepared in duplicate whenever possible. The participation of two employees in each cash receipts transaction is desirable. For example, one person opens the mail, prepares a list of checks received, and forwards one copy of the list to the accounting department and another copy with the checks to the cashier who will deposit them.

5 Good internal control over *cash disbursements* requires that all payments (except those from petty cash) be made by prenumbered checks. The officials authorized to sign checks should not have authority to approve invoices for payment or to make entries in the accounting records. Before an official signs a check, he should require that supporting documents justifying the payment be presented to him. These documents should be stamped "Paid," and the checks should be mailed without going back to the person who prepared them.

6 One widely used means of controlling cash disbursements is the *voucher system*. A *voucher* (a serially numbered form) is prepared for each expenditure. Approval signatures are placed on the voucher to show that the expenditure was authorized, the goods or services received, the invoice

prices verified, and the proper accounts debited and credited. A completed voucher must accompany every check submitted for signature. Before signing the check, the official authorized to make cash disbursements will review the voucher to determine that the expenditure has been approved.

7 Internal control is strong in a voucher system, because each expenditure must be verified and approved before a check is issued, and because the function of signing checks is separated from the functions of approving expenditures and recording cash transactions.

8 As previously stressed, it is desirable that all cash payments be made by check; however, in every business some small expenditures are necessary for which it is not practicable to issue checks. Taxi fares, collect telegrams, and postage stamps are common examples. To control these small payments not being made by check, almost every business establishes a *petty cash fund*. A check is written for perhaps $50 or $100 and is cashed, and the cash is kept on hand for use in making small expenditures. A receipt or *petty cash voucher* should be obtained and placed in the fund to replace each cash payment. Therefore the fund always contains a constant amount of cash and vouchers. The expenses are recorded in the accounts when the fund is replenished, perhaps every two or three weeks. The entry for the replenishment check will consist of debits to the proper expense accounts and a credit to Cash.

9 Each month the bank will provide the depositor with a *statement* of his or her account, showing the beginning balance, dates and amounts of deposits, deductions for checks paid, any other charges, and the ending balance. All paid checks are returned to the depositor with the bank statement. When numerous checks are being deposited daily, it is inevitable that occasionally one will *bounce*; that is, the drawer of the check will have insufficient funds on deposit to cover it. The check will be marked *NSF* (not sufficient funds), charged back against the depositor's account, and returned to the depositor. An NSF check should be regarded as a receivable rather than cash, until it is collected directly from the drawer, redeposited, or determined to be worthless.

10 The amount of cash which appears on the balance sheet of a business should be the correct amount of cash owned at the close of business on that date. To determine this amount, it is necessary to **reconcile** the monthly bank statement with the balance of cash as shown by the depositor's accounting records. The balance shown on the bank statement will usually not agree with that shown on the depositor's books because certain transactions will have been recorded by one party but not by the other. Examples are outstanding checks, deposits in transit, service charges, NSF checks, and errors by the bank or by the depositor.

11 The *bank reconciliation* will identify the items which cause the balance of cash per the books to differ from the balance shown on the bank statement, and it will show the adjusted or correct amount of cash. Those reconciling items which have not yet been recorded by the depositor (or which reflect errors on the depositor's part) must be entered on the books to make the accounting records correct and up-to-date at the end of the period.

12 Many companies invest cash not needed for current operations in high-grade marketable equity securities, such as government bonds and the bonds and stocks of large corporations. Investments in marketable equity securities are preferable to holding idle cash because of the interest or dividend revenue which they produce. Marketable equity securities may be purchased or sold at quoted market prices through organized securities exchanges, such as the *New York Stock Exchange*.

13 The market price of stocks is quoted in dollars per share. Bond prices are quoted as a *percentage* of the bond's maturity value (or face value), which usually is $1,000. Thus, a bond quoted at 102 has a market value of $1,020.

14 Investments in marketable equity securities originally are recorded in the accounting records at cost. Commissions paid to a broker for purchase of securities are included in cost of the investment. When investors buy bonds between interest-payment dates, they pay the current market price of the bond plus the interest accrued since the last interest date. This payment for interest is not part of the cost of the

bond, but is debited to a separate account and collected as part of the next semi-annual interest payment from the issuing corporation. Interest accrues from day to day on bonds, but dividends do not accrue on stock. Usually cash dividends are not recognized as earned until the date of receipt.

15 When marketable equity securities are sold, any difference between the sales price and the cost of the securities should be recognized as a gain or a loss. Since bonds sell at the quoted market price *plus accrued interest*, the seller will receive any interest which has accrued since the last interest payment date. When an investment in bonds is sold, the seller should credit *Interest Revenue* for any portion of the proceeds which represents accrued interest.

16 Gains and losses on the sale of marketable securities, as well as interest and dividends earned, are all nonoperating income. These items should be shown separately on the income statement after the determination of income from operations.

17 In the balance sheet, most companies classify their investments in marketable equity securities as current assets. If a company has a definite intention to hold certain securities on a long-term basis, however, it may elect to classify these securities as a noncurrent asset under a caption such as Long-Term Investments. When securities owned are *not readily marketable* or are held for the *purpose of exercising control* over the issuing company, they must be classified as long-term investments.

18 A short-term investment in bonds generally is carried in the accounting records at cost until the bonds are sold. If bonds are held as a long-term investment, the valuation procedures become more complex and will be discussed in Chapter 13.

19 Investments in marketable equity securities (stocks) are valued in the balance sheet at the *lower of aggregate cost or market value at the balance sheet date*. In applying this lower-of-cost-or-market rule, the total cost of the entire portfolio of marketable equity securities is compared with its cost, and the lower of these two amounts is used as the balance sheet valuation.

20 The carrying value of the portfolio is reduced to a market value below cost by an entry debiting *Unrealized Loss on Marketable Securities* and crediting *Valuation Allowance for Marketable Securities*. The loss from decline in market value is termed *unrealized* to distinguish it from a loss which is realized by an actual sale of the securities. The valuation allowance is a *contra-asset* account; it appears in the balance sheet as a *deduction from Marketable Securities*, thus reducing the carrying value of the portfolio to its market value.

21 The balance of the valuation allowance is adjusted at the end of every accounting period. If the valuation allowance must be increased because of further declines in market value, the adjusting entry will recognize an additional unrealized loss. If market prices have increased since the last balance sheet date, the adjusting entry will reduce or eliminate the valuation allowance and recognize an *unrealized gain*.

22 The amount of unrealized gain which can be recognized is limited to that which results from eliminating the credit balance of the valuation allowance. In brief, when marketable equity securities have been written down to a market value below cost, they can be written back up to original cost if the market prices recover. However, the rules of the FASB *do not* permit recognition of any market rises *above* original cost.

23 Lower-of-cost-or-market adjustments affect the carrying value of the portfolio as a whole, but do not change the carrying values of specific investments, within that portfolio. These adjustments, therefore, have *no effect* upon the gain or loss recognized when an investment is sold. When specific securities are sold, the gain or loss realized from the sale is determined by comparing the *cost* of the securities (without regard to lower-of-cost-or-market adjustment) to their selling price.

24 The lower-of-cost-or-market adjustments described above are *not acceptable* for determining income subject to income taxes. The only gains and losses recognized for income tax purposes are realized gains and losses resulting from sale of an investment.

25 The unrealized gains and losses resulting from application of the lower-of-cost-or-market rule are presented differently in the financial statements, depending upon wheth-

er the securities are classified as a current asset or a long-term investment. When the securities are considered a current asset, any unrealized gains or losses are shown in the income statement. Unrealized gains and losses on long-term investments *do not appear in the income statement;* they are closed directly into an account called Unrealized Loss on Long-Term Investments, which appears in the balance sheet as a *reduction in stockholders' equity*.

26 Many accountants are convinced that investments in securities should be valued in the balance sheet at *current market price*. This value is the most significant to the banker or other user of the balance sheet in judging financial strength and debt-paying ability. Moreover, the market value is readily obtainable and can be objectively verified. Remember, valuation of marketable equity securities at current market prices is *not* in accordance with current accounting practice.

TEST YOURSELF ON THE CONTROL OF CASH TRANSACTIONS

True or False

For each of the following statements, circle the T or the F to indicate whether the statement is true or false.

T F **1** The balance sheet item of Cash includes amounts on deposit with banks, and also currency, money orders, and customers' checks on hand.

T F **2** Reconciling a bank account means determining that all deductions shown on the bank statement represent checks issued by the depositor in the current period.

T F **3** No entry is made in the accounting records at the time a small payment is made from the petty cash fund.

T F **4** Internal control over cash should include measures to prevent fraud or loss, to provide accurate records of cash transactions, and to assure the maintenance of adequate but not excessive cash balances.

T F **5** Internal control over cash receipts is most effective when one person is made solely responsible for receiving and depositing cash and making related entries in the accounting records.

T F **6** All cash receipts should be deposited intact in the bank daily, and all material cash payments should be made by check.

T F **7** The purpose of preparing a bank reconciliation is to identify those items which cause the balance of cash per the bank statement to differ from the balance of cash per the ledger, and thereby to determine the correct cash balance.

T F **8** In preparing a bank reconciliation, outstanding checks should be deducted from the balance shown on the bank statement, and deposits in transit (or undeposited receipts) should be added to the bank balance.

T F **9** After preparing a bank reconciliation, journal entries should be made to record each of the items shown as adjustments to the balance per depositor's records.

T F **10** The Petty Cash account should be debited when the fund runs low and a check is drawn to replenish it.

T F **11** The principal advantage of a *voucher system* is that it provides strong internal control over the making of expenditures and the payment of liabilities.

T F **12** A voucher is a document which shows that the necessary steps to verify the propriety of an expenditure have been performed and that a cash disbursement is justified.

T F **13** The quoted market price of marketable securities is established every morning by an agency of the federal government.

T F **14** A company which has owned marketable equity securities for more than one year must classify the investment as a noncurrent asset.

T F **15** When an investment in bonds is sold between interest dates, the seller forfeits the interest which has accrued since the last interest payment date.

T F **16** Investments in marketable equity securities are valued at the lower of aggregate cost or market value, while investments in marketable debt securities generally are valued at cost.

T F **17** Jay Corporation purchased marketable equity securities at a cost of $1 million, but at the next balance sheet date the market value of the securities had dropped to $950,000. If Jay Corporation reduces the carrying value of the securities to market, it may deduct a $50,000 unrealized loss on its income tax return.

(T) F 18 An unrealized loss relating to an investment in marketable equity securities is deducted in the income statement if the investment is classified as a current asset, but does not reduce net income if the investment is classified as long-term.

(T) F 19 Interest revenue is recognized as it accrues, but dividend revenue generally is not recognized until the cash is received.

T F 20 Under the rules of the FASB, the amount of unrealized gain which an investor can recognize on an investment in marketable equity securities is limited to the amount of unrealized losses recognized in prior periods.

(T) F 21 Many accountants believe that investments in marketable securities should be shown in the balance sheet at current market value and that changes in market value should be recognized as gains and losses. However, this approach is not in accordance with current practice.

Completion Statements

Fill in the necessary words or amounts to complete the following statements:

1 An adequate system of internal control over cash should include separating the function of handling cash from the _posting of balance_ .

2 Cash frauds often begin with temporary unauthorized "borrowing" by employees of cash received from customers. One effective step in preventing such irregularities is to insist that each day's cash receipts be _____ _____ in the bank.

3 If duties relating to cash handling and the maintenance of accounting records are sufficiently subdivided so that the work of one person or department serves to verify that of another, then the permanent con-

cealment of fraud is possible only through the _joint collusion_ .

4 Among the most common reconciling items in a bank reconciliation are _outstanding Check_ , which should be deducted from the balance shown by the bank, and _unrecorded deposits_ , which should be added to the balance shown by the bank statement.

5 The abbreviation *NSF* applied to a check returned by a bank means _Not suff. funds_ , and calls for an entry on the depositor's books debiting _accts receivable_ .

6 In the preparation of a bank reconciliation, various reconciling items are added to or deducted from the balance per the bank statement or the balance per the depositor's records. Outstanding checks should be _sub from_ the balance per the _bank statement_ . Deposits in transit should be _added to_ the balance per the _bank statement_ . Bank service charges should be _subtracted_ the balance per the _deposits records_ . Collections made by the bank in behalf of the depositor should be _added to_ the balance per the _dep records_ .

7 When a voucher system is in use, the recording and payment of the monthly telephone bill would require two entries: (a) an entry in the _Voucher Reg_ debiting _tele expense_ and crediting _Voucher Payable_ ; and (b) an entry in the _Check Reg_ debiting _Voucher Payable_ and crediting _Cash_ .

8 In a voucher system, every cash disbursement must be authorized by personnel of the _accting_ department but the related check must be signed by an officer

of the _finance_ department. After a check is signed, it should be mailed directly to the _payee_ ; the related voucher should be _perforated_ and returned to the _accounting_ department.

9 The bonds of Artic Oil Co. are selling at a market price of $925. The market quotation as shown in the newspaper for these bonds would be _92 ½_ .

10 When a company purchases bonds between interest dates, the excess of its payment over the price of the bond and the commission will be debited to an account entitled _Accrued Bond Int., Receivable_ .

11 In managing an investment portfolio, an investor seeks to maximize _return_ while minimizing _risk_ . Purchasing securities of companies in different industries is called _Diversifying_ and is one means of reducing _risk_ .

Multiple Choice

Choose the best answer for each of the following questions and enter the identifying letter in the space provided.

_____ 1 Which of the following practices is undesirable from the standpoint of maintaining adequate internal control over cash?
a Appointing as custodian of a petty cash fund an employee who has no responsibility with respect to maintenance of accounting records.
b Recording overages and shortages from errors in handling over-the-counter cash receipts in a ledger account, Cash Over and Short.
c Authorizing the cashier to make bank deposits.
d Authorizing the official who approves invoices for payment to sign checks.

_____ 2 Checks received through the mail should be:
a Transmitted to the accounts receivable department without delay.
b Deposited by the mail-room employee.
c Listed by the mail-room employee and forwarded to the cashier; a copy of the list should be sent to the accounts receivable department.
d Handled first by the accounts receivable

department, which after making appropriate entries in the accounts should turn over the checks to the cashier to be made part of the daily bank deposit.

_____ 3 When a bank reconciliation has been satisfactorily completed, the only related entries to be made on the depositor's books are:
a To record items which explain the difference between the balance per the books and the adjusted cash balance.
b To reconcile items which explain the difference between the balance per the books and the balance per the bank statement.
c To correct errors existing in the bank statement.
d To record outstanding checks and bank service charges.

_____ 4 Which of the following is *not* a significant element of internal control over cash disbursements?
a Perforating or stamping "Paid" on supporting invoices and vouchers.
b Using serially numbered checks and accounting for all numbers in the series.
c Use of a Cash Over and Short account.
d Establishment of a petty cash fund.

_____ 5 Which of the following is *not* a significant element of internal control over cash receipts?
a Prelisting customers' remittances received in the mail.
b Establishing a petty cash fund.
c Depositing each day's cash receipts intact in the bank.
d Prenumbering sales tickets.

_____ 6 Which of the following statements describes an advantage of the use of a voucher system?
a Assures that every expenditure is reviewed and verified before payment is made.
b Provides automatically a comprehensive record of business done with particular suppliers.
c Provides a highly flexible system for handling unusual transactions.
d Reduces the number of checks that will be written during any given period.

_____ 7 Dart Co. bought $10,000 (maturity value) of 12% bonds at a price of 92. The brokerage commission was $30 and accrued interest amounted to $200. Dart Co. should debit investment in Bonds:
a $9,200
b $9,230
c $9,430
d Some other amount

8 Which of the following investments should *not* be classified as a marketable security:

a U.S. government bonds which will not mature for several years.

b Stock issued by a public utility company.

c Stock that has paid no dividends for several years.

d Stock held for the purpose of exercising control over the issuing company.

_____ **9** Under current accounting practice:

a The same valuation concepts are applied to marketable debt securities and marketable equity securities.

b The same income is recognized from an investment in common stock regardless of whether the shares are held for temporary investment or for purposes of controlling the issuing company.

c All marketable equity securities owned for more than one year should be classified as noncurrent assets.

d The treatment accorded to fluctuations in the market value of securities owned depends upon whether the market value is above or below cost.

_____ **10** The only securities owned by Gear Company are 1,000 shares of Delta Corporation common stock, which were purchased in Year 2 at a price of $45 per share plus a total broker's commission of $300. At December 31 of Year 2, the market price of Delta Corporation stock was $40 and at December 31 of Year 3 the price was $55. The carrying value of the investment in Gear Company's balance sheet at December 31 of each year is:

a $45,300 at December 31 of both years.

b $40,000 at December 31 of Year 2 and $45,300 at December 31 of Year 3.

c $40,000 at December 31 of Year 2 and $55,000 at December 31 of Year 3.

d None of the above.

Exercises

1 The following entries, in general journal form, concern the establishment and operation of a petty cash fund. You are to use the information contained in the explanation portions of the entries to complete the journal entries in proper form.

	Debit	Credit
Sept. 11		
To record the establishment of a $300 petty cash fund.		
Sept. 30		

To replenish the petty cash fund for the following:
postage, $48; travel, $26; and miscellaneous expense, $55.

2 You are to fill in the missing portions of the bank reconciliation shown on this page for the Hunter Corporation at July 31, 19___, using the following additional information:

a Outstanding checks: no. 301, $2,500; no. 303, $600; no. 304, $1,800; no. 306, $1,282.

b Service charge by bank, $6.

c Deposit made after banking hours on July 31, $1,950.

d A $264 NSF check drawn by our customer Jay Kline, deducted from our account by bank and returned to us.

e An $1,800 note receivable left by us with bank for collection was collected and credited to our account. No interest involved.

f Our check no. 295, issued in payment of $580 for office supplies, was erroneously written as $688 but was recorded in our accounts as $580.

HUNTER CORPORATION
Bank Reconciliation
July 31, 19___

Balance per depositor's records, July 31, 19___	$11,364
Add:	
Note receivable	1800
	13164
Deduct:	
SC	−6
NSF	264
OVERFLOW	108
Adjusted balance	$12786
Balance per bank statement, July 31, 19___	$17,018
Add:	
Deposit	1950
	18968
Deduct:	
Adjusted balance (as above)	$12786

3 On September 1, Year 5, National Company bought $100,000 par value of World Airlines 12% bonds at a price of 87¾ and accrued interest, plus a brokerage commission of $500. Interest dates of the bonds were August 1 and February 1. On April 1, Year 6, the National Company sold the bonds at a price of 91.

Complete the journal entries for the several transactions relating to the bonds as indicated below.

3	General Journal		
Year 5			
Sept. 1	Accrued Bond Interest Receivable		
	Purchased $100,000 par value of World Airlines 12% bonds		
	at 87¾ and accrued interest, plus commission of $1,000.		
Dec. 31			
	To accrue bond interest earned to Dec. 31 ($100,000 × 12% × $\frac{4}{12}$).		
Year 6			
Feb. 1			
	Received semiannual bond interest on World Airlines bonds ($100,000		
	× 12% × ½).		
Apr. 1			
	To accrue interest to date of sale of investment in World Airlines		
	bonds ($100,000 × 12% × $\frac{2}{12}$).		
Apr. 1			
	To record sale of $100,000 par value of World Airlines 12% bonds		
	at 91 plus accrued interest of $2,000 and minus commission of		
	$500.		

4 Milestone Corporation acquired a portfolio of marketable equity securities in Year 1. The portfolio is regarded as a current asset, and securities are frequently purchased and sold from the portfolio. The cost and market value of the portfolio is shown below for the first three years:

	Cost	Market Value Dec. 31
Year 1	$325,000	$301,000
Year 2	270,000	255,000
Year 3	310,000	330,000

On January 2, Year 4, the company sold from the portfolio securities which had cost $45,000. The sales proceeds amounted to $52,000. Prepare the adjusting entry at the end of each of the three years to value the portfolio at the lower of cost or market. Also prepare the entry on January 2, Year 4, to record the sale of securities.

4   **General Journal**

Year 1			
Dec. 31			

8

RECEIVABLES AND PAYABLES

(handwritten note at top right:) Bad Debts Debit Allow for Doubtful Acctd. credit Accts Recievb

HIGHLIGHTS OF THE CHAPTER

1 An important factor in the growth of the American economy has been the increasing tendency to sell goods on credit. In most large businesses, the major portion of total sales is actually sales on credit. Since every credit sale creates some sort of receivable from the customer, it follows that accounts receivable and/or notes receivable will be large and important assets on the balance sheets of most businesses.

2 A business can increase sales by giving its customers easy credit terms. But no business wants to sell on credit to customers who will be unable to pay their accounts. Consequently, many businesses have a credit department which investigates the credit records of new customers to see if they are acceptable credit risks.

3 A few accounts receivable will prove to be uncollectible. As long as the portion of uncollectible accounts is relatively small, it is to the advantage of the business to go ahead and incur these losses because the extension of credit to customers is also bringing in a lot of profitable business. The losses from accounts that do prove uncollectible are an *expense* resulting from the use of credit to increase sales.

4 A most fundamental accounting principle is that *revenue must be matched with the expenses incurred in securing that revenue.* Uncollectible Accounts Expense is caused by selling goods or services to customers who fail to pay their bills. The expense is therefore incurred in the *period the sale is made*

even though the receivable is not determined to be uncollectible until some following period. At the end of each accounting period before preparing financial statements, we must therefore *estimate* the amount of uncollectible accounts expense. This estimate is brought on the books by an adjusting entry debiting *Uncollectible Accounts Expense* and crediting *Allowance for Doubtful Accounts.* The allowance for Doubtful Accounts is a *contra-asset account;* it appears in the balance sheet as a deduction from Accounts Receivable and thus leads to an *estimated realizable value* for receivables.

5 Allowance for Doubtful Accounts is sometimes called *Allowance for Bad Debts.* Uncollectible Accounts Expense is sometimes referred to as *Bad Debts Expense.*

6 Since the allowance for doubtful accounts is necessarily an estimate rather than a precise calculation, there is a fairly wide range of reasonableness within which the amount may be set. The factor of *conservatism* which historically has been of considerable influence on accounting practice implies a tendency to state assets at their minimum values rather than in a purely objective manner. Establishing a relatively large allowance for doubtful accounts also means recording a relatively large amount of uncollectible accounts expense, thus tending to minimize net income for the current period.

7 Two methods of estimating uncollectible accounts expense are in wide use. The first method, which we call the *balance sheet approach,* relies on aging the *accounts receivable* and thereby arriving at the total amount

estimated to be uncollectible. The allowance for uncollectible accounts is then adjusted (usually increased) to this estimated uncollectible amount, after *giving consideration to the existing balance* in the allowance account.

8 The alternative method of estimating uncollectible accounts expense stresses that the *expense* is usually a fairly constant *percentage of sales* (or of sales or credit). Therefore the amount of the adjustment is computed as a percentage of the period's sales *without regard to any existing balance* in the allowance account. This method is often called the *income statement approach* to estimating uncollectible accounts expense.

9 An *aging schedule* for accounts receivable is a list of the balances due from all customers, with each amount placed in a column indicating its age. Thus, we might use columns with headings such as Not Yet Due, Past Due 1 to 30 Days, Past Due 31 to 60 Days, etc. Each column total should be computed as a percentage of total receivables. Changes in the percentages from month to month indicate whether the quality of receivables is improving or deteriorating.

10 When a customer's account is determined to be uncollectible, it should immediately be written off. The write-off consists of a debit to the Allowance for Doubtful Accounts and a credit to Accounts Receivable. The credit will be posted to the customer's account in the subsidiary ledger as well as to the controlling account in the general ledger. Since the write-off reduces both the asset Accounts Receivable and the contra-asset Allowance for Doubtful Accounts, *there is no change in the net carrying value of receivables.* Neither is there any recognition of expense at the time of the write-off. The write-off merely confirms the validity of our earlier estimate in recording uncollectible accounts expense in the period the sale was made.

11 The *direct charge-off method* of recognizing uncollectible accounts expense does not recognize any expense until a particular account receivable is determined to be uncollectible. At that point the receivable is written off with an offsetting debit to Uncollectible Accounts Expense. An allowance account is not used. There is little theoretical support for the direct charge-off method because it makes no attempt to match revenue with the expenses associated with that revenue. This method is not widely used.

12 Making credit sales to customers who use major credit cards avoids the risk of uncollectible accounts because the account receivable is paid promptly by the credit card company. Making sales through credit card companies also has the advantages of eliminating the work of credit investigations, billing, and maintaining an accounts receivable subsidiary ledger. However, credit card companies charge a fee equal to a percentage (usually 3 to 7%) of each credit sale.

13 In analyzing financial statements it is common practice to consider the relationship between average receivables and annual credit sales. For example, if annual credit sales were $2,400,000 and average receivables were $600,000, receivables would represent one-fourth of a year's sales (90 day's sales). If the credit terms are, say, 30 days, it is apparent that many receivables are past due, that the *turnover* of receivables is too slow, and that corrective action is needed.

14 *Installment sales* typically require a small down payment and a long series of monthly payments, perhaps extending over several years. For income tax purposes, a business is permitted to spread the profit on an installment sale over the period of collection in proportion to the cash received. For financial statements, however, the installment basis of measuring income has been prohibited by the American Institute of Certified Public Accountants. The principle of matching revenue with related expenses is best achieved by recognizing the entire gross profit in the period of the sale and by establishing an allowance for doubtful accounts.

15 A promissory note is an unconditional promise in writing to pay on demand or at a future date a definite sum of money. Most notes are for periods of a year or less and are therefore classified as current assets by the payee and as current liabilities by the maker of the note. Most notes bear interest (a charge made for the use of money). Interest rates are stated on an annual basis, and a 360-day year is usually assumed. The formula is: *Principal* $\times$ *rate of interest* $\times$ *time* = *interest.* (*Prt* = *i.*)

16 The face amount of each note receivable is debited to the Notes Receivable account in the general ledger. The notes themselves when properly filed are the equivalent of a subsidiary ledger. An adjusting entry for interest accrued on notes receivable is necessary at the end of the period. The entry will debit Accrued Interest Receivable and will credit Interest Revenue. When the note is collected in the following period, the entry will be a debit to Cash offset by a credit to Notes Receivable for the face amount of the note, a credit to Accrued Interest Receivable for the amount of the accrual, and a credit to Interest Revenue for the remainder of the interest collected.

17 If the maker of the note defaults (fails to pay as agreed), an entry should be made to transfer the note and any interest earned to an account receivable. If both parties agree that a note should be renewed rather than paid at maturity, an entry should be made debiting and crediting the Notes Receivable account and explaining the terms of the new note.

18 Notes receivable are often *discounted*, that is, sold to a financial institution, with the seller endorsing the note and thereby agreeing to make payment if the maker defaults. The purpose is to obtain cash quickly.

19 When a company endorses a note and discounts it to a bank, the company promises to pay the bank if the maker of the note fails to do so. This liability of the endorser is known as a *contingent liability*. A contingent liability is a potential liability which will either develop into a real liability or be eliminated, depending upon some future event. Contingent liabilities are disclosed in *footnotes* to the balance sheet and are not included in the regular liability section.

20 To compute the amount of cash obtainable by discounting a note receivable, first compute the maturity value of the note (principal plus interest due at maturity). Then, deduct from the maturity value the discount or interest charged by the bank. This discount is calculated by multiplying the bank's rate of interest times the maturity value for the number of days between the date of discounting and the date of maturity.

21 *Current liabilities* are amounts payable to creditors within one year or the operating cycle, whichever is longer. A company's debt-paying ability is judged, in part, by the relationship of its current assets to its current liabilities. Some examples of current liabilities are notes payable, accounts payable, cash dividends payable, and various types of accured liabilities.

22 A note payable may be issued as evidence of indebtedness to banks or to other creditors. When money is borrowed from the bank, two approaches may be used in drawing up the note: (a) the note may be drawn for the *principal amount,* and interest stated separately, to be paid at maturity, or (b) the note may be drawn for the *amount borrowed plus the interest to be paid at maturity*. When the latter procedure is followed, the rate of interest (or the amount of interest) is not separately listed on the note.

23 When the note is drawn for the principal amount borrowed, Cash is debited and Notes Payable is credited at the time the note is issued. The entry to record the payment of principal and interest requires a debit to Notes Payable for the amount of principal, a debit to Interest Expense for the interest paid, and a credit to Cash.

24 When the note is drawn for the *amount being borrowed plus the interest,* the note is for an amount larger than the immediate liability because the note includes interest *not yet owed* to the creditor. When such a note is drawn, Cash is debited for the amount received, *Discount on Notes Payable* is debited for the interest not yet owed, and Notes Payable is credited for the face amount of the note. Discount on Notes Payable is a *contra-liability* account and is subtracted from Notes Payable on the balance sheet, so that the net liability reflects only the amount owed at present.

25 When the note is paid, the interest has been earned by the creditor. The balance of the Discount on Notes Payable account is therefore recognized as interest expense (debit Interest Expense; credit Discount on Notes Payable). Notes Payable is debited and Cash is credited to record the payment of the note.

26 If a note is not repaid in the same period it was issued, it will be necessary to recognize the interest which has accrued (become owed) on the note during each period. If the note is drawn only for the principal amount, the interest which has accrued during the period is recognized by a debit to Interest Expense and a credit to the liability account Accrued Interest Payable. If the interest was included in the face of the note, the interest which accrues each period is transferred from Discount on Notes Payable (interest not yet owed) to Interest Expense. This entry would debit Interest Expense and credit (reduce) the contra-liability account Discount on Notes Payable.

27 When a note receivable is drawn to include future interest charges in the face amount of the note, the amount of the unearned interest should be credited to a *contra-asset* account entitled *Discount on Notes Receivable*. The interest which is earned each period is then transferred from Discount on Notes Receivable (representing the unearned interest) to the revenue account, Interest Revenue. The journal entry will debit (reduce) the contra-asset account Discount on Notes Receivable and credit Interest Revenue.

28 The concept of *present value* is based on the time value of money. Your would probably prefer to receive $1,000 today rather than $1,000 one year from today. If you invested $1,000 today, it would grow to a larger amount during the next year. The concept of present value applies to those long-term notes receivable and notes payable which do not bear any stated rate of interest or which bear an unrealistically low rate of interest. A portion of such long-term notes should be *assumed to represent an interest charge*.

29 If a business buys equipment by issuing a long-term note payable bearing no interest, the present value concept should be used. This will require a debit to Equipment for the present value of the note and a debit to Discount on Notes Payable for the excess of the face amount of the note over its present value. These two debits are offset by a credit to Notes Payable for the face amount of the note. The amount in the Discount on Notes Payable account will be transferred to Interest Expense over the life of the note.

30 A company selling an asset and receiving a long-term, non-interest-bearing note in payment should also use the present value concept in recording the transaction. A contra-asset account, Discount on Notes Receivable, is credited with the difference between the face amount of the note and its present value. The amount of the discount will be transferred to Interest Revenue over the life of the note.

31 A great deal of merchandise is sold on the installment plan, calling for regular payments over many months. Substantial interest charges are usually included in the installment contract signed by the customer. The transaction is recorded by a debit to Installment Contracts Receivable for the face amount of the contract. This debit is offset by a credit to Sales for the *present value* of the future payments and by a credit to Discount on Installment Receivables for the unearned finance charges. The amount credited to this contra-asset account will be transferred to Interest Revenue over the collection period. Thus the interest charges in a contract calling for 36 monthly payments will be earned over a period of 36 months.

TEST YOURSELF ON RECEIVABLES AND PAYABLES

True or False

For each of the following statements, circle the T or the F to indicate whether the statement is true or false.

T F 1 The practice of estimating uncollectible accounts expense at the end of each accounting period is designed to match revenue and expenses so that all expenses associated with the revenue earned in the period are recognized as expense in that same period.

T F 2 During the first year of its existence, Cross Company made most of its sales on credit but made no provision for uncollectible accounts. The result would be an overstatement of assets and owners' equity, an understatement of expense, and an overstatement of net income.

T F 3 Conservatism in the valuation of accounts receivable would call for holding the amount entered in Allowance for Doubtful Accounts to a bare minimum.

T F 4 The *balance sheet* approach to estimating uncollectible accounts expense emphasizes the aging of accounts receivable and the adjustment of the allowance account to the level of the estimated uncollectible amount.

T F 5 The *income statement* approach to estimating uncollectible accounts expense does not require the use of an allowance account.

T F 6 When the year-end provision for uncollectible accounts expense is estimated as a percentage of sales, the estimate is recorded without regard for the existing balance in the allowance account.

T F 7 The *direct charge-off* method does not cause receivables to be stated in the balance sheet at their estimated realizable value.

T F 8 When a given account receivable is determined to be worthless, it should be written off the books by an entry debiting Uncollectible Accounts Expense and crediting the Allowance for Doubtful Accounts.

T F 9 When a company collects an account receivable previously written off as worthless, an entry should be made debiting Accounts Receivable and crediting Allowance for Doubtful Accounts. A separate entry is then made to record collection of the account.

T F 10 The write-off of an account receivable determined to be worthless by debiting the Allowance for Doubtful Accounts will not affect the net carrying value of the receivables in the balance sheet.

T F 11 Annual credit sales divided by the amount of average accounts receivable indicates how long it takes to convert receivables into cash.

T F 12 X Co. sells merchandise on 30-day accounts and also on a 36-month installment plan. Under both methods, the amount debited to a receivable account will be equal to the amount credited to the sales revenue account.

T F 13 A retailer who sells to a customer using a national credit card will have an uncollectible account if the customer never pays the credit card company.

T F 14 When a company accepts a interest-bearing note from a customer, the accounting entry should include a debit for the principal plus the interest specified in the note.

T F 15 When a non-interest-bearing note receivable is discounted with a bank, the cash proceeds will usually be equal to the maturity value of the note.

T F 16 Interest may be stated separately or included in the face amount of a note payable.

T F 17 In reporting notes payable in the balance sheet, the Discount on Notes Payable account should be subtracted from the balance in the Notes Payable account.

T F 18 If the interest is not included in the face amount of a note payable, accrued interest at the end of a period should be recognized in a separate liability account; if the interest is included in the face amount, accrued interest should be recognized by decreasing the Discount on Notes Payable account.

T F 19 Contingent liabilities may not become real liabilities and need not be disclosed in the financial statements or footnotes to the statements.

T F 20 When a retail store sells merchandise to a customer who uses a bank credit card (such as Visa or Mastercard), the account to be debited is Cash rather than Accounts Receivable.

T F 21 When a company discounts a note receivable at its bank, the amount of cash received may be either more or less than the face value of the note.

T F 22 The concept of present value is applied to long-term notes receivable and payable rather than to short-term notes.

T F 23 The present value of a sum of money due several years in the future is always larger than the future amount.

T F 24 When a company sells goods in exchange for a long-term, non-interest-bearing note receivable, the valuation of the note at its present value is necessary to avoid an overstatement of assets, net income, and owners' equity.

Completion Statements

Fill in the necessary words or amounts to complete the following statements:

1 The accounting principle which underlies the practice of estimating uncollectible accounts expense each period is known as   _____.

250 = 10,000 2/12

This process is essential to the periodic determination of _net_ _income._

2 If the Allowance for Doubtful Accounts is understated, the net realizable value of accounts receivable will be _overstated_, owners' equity will be _overstated_, and net income will be _overstated._

3 The income statement approach to uncollectible accounts emphasizes estimating _Uncollectible Accts Exp_ for the period, while the balance sheet approach emphasizes estimating the proper level for the _Allow_ _for Doubtful_ _Account._

4 Bitterroot Company obtained a $16,000 note receivable from a customer and discounted it at the bank the same day, receiving a sum of $15,940. The entry to record the discounting would be a debit to Cash for $ _15,940_ , a _debit_ to _Interest Expense_ for $ _60_ , and a credit to Notes Receivable for $ _16,000_ .

5 If the interest on a 60-day note with a face value of $10,000 amounts to $250, the rate of interest is _15_ % per annum.

6 The entry to record interest accrued on notes receivable at the year-end consists of a debit to _Accrued Int Receivable_ and a credit to _Int_ _Revenue_. Of these accounts, the one to be closed into the Income Summary is _Int. Rev._ .

7 The Inn Place made credit sales of $4,200 to customers using Global Express credit cards. Global Express charges retailers a fee of 4%. The entry to record collecting the cash from these credit sales would be a debit to Cash for $ _4032_, a _debit_ to _____ _____ _Expense_ for $ _168_ , and a _credit_ to _Acct Rec_ for $ _4200_ .

8 Discount on Notes Payable is a _Contra liability_ _____ account which should be _deducted_ from the face value of notes payable in the liability section of the balance sheet. The amount of the Discount on Notes Payable will eventually be recognized as _Interest_ _expense_ .

9 Discount on Notes Receivable is a _Contra_ _asset_ account which should be _____ _____ from the face value of _____ _____ . The amount of the Discount on Notes Receivable will eventually be recognized as _____ _____ .

10 Company A borrows $10,000 cash and signs a note for $10,150, due in 60 days. On the same day, Company B borrows $10,000 cash and signs a note for $10,000 plus 9% interest, due in 60 days. Both companies prepared financial statements 30 days after borrowing the money. The liability relating to the loan for Company A (Note Payable less remaining Discount on Notes Payable) would be $ _10,075_ the liability for Company B (Notes Payable plus Accrued Interest Payable) would be $ _1075_ . At the maturity of the notes, Company A must pay $ _10,150_ and Company B must pay $ _10,147.90_ to the lender.

Multiple Choice

Choose the best answer for each of the following questions and enter the identifying letter in the space provided.

_d_ 1 When an allowance for the estimating of uncollectible accounts is in use, the writing off of an individual account receivable as worthless will:

a Be recorded by a debit to Uncollectible Accounts Expense.

b Increase the balance in the allowance account.

c Decrease the debit balance in the allowance account.

d Have no effect on the working capital of the company.

_a_ 2 Bryan Company, after aging its accounts receivable, estimated that $3,500 of the $125,000 of receivables on hand would probably prove uncollectible. The Allowance for Doubtful Accounts contained a credit balance of $2,300 prior to adjustments. The appropriate accounting entry is:

a A debit to Uncollectible Accounts Expense and a credit to Allowance for Doubtful Accounts for $1,200.

b A debit to Uncollectible Accounts Expense and a credit to Allowance for Doubtful Accounts for $3,500.

c A debit to Uncollectible Accounts Expense and a credit to Allowance for Doubtful Accounts for $5,800.

d A debit to Allowance for Doubtful Accounts and a credit to Accounts Receivable for $3,500.

3 Pine Company uses the income statement approach in estimating uncollectible accounts expense and has found that such expense has consistently approximated 1% of net sales. At December 31 of the current year receivables total $150,000 and the Allowance for Doubtful Accounts has a credit balance of $400 prior to adjustment. Net sales for the current year were $600,000. The adjusting entry should be:

a A debit to Uncollectible Accounts Expense and a credit to Allowance for Doubtful Accounts for $5,600.

b A debit to Uncollectible Accounts Expense and a credit to Allowance for Doubtful Accounts for $6,400.

c A debit to Allowance for Doubtful Accounts and a credit to Accounts Receivable for $6,000.

d A debit to Uncollectible Accounts Expense and a credit to Allowance for Doubtful Accounts for $6,000.

4 The presence of the account Discount on Notes Payable indicates that:

a Money was borrowed on a short-term basis at a rate in excess of the going market rate.

b Assets were increased at the time of borrowing by an amount in excess of the cash received.

c Interest has been paid in advance of the due date.

d A note payable has been issued for an amount equal to the sum of the principal and interest payable on the maturity date of the note.

5 The presence of the account Discount on Notes Receivable indicates that:

a A contingent liability exists.

b The face amount of a note receivable includes the interest receivable at the maturity date.

c Interest expense will be incurred in future periods.

d Total liabilities are less than if the discount had not been recorded.

6 Mann Company accepts numerous notes receivable from its customers. When the maker of a note defaults, Mann Company should:

a Transfer the principal of the note to Accounts Receivable and write off the accrued interest as a loss.

b Make no accounting entry if the maker of the defaulted note will sign a renewal note on equally favorable terms.

c Debit Accounts Receivable for the principal of the note plus interest earned, offset by credits to Notes Receivable and Interest Revenue.

d Record a contingent liability for the maturity value of the note.

7 Carl sold equipment today and received in payment a 10-year note receivable bearing interest at 1% a year. If Carl's accounting for this transaction follows the concept of *present value:*

a Discount on Notes Receivable will be debited for the difference between the present value the note and its maturity value.

b The note will be recorded at its face value or its maturity value, whichever is lower.

c The Notes Receivable account will increase each year by 1% through use of an annual adjusting entry.

d An amount will be recorded as Discount on Notes Receivable at the date of acquiring the note and transferred gradually to Interest Revenue over the 10-year life of the note.

8 Ace Company is arranging to borrow $50,000 from its bank for a period of 6 months at an annual interest rate of 12%. The bank has agreed that Ace Company may sign either of two forms of promissory note: a note for $50,000 with interest stated separately or a note with interest included in the face amount.

a The cost borrowing will be the same with either form of note, but Ace Company's balance sheet will show a large total amount of liabilities if interest is included in the face amount of the note.

b The cost of borrowing will be less if the interest is stated separately.

c An account for Discount on Notes Payable should be used regardless of which form of note is selected.

d The amount of interest expense will be the same and the total liability related to the bank loan will be the same regardless of which form of note is chosen.

Exercises

1 A list of account titles, each preceded by a code letter, appears below. Using this code, indicate the accounts to be debited and credited in properly recording the 10 transactions described. In some cases more than one account may be debited or credited.

(Note that *X designates any account not specified in the list.*)

A Cash
B Notes Receivable
C Accounts Receivable
D Allowance for Doubtful Accounts
E Notes Payable
F Discount on Notes Payable
G Accrued Interest Payable
H Uncollectible Accounts Expense
I Interest Expense
J Credit Card Discount Expense
X Any account not listed

2 Compute the interest on the following amounts using the assumption of a 360-day year.

a $12,000 at 14% for 60 days: $ _____

b $ 8,400 at 18% for 75 days: $ _____

c $ 4,000 at 12% for 90 days: $ _____

d $ 9,000 at 12½% for 120 days: $ _____

e $13,000 at 15% for 180 days: $ _____

Transactions	Account(s) Debited	Account(s) Credited
Example: Sold merchandise, receiving part cash and the balance on account.	A, C	X
1 Wrote off the account of J. Smith as uncollectible.	D	C
2 Borrowed $5,000 from a bank, signing a note for the amount of $5,000, with interest stated at 16%.	A	E
3 Collected cash from a national credit card company (not a bank) for credit card sales made this week.	A J	C
4 Discounted at bank a non-interest-bearing note receivable on same day note was received.	A I	B
5 Reinstated the account of J. Smith, written off in **1** above, when Smith promised to make payment.	C	D
6 Recognized interest expense for the period relating to $5,000 note payable in **2** above. Note not yet due.	I	G
7 Borrowed from a bank, signing a note in which the face amount included the interest.		
8 Collected the J. Smith account in full.		
9 Paid the $5,000 note originating in **2** above and all interest due, 20 days after making the adjusting entry in **6** above.		
10 Recognized interest expense for the period relating to note originating in **7** above. Note not yet due.		

9

INVENTORIES

HIGHLIGHTS OF THE CHAPTER

1 In previous chapters you have become familiar with the use of a dollar amount for inventory in both the balance sheet and the income statement; however, the amount for inventory has been given without much discussion as to its source.

2 In this chapter we consider what goods are properly included in inventory, how the cost of the ending inventory is computed, and what the advantages and disadvantages are of several alternative methods of valuing inventory.

3 In a retail or wholesale business, inventory consists of *all goods owned and held for sale* in the regular course of business.

4 The *cost of goods available for sale* minus the *ending inventory* equals the *cost of goods sold*. When we assign a value to the ending inventory, we are thereby also determining the *cost of goods sold* and therefore the *gross profit on sales*.

5 The ending inventory of one year is the beginning inventory of the next year. Therefore an error in the valuation of ending inventory will cause the income statement of two successive years to be in error by the full amount of the error in inventory valuation.

6 a When *ending* inventory is understated, net income will be understated.

b When *ending* inventory is overstated, net income will be overstated.

c When *beginning* inventory is understated, net income will be overstated.

d When *beginning* inventory is overstated, net income will be understated.

7 In other words, an inventory error is *counterbalancing* over a two-year period. If ending inventory is overstated, the income for the current year will be overstated, but income for the following year will be understated by the same amount. The reverse is also true: if ending inventory is understated, the income for the current year will be understated but income for the following year will be overstated.

8 An error in inventory valuation will cause several parts of the financial statements to be in error. On the income statement, the cost of goods sold, the gross profit on sales, and the net income will all be wrong by the full amount of the inventory error. On the balance sheet of the year in which the inventory error occurs, the owners' equity, the total current assets, and the balance sheet totals will also be in error.

9 Since an error in inventory has a counterbalancing effect on income over a two-year period, the owners' equity and the balance sheet totals will be correct at the end of the second year.

10 Taking a physical inventory is common practice at the end of each year. This means counting the merchandise owned, multiplying the quantity of each item by the unit cost to get a dollar value, and adding these values together to arrive at a total dollar figure for inventory.

11 Inventory includes all goods owned regardless of location. Title passes from seller to buyer when delivery is made. For goods in transit at year-end, we must consider the terms of shipment. If the terms of shipment are *F.O.B. shipping point*, the goods in transit

are the property of the buyer. If the terms are *F.O.B. destination*, the goods remain the property of the seller while in transit.

12 The primary basis of accounting for inventory is *cost*, which includes transportation-in (the cost incurred in bringing the merchandise to the point where it is to be offered for sale).

13 When several lots of identical merchandise are purchased at different prices during the year, which price should be considered as the cost of the units remaining in the year-end inventory? We shall consider four alternative valuation methods: (a) specific identification, (b) average cost, (c) first-in, first-out, and (d) last-in, first-out.

14 The specific identification method may be used if the units in the ending inventory can be identified as having come from specific purchases.

15 The average-cost method is computed by dividing the total *cost* of units available for sale by the number of units available for sale. This *weighted-average unit cost* is then multiplied by the number of units in the ending inventory.

16 The first-in, first-out method (*fifo*) is based on the assumption that the first merchandise acquired is the first sold. Therefore, ending inventory consists of the most recently acquired goods and is valued at the prices paid in the more recent purchases.

17 The last-in, first-out method (*lifo*) assumes that the most recently acquired goods are sold first and that the ending inventory consists of the "old" merchandise acquired in the earliest purchases. Thus, the prices applied in valuing the ending inventory are the prices paid on the earliest purchases. The more recent prices are considered to apply to the cost of the goods sold.

18 During a period of changing prices, each of these four alternative inventory methods will lead to different figures for cost of goods, gross profit on sales, net income, and owners' equity. However, all are acceptable because they are merely alternative methods of measuring *cost*.

19 During a period of rising prices, the *lifo* method will lead to the smallest inventory value, the lowest net income, and the lowest income tax. This is because the more recent (and higher) costs are considered to be the cost of the units sold and the earlier (and lower) purchase prices are considered

to be the cost of the unsold units comprising the ending inventory. Supporters of lifo argue that income is most accurately measured by **matching** the **current** cost of merchandise against **current** sales prices regardless of which physical units of merchandise are actually delivered to customers.

20 The *fifo* method produces a realistic balance sheet amount for inventory close to current replacement cost, whereas the *lifo* method produces a balance sheet value for inventory reflecting prices in the distant past.

21 *Inflation complicates the measurement of net income.* During a period of rising prices, the cost of replacing goods sold exceeds the historical cost of goods sold as reported in the income statement. Many accountants and business executives believe that the use of historical costs tends to *overstate* net income because the business must pay a higher cost (the replacement cost) than is deducted from revenue (the historical cost) with respect to goods sold.

22 The excess of the replacement cost of goods sold over their historical cost is termed *inventory profit*. Inventory profit is a restricted type of income, since it must be reinvested in inventory just to maintain inventory levels and therefore is not available for distribution to the owners. During a period of inflation, fifo results in a lower historical cost of goods sold than does lifo. Thus, fifo causes a larger amount of inventory profit to be included in reported net income.

23 To show the effects of inflation, the FASB requires large corporations to disclose what it would cost to replace their inventories at current prices and what their cost of sales would be if computed by using the replacement cost of the goods sold. When we consider the cost of replacing goods sold to customers, it appears that many companies have been much less profitable than their financial statements (based on historical costs) have indicated.

24 Continuing inflation and high income tax rates have led to increased interest by business managers in lifo. The lifo method causes reported net income to reflect the increasing cost of replacing the goods sold during the year and also tends to avoid basing income tax payments on an exaggerated measurement of taxable income.

25 If the utility of inventory falls below cost because of deterioration, price-level declines, or other reasons, it may be valued at the *lower-of-cost-or-market*. The word *market* in this context means *replacement* cost. The justification is prompt recognition of any loss which may have occurred. In no case should inventory be carried at more than its *net realizable value*.

26   The lower-of-cost-or-market rule may be applied to each item in the inventory, or to each category of inventory, or to the inventory as a whole.

27   The *gross profit method* of estimating inventories is useful when inventory is lost by fire or theft, or when it is desired to prepare monthly financial statements without incurring the expense of taking a physical inventory.

28   To apply the gross profit method, obtain from the ledger the figures for beginning inventory, purchases, and sales. Cost of goods sold is then computed by reducing the sales figure by the usual gross profit rate of prior periods. The difference between the cost of goods available for sale and the computed cost of goods sold represents the estimated ending inventory.

29   In retail stores, the merchandise is marked with the retail selling price. It is therefore convenient to use the *retail method of inventory*, which consists of pricing the inventory at selling price and then reducing it to cost by applying the ratio prevailing in the current period between cost and selling price. To use the retail method of inventory, it is necessary to maintain records of the beginning inventory and of the purchases in terms of selling price as well as of cost.

30   Whatever method of inventory is selected, it should be followed consistently from period to period to avoid distorting reported income merely because of changes in accounting method.

31   Up to this point, we have emphasized the *periodic inventory system* in which inventory is not known from day to day but determined by taking a physical inventory periodically. The alternative is a *perpetual inventory system* which provides a continuous running balance of inventory.

32   In a perpetual inventory system, purchases are debited directly to the Inventory account rather than to a Purchases account. A sale of merchandise requires two entries: (a) a debit to Cash (or Accounts Receivable) and a credit to Sales for the sales price and (b) a debit to Cost of Goods Sold and a credit to Inventory for the *cost* of the merchandise. To avoid making a large number of entries in the general journal, we can enter a special column in the sales journal to show the cost of the goods sold in each transaction. At the end of each month the total of this "cost" column can be posted as a debit to Cost of Goods Sold and a credit to Inventory.

33   There are several advantages to a perpetual inventory system. Internal control is strengthened because management will become aware of any shortages when the physical count of inventory is compared with the perpetual inventory records. Since the perpetual inventory records always show the amount which should be on hand, a physical inventory may be taken at dates other than year-end. Also, monthly or quarterly financial statements can readily be prepared from the perpetual inventory records without the need for a physical inventory. Although more costly to operate, the perpetual inventory system is appropriate for a business dealing in goods of high unit value.

TEST YOURSELF ON INVENTORIES

True or False

For each of the following statements, circle the T or the F to indicate whether the statement is true or false.

T F   1   A major objective of accounting for inventories is proper measurement of net income.

T F   2   An error in the valuation of inventory at the end of the period will cause errors in net income for two periods.

T F   3   Taking the inventory refers to the physical count to determine the quantity of inventory on hand; pricing the inventory means determining the cost of the inventory on hand.

T F   4   If the terms of shipment are F.O.B. shipping point, the goods in transit should normally belong to the seller.

T F   5   Errors in the valuation of inventory are counterbalancing; an error which causes an overstatement of net income this period will cause an understatement next period.

T F   6   Inventories are usually valued at cost, but the cost figure for an inventory can differ significantly depending upon what inventory method is used.

T F 7 The recording of a sale in the wrong period will have no effect on the net income for each period if the goods are excluded from inventory in the period in which the sale is recorded.

T F 8 An overstatement of ending inventory will cause an understatement of net income.

T F 9 The specific identification method of inventory valuation is particularly appropriate for low-priced, high-volume articles.

T F 10 The average-cost method places weight more on the prices at which large purchases were made than on the prices at which small purchases were made.

T F 11 Using the first-in, first-out (fifo) method during a period of rising prices implies that the cheaper goods have been sold and the more costly goods are still on hand.

T F 12 If we consider the "true" cost of sales to be the replacement cost of goods sold, income statements using historical costs tend to understate net income during periods of inflation.

T F 13 During a period of rapid inflation, using lifo will maximize reported net income.

T F 14 Using the lifo method implies that the ending inventory consists of the most recently acquired goods.

T F 15 Inventory profits result from increasing the selling price of merchandise.

T F 16 The use of the lower-of-cost-or-market rule produces a conservative inventory valuation because unrealized losses are treated as actually incurred.

T F 17 The gross profit method permits a business to estimate ending inventory without actually taking a physical count of the goods on hand.

T F 18 The retail method of inventory valuation permits us to take and price the physical inventory at current retail prices rather than look up invoices to determine the cost of goods on hand.

T F 19 Consistency in the valuation of inventories requires that a method once adopted cannot be changed unless the company is sold.

T F 20 A perpetual inventory system is easier and less expensive to operate than is a periodic inventory system.

T F 21 In a perpetual inventory system, ledger accounts for inventory and the cost of goods sold are continuously updated for purchases and sales of merchandise.

Completion Statements

Fill in the necessary words or amounts to complete the following statements:

1 If goods are shipped F.O.B. destination, the _____ to the goods while in transit belongs to the _____ and the goods should be excluded from the inventory of the _____ .

2 Ending inventories are *overstated* as follows: Year 1 by $20,000; Year 2 by $8,000; and Year 3 by $15,000. Net income for each of the three years was computed at $25,000. The corrected net income figure (ignoring the effect of income taxes) for each of the three years is: Year 1, $_____ ; Year 2, $_____ ; Year 3, $_____ .

3 The four most commonly used inventory valuation methods are: _____ _____ , _____ _____ , _____ , and _____ .

4 One of the most significant recent developments in accounting practice is the requirement by the FASB that large corporations disclose the _____ cost of their inventories and their cost of sales computed by using the _____ cost of goods sold. This disclosure indicates that income statements using _____ cost may have been (overstating, understating) _____ _____ the profitability of many companies during periods of inflation.

5 Inventory profits represent the difference between the historical cost of goods sold and the _____ _____ of goods sold. Inventory profits are a restricted type of income because they must be _____ in _____ and because they are not available to finance dividends or expansion. During a period of rising prices, companies using the _____ inventory method might be expected to have the largest inventory profits.

6 The lower-of-cost-or-market rule results in the recognition of a _____ in the _____ cost of inventory. However, an _____ in the _____ cost would not be recognized.

7 During a period of rising prices, using the _____ method implies that the cheaper goods are still on hand while the more expensive ones were sold.

8 The method of inventory valuation frequently used by retail stores is first to value the inventory at _____ and then to convert this amount to a _____ figure by applying the _____ of cost to selling prices during the current period.

9 In a perpetual inventory system, purchases are recorded by a debit to _____ and a credit to Accounts Payable. Sales are recorded by two entries: (a) a debit to Accounts Receivable and a credit to _____ for the _____ price of the merchandise and (b) a debit to ____ _____ _____ ____ and a credit to _____ for the _____ of the goods.

Multiple Choice

Choose the best answer for each of the following questions and enter the identifying letter in the space provided.

_____ **1** Which of the following items would **not** be included in inventories on the balance sheet?
a Raw materials used in manufacture of chemicals.
b Building materials used in construction.
c Cars left by customers at an auto repair shop.
d Goods purchased but not yet delivered to premises (title passed).

_____ **2** An overstatement of $1,000 in the inventory at the end of Year 4 would:
a Understate the beginning inventory of Year 5.
b Have no effect on net income of Year 3.
c Overstate purchases for Year 5.
d Have no effect on net income of Year 4.

_____ **3** Which of the following is **not** an acceptable inventory method?
a Lower of cost or market.
b Sales value.

c Specific identification.
d First-in, first-out.

_____ **4** During a period of rising prices, which inventory pricing method might be expected to give the lowest valuation for inventory on the balance sheet and the lowest net income figure?
a Cost on a lifo basis.
b Cost on a fifo basis.
c Weighted-average cost.
d Fifo, lower of cost or market.

_____ **5** The gross profit method of estimating inventories:
a Is a useful means of determining the rate of gross profit without taking a physical inventory.
b Is a useful means of verifying the reasonableness of a physical inventory count.
c Provides information about the number of units in the ending inventory.
d Provides information about changes in the rate of gross profit.

_____ **6** *Net realizable value*, as the term is used in relation to inventory valuation, means:
a Replacement cost of the goods in inventory.
b Cost of the goods on a fifo basis increased by anticipated selling expenses.
c Selling price of the goods minus anticipated selling expenses.
d Sales price of the goods minus anticipated selling expenses and profit margin.

_____ **7** Goods costing $750 are sold for $1,000 at the end of Year 1, but the sale is recorded in Year 2. The goods *were* included in the ending inventory at the end of Year 1. The most likely effect of this error is:
a Net income for Year 1 was understated by $1,000.
b Net income for Year 2 was overstated by $250.
c Beginning inventory for Year 2 is understated by $750.
d Net income for Year 1 was overstated by $250.

Exercises

1 In each of the situations described below, indicate the effect of the error on the various elements of financial statements prepared at the end of the current year, using the following code:

O = overstated, U = understated, NE = no effect

	Situation	Revenues	Costs and/or Expenses	Net Income	Assets	Liabilities	Owners' Equity
a	No record made of goods purchased on credit and received on Dec. 31. Goods omitted from inventory.						
b	Made sale in late December; goods were delivered on Dec. 31 but were also included in inventory on Dec. 31.						
c	In taking the physical inventory, some goods in a warehouse were overlooked.						
d	A purchase made late in year was recorded properly on the books, but the goods were not included in the ending inventory.						

2 The following inventory information is available for the month of May:

	Units	Total Cost
Beginning inventory, May 1	500	$5,000
Purchase, May 3	400	4,400
Purchase, May 10	800	9,600
Purchase, May 21	300	3,900

The replacement cost of each unit on May 31 is $12.50. Sales amounted to 1,500 units at an average price of $16.10.

Compute the cost of the ending inventory of 500 units and the cost of goods sold under each of the following inventory methods:

		Inventory	Cost of Goods Sold
a	Fifo—cost	$ _____	$ _____
b	Fifo—cost or market, whichever is lower . .	$ _____	$ _____
c	Lifo—cost	$ _____	$ _____
d	Average—cost	$ _____	$ _____

CGS=1,147

3 On July 20, 19__, the accountant for B Company is in the process of preparing financial statements for the year ending June 30, 19__. The physical inventory, however, was not taken until July 10, 19__, and the accountant finds it necessary to establish the approximate inventory cost at June 30, 19__, from the following data:

Physical inventory, July 10, 19__	$30,000
Transactions for period July 1—July 10:	
Sales	15,200
Sales returns	400
Purchases	17,500
Purchases returns	550

The gross profit on sales of the past couple of years has averaged 22.5% of net sales. In the space below, compute the approximate inventory cost at June 30, 19__.

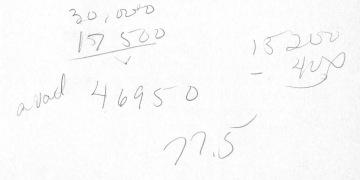

30,000
157,500
avail 469,500

15,200
- 400

22.5

10

PLANT AND EQUIPMENT, DEPRECIATION, NATURAL RESOURCES, AND INTANGIBLE ASSETS

HIGHLIGHTS OF THE CHAPTER

1 The term *plant and equipment* is used to describe long-lived assets used in the operation of the business and not held for sale to customers. The term *fixed assets* has been used to describe plant assets but is now used less frequently.

2 A plant asset is a *stream of services* to be received by the owner over a long period of time. As the services are received, a portion of the asset is consumed and should be recognized as an expense (depreciation).

3 The major categories of plant and equipment include:

a Tangible plant assets, such as land, buildings, and machinery. Most of these assets are *subject to depreciation*, whereas land, for example, is generally *not subject to depreciation*.

b Intangible assets, such as patents, copyrights, trademarks, franchises, organization costs, leaseholds, and goodwill. The term *intangible assets* is used to describe noncurrent assets which have *no physical form*. The cost of intangible assets is subject to *amortization*.

4 The major accounting problems relating to plant and equipment are:

a Determining the cost of the plant asset.

b Procedures for allocating the cost of a plant asset to accounting periods.

c Recording costs (such as repairs) incurred in using plant assets.

d Recording the disposal of plant assets.

5 All *reasonable* and *necessary* expenditures incurred in acquiring a plant asset and placing it in use should be recorded in an asset account. The cost may include the list price, sales or use taxes paid, freight and handling costs, installation costs, and insurance prior to the time that the asset is placed in service.

6 Cash discounts reduce the net cost of the asset. Interest paid when an asset is purchased on the installment plan should be recorded as an expense rather than as part of the cost of acquiring the asset.

7 The cost of land may include real estate commissions, escrow fees, title insurance fees, delinquent taxes (including penalties and interest), etc. *Special assessments* for street paving or other improvements should be added to the cost of the land. Separate ledger accounts are always maintained for land and buildings. Certain land-improvement cost, such as fences, driveways, parking lots, sprinkler systems, and landscaping, have a limited life and should be recorded in a separate account and depreciated.

8 When a building is purchased, the total cost includes the price paid plus all incidental costs, such as termite inspection fees, legal fees, and major repairs necessary before the building is occupied. When a building is constructed by the owner, the total cost of the building includes all direct expenditures (labor, materials, building permit, etc.) plus a reasonable estimate of indirect costs (overhead).

9 A *capital expenditure* is one that will benefit many accounting periods; a *revenue expend-*

iture is one that will benefit only the current accounting period. Capital expenditures are recorded in asset accounts and are deducted from revenue through the process of depreciation; revenue expenditures are recorded in expense accounts as incurred.

10 *Depreciation* is the process of *allocating the cost of plant assets* to the periods in which services are received from the assets. A separate depreciation expense account should be maintained for each major group of depreciable assets, and the total amount of depreciation expense for the fiscal period should be disclosed in the income statement.

11 Depreciation is *not* a process of assigning a market value (or realizable value) to plant assets, nor is it a process of accumulating a fund for the replacement of assets when they become worn out or obsolete. Depreciation is an *allocation process*: The cost of an asset, less residual value, is allocated to the years that are benefited from the use of the asset.

12 The balance in the Accumulated Depreciation account represents the portion of the historical cost of plant assets which has expired to date; this account does *not* represent a fund of cash accumulated to replace plant assets.

13 The two major causes of depreciation are:
a Physical deterioration from use.
b Obsolescence due to technological changes or changing needs of the company.

14 The methods of computing periodic depreciation are:
a Straight-line:

$$\frac{\text{Cost} - \text{residual value}}{\text{Estimated years of useful life}}$$

b Units of output:

$$\frac{\text{Cost} - \text{residual value}}{\text{Total estimated units of output}} \times \begin{array}{c}\text{units}\\\text{produced}\end{array}$$

c Fixed-percentage-on-declining balance: Book value of the asset multiplied by a rate which is usually twice the straight-line rate.
d Sum-of-the-years'-digits: Cost minus residual value multiplied by a fraction, of which the numerator is the remaining years of useful life and the denominator is the sum of the years of useful life.

15 The *straight-line method* is the simplest and the most widely used method of computing depreciation. Under this method an *equal portion* of the cost of the asset (less residual value) is allocated to each period of use. This method is most appropriate when usage of an asset is fairly uniform from period to period.

16 When the usage of an asset fluctuates and output can be estimated in terms of some unit (such as tons produced or miles driven), a more equitable allocation of a plant asset can be obtained by computing depreciation on the basis of output. Cost (less residual value) is divided by estimated output to obtain a depreciation *rate per unit*. Depreciation for a period is computed by multiplying the rate per unit by the number of units produced.

17 Under *accelerated depreciation* methods, larger amounts of depreciation are recorded in the early years of use and reduced amounts in later years. Accelerated methods are particularly appropriate when obsolescence is more significant than physical deterioration in rendering the asset less useful or productive. In some cases the use of an accelerated depreciation method tends to equalize the total expense of using an asset because decreasing periodic depreciation charges are offset by increasing repair outlays as the asset gets older.

18 A business need not use the same method of depreciation for all its assets. Also, different methods may be used for tax purposes than are being used in the accounting records and financial statements.

19 For income tax purposes, assets acquired after January 1, 1981, may be depreciated by a special method called the Accelerated Cost Recovery System (ACRS). ACRS is an accelerated method for three reasons: (1) the rate table published by the IRS allows for writing-off higher percentages in the early years, (2) ACRS makes no provision for a salvage value, and (3) assets generally may be written off over a period shorter than their actual useful lives.

20 ACRS is used for income tax purposes only; it generally *is not* acceptable for financial reporting purposes.

21 Depreciation rates are based on estimates of useful life. If the estimate of useful service life is found to be in error, the estimate should be revised, and the *undepreciated cost of the asset should be allocated over the years of remaining useful life.* A change in annual depreciation expense may also result from a change in the *estimate of residual value* or from a change in the *method* of computing depreciation.

22 In an economy characterized by inflation, the current replacement cost of plant assets may be much greater than their historical cost. Supporters of *replacement cost accounting* argue that income is *overstated* when depreciation expense is based upon historical cost because these costs are less than the *current value* of the asset services being used up.

23 The criticism of historical cost is a convincing one. For this reason, the SEC now requires large corporations to *disclose* the estimated replacement cost of their plant assets and the depreciation expense computed using these costs. This rule does *not* mean that replacement cost is used *instead* of historical cost; rather, the current replacement cost data are presented in a footnote as *additional supplementary information*.

24 When units of plant and equipment wear out or become obsolete they must be discarded, sold, or traded in. To record the disposal of a depreciable asset, the cost of the asset must be removed from the asset account, *and the accumulated depreciation* (on that asset) *must be removed* from the contra-asset account.

25 The *book value*, or carrying value, of a depreciable asset is its cost minus accumulated depreciation. If the asset is sold for a price above book value, there is a *gain* on the sale. If the asset is sold for less than book value, there is a *loss*.

26 When a depreciable asset is sold, the amount of the gain or loss is determined by comparing the book value of the asset sold with the amount received from the sale. The amount of a gain would be *credited* to a *Gain on Disposal of Plant Assets* account, and a loss would be *debited* to *Loss on Disposal of Plant Assets*.

27 For purposes of determining taxable income, no gain or loss is recognized when a depreciable asset is *traded in* on a similar asset. The cost of the new asset is recorded as the sum of the *book value of the old asset plus any additional amount paid* (or to be paid) for the new asset.

28 Income tax regulations and financial accounting rules are alike in not recognizing a gain on an exchange of similar plant assets, but they differ when the exchange results in a loss. A loss on an exchange of similar plant assets may not be deducted for tax purposes, but it *should be recognized* in the financial statements. An exchange results in a loss when the trade-in allowance given on the old asset is less than its book value.

29 Natural resources, such as mines or timber stands, are physically extracted and converted into inventory. These assets are recorded at cost and reported separately in the balance sheet.

30 *Depletion* is the process of *allocating the cost* of a natural resource to the units removed. The depletion rate is computed by dividing the cost of the natural resource by the estimated number of units available to be removed. The rate is then multiplied by the number of units removed during a period to determine the total depletion charge for the period.

31 For tax purposes, the IRS permits companies in some industries to take a deduction for depletion expense equal to a specified percentage of revenue from production of mineral deposits. This *percentage depletion* is used *only for tax purposes* and is not acceptable in financial statements.

32 *Intangible assets* are those noncurrent assets which do not have physical substance but which contribute to the process of earning revenue. Intangibles are recorded at cost and should be *amortized* over their useful lives. It is often difficult to estimate the useful life of an intangible asset, but the maximum amortization period *may not exceed 40 years*. Intangible assets generally are amortized by the straight-line method.

33 *Goodwill* is the market value of a going business *in excess of* the fair market value of the other identifiable assets of the business. It represents the *present value* of expected future earnings *in excess of* the normal return on the net identifiable assets of the business. The term *net identifiable assets* refers to all assets except goodwill minus liabilities.

34 Goodwill may exist in many businesses, but it should be recorded in the accounts *only when it is purchased*.

35 The following three methods may be used in *estimating* the value of goodwill owned by a business unit:

a Negotiated agreement between buyer and seller. If a business with net assets (at market value) of $80,000 is sold for $100,000, this suggests that goodwill of $20,000 is possessed by this business.

b A multiple of the amount by which the average annual earnings exceed normal earnings. If the normal earnings are estimated at $20,000 and average annual earnings are $22,500, goodwill may be estimated at, say, five times excess earnings ($22,500 −$20,000), or $12,500.

c The capitalized value of excess earning power. For example, if excess earnings amount to $5,000 and the capitalization rate agreed upon is 20%, the goodwill would be estimated at $25,000 ($5,000 ÷ .20 = $25,000).

TEST YOURSELF ON PLANT AND EQUIPMENT; DEPRECIATION

True or False

For each of the following statements, circle the T or the F to indicate whether the statement is true or false.

T F 1 In a broad sense, the cost of a machine or a building may be viewed as a long-term prepaid expense.

T F 2 An auto owned by a glass manufacturer would be reported under Plant and Equipment, while glass owned by an auto manufacturer would be classified as Inventory.

T F 3 The cost of land that is entered in the books should not include any transaction costs, such as real estate commissions paid.

T F 4 *Capital expenditures* are those disbursements which are allocated to several accounting periods; *revenue expenditures* are charged off as current expenses.

T F 5 The cost of a plant asset should include all costs necessary to get the asset ready for use, including the cost of the units spoiled in production while the asset was being adjusted and tested.

T F 6 A small expenditure, such as $10 for a set of spark plugs, may reasonably be charged to expense even though the expenditure may benefit several periods.

T F 7 Obsolescence may be a more significant factor than wear and tear through use in putting an end to the usefulness of many depreciable assets.

T F 8 Depreciation expense for a period should be a reasonably good estimate

of the change in the fair market value of an asset during the period.

T F 9 If the price of construction goes up by 25% during Year 1, and amount of depreciation on a building already owned will be increased, but not necessarily by 25%.

T F 10 In practice, the residual value of an asset is often ignored in estimating annual depreciation expense.

T F 11 The units-of-output method of depreciation yields similar results to *accelerated* methods of depreciation when the rate of output increases steadily over a period of years.

T F 12 The Accumulated Depreciation account is a fund established for the replacement of assets, but it will not be large enough to cover the cost of replacement during a period of inflation.

T F 13 The fixed-percentage-on-declining-balance method of depreciation has a "built-in" residual value and can never allocate 100% of the original cost of an asset to expense.

T F 14 A company organized after January 1, 1981 should use the ACRS method of depreciation in its financial statements even if another method is used for income tax purposes.

T F 15 When it becomes evident that a plant asset will have a useful life longer than had been originally estimated, the depreciation rate will be revised according to the new estimate of useful life.

T F 16 If depreciation were based upon current replacement costs rather than historical costs, most companies would report lower net income.

T F 17 Whenever a depreciable asset is sold, both the cost of the asset and the accumulated depreciation must be removed from the accounts.

T F 18 For both tax purposes and preparing financial statements, no gain is recognized when the trade-in allowance on a plant asset exceeds its book value.

T F 19 For both tax purposes and preparing financial statements, no loss is recognized when the trade-in allowance on a plant asset is less than its book value.

T F 20 Depletion refers to the allocation of the cost of an intangible asset over the periods that benefits are received.

T F̶ 21 Intangible assets are assets that cannot be sold.

T̶ F 22 The systematic write-off of intangible assets to expense is known as amortization.

T̶ F 23 Goodwill is the present value of future earnings in excess of the normal return on net identifiable assets.

T F̶ 24 When a business has superior earnings for many years, goodwill probably exists and should be recorded on the books.

T̶ F 25 If a buyer of a business pays a price for the business in excess of the fair market value of the net tangible assets, the buyer may record goodwill as one of the assets being acquired.

Completion Statements

Fill in the necessary words or amounts to complete the following statements:

1 The two causes of depreciation are: (a) ___physical deterioration___ and (b) ___obsolescence___ .

2 If a ___capital___ expenditure is erroneously recorded as a ___revenue___ expenditure, net income will be ___understated___ in the current period, and overstated in every future period in which depreciation should have been recognized.

3 Net income for three consecutive years was reported as follows:

Year 1 . . . . $30,000
Year 2 . . . . $39,000
Year 3 . . . . $40,000

At the beginning of Year 1 a capital expenditure of $15,000 for a new machine, which should have been depreciated over a five-year life using the sum-of-the-years'-digits method, was erroneously charged to repair expense. The correct net income for the three years should have been as follows:

Year 1, $ ___40,000___ ;Year 2, $ ___35,000___ ;
Year 3, $ ___37,000___ .

4 The ACRS method of depreciation is used on assets acquired after January 1, ___1981___ . This method is allowable for ___income tax___ purposes and is (widely used, not acceptable) ___N A___ for use in financial statements.

5 Supporters of replacement cost accounting argue that net income is the excess of revenue over the ___replace cost___ of the resources used up in producing that revenue. This argument suggests that the current practice of basing depreciation expense upon ___original cost___ cost tends to (overstate, understate) ___overstate___ net income.

6 The entry to record the disposal of a depreciable asset will always include a credit to the asset account for the ___original cost___ of the asset, and a debit to the ___accumulated depreciation___ account.

7 Tax regulations provide that the cost of new equipment shall be the sum of the ___book value___ of any old equipment traded in plus any ___additional amt___ paid or to be paid in acquiring the new equipment.

8 The cost of intangible assets should be ___depreciated___ by the ___amortization___ method over a period not to exceed ___40___ years.

Multiple Choice

Choose the best answer for each of the following questions and enter the identifying letter in the space provided.

___c___ 1 Big Company purchased land for $80,000 subject to delinquent property taxes of $4,000. These taxes were paid immediately by Big Company along with interest of $320 on the delinquent taxes. The cost of this land should be recorded by Big Company at:
a $80,000
b $84,000
c $84,320
d Some other amount

___a___ 2 The book value or carrying value of a depreciable asset is best defined as:
a The undepreciated cost of the asset.
b The price that the asset would bring if offered for sale.
c Accumulated depreciation on the asset since acquisition.
d Original cost of the asset.

___b___ 3 The straight-line method of depreciation:

a Generally gives best results because it is easy to apply.

b Ignores fluctuations in the rate of asset usage.

c Should be used in a period of inflation because it accumulates, at a uniform rate, the fund for the replacement of the asset.

d Is the best method to use for income tax purposes.

_____ 4 *Accumulated depreciation*, as used in accounting, may be defined as:

a Earnings retained in the business that will be used to purchase another asset when the present asset is depreciated.

b Funds (or cash) set aside to replace the asset being depreciated.

c The portion of the cost of a plant asset recognized as expense since the asset was acquired.

d An expense of doing business.

_____ 5 A and B Companies purchase identical equipment having an estimated service life of 10 years. A Company uses the straight-line method of depreciation, and B Company uses the sum-of-the-years'-digits method. Assuming that the companies are identical in all other respects:

a B Company will record more depreciation on this asset over the entire 10 years than will A Company.

b At the end of the third year, the book value of the asset will be lower on A Company's books than on B Company's.

c A Company's depreciation expense will be greater in the first year than B Company's.

d A Company's net income will be lower in the ninth year than B Company's.

_____ 6 Which of the following is not an intangible asset?

a A patent.

b A trademark.

c An investment in marketable securities.

d Goodwill.

_____ 7 The best evidence of goodwill existing in a business is:

a The appearance of goodwill on the balance sheet.

b Numerous contributions to the charitable organizations.

c A long-standing reputation for manufacturing a high-quality product.

d A long record of earnings greater than those of like-size firms in the same industry.

_____ 8 Lucky Strike Mines recognizes $2 of depletion for each ton of ore mined. This year 750,000 tons of ore were mined, but only 700,000 tons were sold. The amount of depletion that should be deducted from revenue this year is:

a $2,900,000

b $1,500,000

c $1,400,000

d $100,000

_____ 9 Morgan Company has traded in a machine on a similar asset, paying cash for the difference between list price and the trade-in allowance. The trade-in allowance on the old machine was greater than its book value. The cost of the new asset should be recorded as:

a The list price of the new asset.

b The estimated fair value of the old asset plus the cash paid.

c The book value of the old asset plus the cash paid.

d The trade-in allowance on the old asset plus the cash paid.

Exercises

1 A truck with an estimated life of four years was acquired on March 31, Year 1, for $11,000. The estimated residual value of the truck is $1,000, and the service life is estimated at 100,000 miles. Compute depreciation for Year 1 and Year 2 using the following methods:

		Year 1	Year 2
a	Straight-line	$ 1875	$ 2500
b	Output (miles driven: Year 1, 20,000; Year 2, 40,000)	$ 2000	$ 4000
c	Sum-of-the-years'-digits .	$ 3000	$ 3250
d	Fixed-percentage-on declining-balance (twice) the straight-line rate) . . .	$ 4125	$ 3437.5

2 Equipment which cost $6,000 had an estimated useful life of six years and an estimated salvage value of $600. Straight-line depreciation was used. In the space provided, prepare the journal entry (omitting explanation) to record the disposal of the equipment under each of the following assumptions:

a The equipment was sold for $4,000 cash after two years' use.

b After three years' use, the equipment was sold for $3,500 cash.

c After four years' use, the equipment was traded in on a similar equipment with a list price of $8,000. The trade-in allowance was $3,100.

General Journal		
a		
b		
c		

3 The Golden Calf, a Las Vegas gambling casino, had net tangible assets of $8,000,000 and earned an average net income of $2,080,000 per year. Other Las Vegas casinos averaged a net income equal to 20% of their net tangible assets. An investment group negotiating to buy the Golden Calf offers to pay $8,000,000 for the casino's net tangible assets, plus an amount for goodwill.

The investment group determined the amount to be paid for goodwill by capitalizing the Golden Calf's annual earnings in excess of the industry average earnings at a rate of 25%. Compute the *total price* the investment group is offering to pay for the Golden Calf.

Computations:

Answer: $_____

11

FORMS OF BUSINESS ORGANIZATION

HIGHLIGHTS OF THE CHAPTER

1 Three common forms of business organization found in the American economy are: the single proprietorship, the partnership, and the corporation.

2 In a single proprietorship, a *Capital account* and a *Drawing account* are maintained in the ledger to show the equity of the owner. The Capital account is credited with the amount invested by the owner and with the net income earned by the business. The Capital account is debited when net losses are incurred. Withdrawals by the owner are debited to a Drawing account, which is closed into the Capital account at the end of the accounting period.

The same procedures are followed for a partnership, except that separate capital and drawing accounts are maintained for each partner.

3 The income statement for a single proprietorship does not include any salary expense for the owner or any income tax expense. The income statement for a partnership shows the amount of net income allocated to each partner but does not report an income tax expense since a partnership, like a single proprietorship, is not a taxable entity.

4 The principal characteristics of the partnership form of organization are:
a Ease of formation.
b Limited life. (A partnership is dissolved whenever there is a change in partners.)
c Mutual agency. (Each partner has the right to bind the partnership to a contract.)

d Unlimited liability. (Each partner may be personally liable for all the debts of the partnership.)
e Co-ownership of partnership property and profits.

5 *Advantages of the partnership* form of organization are:
a It brings together sufficient capital to carry on a business.
b It combines special skills of the several partners.
c It offers freedom and flexibility of action.
d It may result in income tax advantages to the partners.

6 *Disadvantages of the partnership* form of organization are:
a A partnership may be terminated upon death or withdrawal of a partner.
b Each partner is personally responsible for partnership debts.
c The partnership is bound by the acts of any partner as long as these acts are within the scope of normal operations.
d The partnership is less effective than a corporation for raising large amounts of capital.

7 A *statement of partners' capital* shows the changes in the partners' capital accounts during a fiscal period. Additional investments made by the partners and their shares of net income are added, and withdrawals are deducted from their beginning capital balances in arriving at their ending capital balances.

8 Factors that partners might consider in arriving at a plan to divide net income include:
a Amount of time each partner devotes to the business.

b Amount of capital invested by each partner.

c Other contributions by each partner to the success of the firm.

9 If the profit- and loss-sharing agreement provides for salary and interest allowances, any *residual* profit or loss must be divided in some ratio. These provisions are followed even if the net income for the year is less than the total of the salary and interest allowances. The excess of the salary and interest allowances over the net income is charged to the partners in the agreed residual profit- and loss-sharing ratio.

10 Salary and interest allowances to partners are merely a *step toward distributing net income*. Such allowances are *not expenses* to be deducted from revenue in arriving at net income.

11 Partnerships are not required to pay income taxes. However, each partner must pay personal income tax on *his or her share* of partnership net income, *regardless of the amount of withdrawals*.

12 The dominant form of business organization in the United States is the *corporation*. A corporation is an "artificial being" which is regarded as a legal person, having a continuous existence apart from its owners. Literally thousands, or even millions of individuals may be the owners of a single corporation; thus the corporation is an ideal means of amassing a great deal of investment capital.

13 A corporation offers certain advantages not found in other forms of business organizations:

a Limited personal liability—the maximum loss by individual stockholders in an unprofitable corporation is limited to the amount of their investment.

b Large amounts of capital may be gathered from the investing public.

c Shares of stock are easily transferable.

d A corporation is separate legal entity with a perpetual existence.

e Corporations are usually run by professional management.

14 Some *disadvantages of the corporate form* of organization are:

a A corporation is a *taxable entity* and must pay a high rate of tax on its net income.

b Corporations are subject to a considerable degree of regulation and disclosure of their business and financial affairs.

c The separation of ownership and management (effective control of corporate affairs) may result in management practices which are detrimental to stockholders.

15 A corporation is organized by filing an application with the appropriate state agency. application contains the articles of incorporation and the list of stockholders and directors. Costs of organizing a corporation are recorded in an *Organization Costs* account and are generally written off as expense over a five-year period.

16 Corporate stockholders have certain *basic rights*:

a To vote for directors.

b To share in profits by receiving dividends (distributions of earnings to the stockholders) declared by the board of directors.

c To share in the distribution of assets if the corporation is liquidated.

d To subscribe to additional shares of stock when the corporation decides to increase the amount of stock outstanding. (This right has been relinquished in some corporations.)

Stockholders *do not* have the right to intervene in the management of a corporation or transact corporation business.

17 The primary functions of the *board of directors* are to manage the corporation and protect the interests of the stockholders. The directors formulate general policies, declare dividends, and review the actions of corporate officers. The board of directors is elected by the stockholders and often includes *outside* directors who are not officers of the corporation.

18 The corporate officers are the active, full-time professional managers of a corporation. Corporate officers usually include a president, several vice-presidents, a controller, a treasurer, and a secretary.

19 Corporations may obtain funds by issuing capital stock, by borrowing money, and by retaining the resources generated from profitable operations. The stockholders' equity in a corporation consists of the capital invested by stockholders (paid-in capital), and the capital acquired through profitable operations (retained earnings). If capital contributed through operations is negative because of losses, a debit balance account called *Deficit* replaces the Retained Earnings account.

20 In order to appeal to a large number of investors, a corporation may issue more than one class of stock. When only one class of stock is issued, it is generally referred to as *capital stock*; when two or more classes of stock are outstanding they usually consist of *common stock* and various types of *preferred stock*.

21 The articles of incorporation specify the number of shares of capital stock which a corporation is authorized to issue and the *par value* (if any) per share. Par value (or stated value) represents *legal capital*—the amount below which stockholders' equity cannot be reduced except by losses. A dividend cannot be declared if it would reduce total stockholders' equity below the par value of the outstanding shares.

22 Capital stock is generally issued for a sum greater than the par (or stated) value; the excess is credited to Paid-in Capital in Excess of Par (or Stated) Value. Stock is almost never issued for less than par value. In the absence of a par or stated value, the entire proceeds are viewed as legal capital and are credited to the Capital Stock account.

23 Most *preferred stocks* have the following features: (a) full dividends to be paid before any dividends on common stock, (b) preferred claim to assets in case of liquidation, (c) callable at the option of the corporation, and (d) no voting power.

24 The dividend preference of most preferred stocks is *cumulative*. This means if any preferred dividends are omitted, these dividends must be *made up* before any dividends can be paid to common stockholders. Omitted dividends on preferred stock are called *dividends in arrears*.

25 Dividends in arrears are not listed as liabilities because no liability to pay a dividend exists unless the dividend has been declared by the directors.

26 A share of *convertible preferred stock* can be exchanged for an agreed number of shares of common stock. A holder of convertible preferred stock has greater assurance of receiving regular dividends than does a holder of common stock, while at the same time sharing in any increase in the value of the common stock.

27 An *underwriter* may help a corporation sell a large stock issue. The underwriter guarantees the issuing company a specific price for the stock, and makes a profit by selling the stock to the public at a higher price.

28 Market value of a share of stock depends on (a) the level of current and projected earnings, (b) the dividend rate per share, (c) the financial condition of the company, and (d) the mood of the stock market.

29 When stock is issued for assets other than cash, the *fair market value* of the noncash asset or the *market value* of the stock should be used as a basis for recording the transaction.

30 Small corporations sometimes allow investors to *subscribe* to stock by agreeing to pay for the stock in installments or at a future date. The issuing corporation debits Subscriptions Receivable and credits Capital Stock Subscribed when the subscription contract is signed.

31 Once stock is issued, most further stock transactions on the open market are between investors and do not affect the corporation which issued the stock.

32 Ownership of stock is evidenced by a *stock certificate* showing the name of the stockholder and the number of shares owned. At the time of issue, the stock certificate is signed by the president and secretary of the issuing corporation and delivered to the stockholder. When the stockholder sells the shares, the certificate is returned to the corporation and canceled. A new certificate is issued to the new owner of the stock.

33 The balance sheet accounts relating to capital stock are actually control accounts. In order to know who the individual stockholders are, the corporation usually maintains a *stockholders' ledger*. This ledger is continually updated for changes in identity of stockholders.

34 For large corporations, a bank or trust company may serve as a *stock transfer agent* and perform the task of updating the stockholders' ledger. Another bank may act as a *stock registrar* who assumes responsibility for issuing stock certificates to stockholders.

TEST YOURSELF ON CORPORATIONS

True or False

For each of the following statements, circle the T or the F to indicate whether the statement is true or false.

T F 1 The owner's equity for a single proprietorship is typically reported in a single account; in a corporation the owners' equity may be reported in three accounts: Capital Stock, Paid-in Capital in Excess of Par, and Retained Earnings.

T F 2 Some states deny the incorporation privilege to persons engaged in certain professions (such as law and public accounting), because the stock issued by a service-type corporation would be too risky for investors.

T F 3 *Mutual agency* means that each partner has the right to bind the partnership to contracts.

T F 4 Each partner's liability for losses incurred by the partnership is limited to his or her investment in the firm.

T F 5 When a profit- and loss-sharing agreement provides for salary and interest allowances to the partners, these salary and interest allowances should be deducted from revenue in arriving at partnership net income.

T F 6 A partner must pay personal income tax on the amount of withdrawals from a partnership, regardless of his or her share of partnership profits or losses.

T F 7 In the absence of a specific agreement, the law requires that partnership profits be divided equally among the partners.

T F 8 Any individual stockholder in a corporation may personally be held liable for all debts incurred by the corporation.

T F 9 A corporation has continuity of existence which permits the business to continue regardless of changes in ownership or the death of a stockholder.

T F 10 A stockholder in a corporation does not have the right to transact corporate business or intervene in the management of the business.

T F 11 Stockholders of a corporation elect the board of directors, which in turn appoints the top officers of the corporation.

T F 12 Organization costs are usually written off as expense in the period when a corporation is organized.

T F 13 The officers of a corporation cannot own stock in that corporation; they are professional managers and not investors.

T F 14 The expression *double taxation* refers to the fact that the net income of a corporation is taxed both by the state in which it is incorporated and by the federal government.

T F 15 When capital stock is sold for a price higher than par value, the Capital Stock account is credited only for the par value of the shares sold.

T F 16 Dividends in arrears refers to bypassed preferred dividends which must be made up before any dividends may be paid on common stock.

T F 17 In case of liquidation, the claims of the preferred stockholders are given preference over the claims of creditors.

T F 18 Common stock of Corporation X pays an annual $1 per share dividend and sells for $15 per share on the open market. The corporation's $1.80 convertible preferred stock is selling for $37 per share and is convertible into two shares of common stock. The holder of 100 shares of the convertible preferred stock should exchange his holdings for 200 shares of common stock because this action will increase his annual dividend revenue from $180 to $200.

T F 19 An underwriter guarantees the issuing corporation a set price for a new issue of stock and then resells the stock to the investing public at a higher price.

T F 20 Subscriptions receivable is a current asset which results from investors subscribing to stock for which they will pay at some future date.

Completion Statements

Fill in the necessary words or amounts to complete the following statements:

1 If the owner of a single proprietorship withdraws merchandise for personal use, the owner's _____ account should be debited for the _____ of the merchandise withdrawn.

2 Income tax expense appears in the income statement of a _____ but does not appear in the income statement of a _____ _____ or a _____ .

3 Carr and Davis agree to share profits in a 2 to 1 ratio *after* allowing salaries of $20,000 to Carr and $28,000 to Davis. Assuming that they earn only $12,000 *before* taking into account the salary allowances, Carr's share of the $12,000 profit will be $_____ and Davis' share will be $_____.

4 A partner invested an additional $14,000 in the partnership during Year 1. His share of partnership net income for Year 1 was $29,000, of which he withdrew only $18,000. The amount of partnership income that the partner must report on his personal income tax return is $_____.

5 Among the disadvantages of the corporate form of organization are (a)_____ _____ and (b)_____ _____.

6 The maximum possible loss of the stockholders in a corporation is limited to_____ _____.

7 When common stock is issued at price above par value, the_____ _____of the shares issued is_____ to the_____ _____ account, and the excess is_____ to an account called_____ _____ _____ _____ _____ _____.

8 Par value represents_____ _____, which cannot be paid as dividends to stockholders.

9 The conversion of preferred stock into common generally requires a debit to_____ _____ and credits to_____ _____ and_____ _____ _____ _____ _____.

10 A corporation had total assets of $400,000 and total liabilities of $150,000 at the beginning of Year 1. At the end of Year 1, it reported total assets of $600,000 and total liabilities of $200,000. During Year 1 it paid dividends of $48,000, representing 60% of its earnings. The total stockholders' equity at the end of Year 1 amounted to $_____, the earnings for Year 1 amounted to $_____, and additional shares of capital stock were issued during Year 1 for $_____.

Multiple Choice

Choose the best answer for each of the following questions and enter the identifying letter in the space provided.

____ 1 Periodic withdrawals by partners are best viewed as:
a Payment for partners' personal services to the partnership.
b Expenses of doing business.
c Taxable income to the partners.
d Distribution of partnership assets to the partners.

____ 2 Smith invests in a partnership some land which cost his father $10,000. The land had a market value of $15,000 when Smith inherited it six years ago, and currently the land is independently appraised at $25,000 even though Smith insists that he "wouldn't take $250,000 for it." The land should be recorded in the accounts of the partnership at:
a $10,000
b $15,000
c $25,000
d $50,000

____ 3 Which of the following best describes the nature of salary and interest allowances in a partnership profit- and loss-sharing agreement?
a Expenses of the business, which should be deducted from revenue in determining net income.
b The amount upon which each partner will have to pay personal income tax.
c A means of distributing net income in relation to services rendered and capital invested by partners.
d A means of determining reasonable monthly withdrawals by each partner.

____ 4 One of the following is *not* a characteristic of the corporate form of organization:
a Limited liability of shareholders.
b Mutual agency.
c Centralized authority.
d Continuous existence.

____ 5 Which of the following is *not* a characteristic of most preferred stock issues?
a Preference as to dividends.
b Participating clause.
c Preference as to assets in event of liquidation.
d No voting power.

____ 6 Which of the following is most relevant in determining the *cost* of assets acquired in exchange for capital stock?
a Par or stated value of the stock.
b Market value of the stock.

c Issuance price of stock already outstanding.

d Estimated useful life of the assets.

7 The Aaron Corporation is authorized to issue 100,000 shares of $10 par value capital stock. It issues one-half of the stock for $25 per share, earns $20,000 during the first three months of operation, and declares a cash dividend of $5,000. The total paid-in capital of the Aaron Corporation after three months of operation is:

a $1,000,000

b $1,020,000

c $1,250,000

d $1,265,000

8 A *deficit* appears on the balance sheet:

a Among the assets.

b As a deduction from total paid-in capital.

c As a deduction from Income Taxes Payable.

d Among the liabilities.

9 One of the following is *not* an officer of a corporation:

a Stock registrar.

b Controller.

c Secretary.

d Treasurer.

10 When stock is sold on a subscription basis and the entire subscription price has been collected, the issuance of the stock is recorded by:

a A debit to Cash and a credit to Capital Stock.

b A debit to Subscriptions Receivable: Capital Stock and a credit to Capital Stock Subscribed.

c A debit to Capital Stock Subscribed and a credit to Capital Stock.

d A debit to Capital Stock and a credit to Subscriptions Receivable: Capital Stock.

Exercises

1 A and B are partners, having capital balances at the beginning of Year 1 of $20,000 and $30,000, respectively. Indicate in the appropriate columns the division of partnership net income between the partners under the specified conditions. If in any case the division results in a deduction from partner's capital, place brackets around your answer to indicate this.

	A's Share	B's Share
First situation: Net income of the partnership is $120,000; partnership agreement provides for:		
a Net income to be divided in the ratio of beginning capitals	$	$
b Interest on beginning capitals at 12%; residual profit or loss divided 70% to A, 30% to B	$	$
c Interest on beginning capitals at 12%; salary to A of $48,000, to B of $36,000, residual profit or loss divided equally	$	$
Second situation: Net loss of the partnership is $16,000; partnership agreement:	$	$
a Is silent as to sharing profits or losses		
b Provides salary to A of $28,000; salary to B of $20,000; residual profit or loss divided 40% to A and 60% to B	$	$

2 Selected account balances for K and L, who share profits 60% to K and 40% to L, are shown at the end of Year 1:

Account	Amount
Income Summary	$25,000 (Cr)
K, Drawing	11,000 (Dr)
L, Drawing	16,000 (Dr)
K, Capital	18,000 (Cr)
L, Capital	17,750 (Cr)

a In the space provided on the following page, prepare the closing entries required at the end of Year 1. Omit explanations.

General Journal

	Income Summary		

b Complete the partially filled-in statement of the partners' capitals shown below for Year 1, assuming that the partners did not invest additional capital in the business during the year.

K&L
Statement of Partners' Capitals
For Year 1

	K	L	Total
Balance, beginning of year . . .	$18,400	$17,750	$36,150
Add: Net income for year . . .			
Subtotal	$	$	$
Less: Withdrawals.			
Balance, end of year	$	$	$

4 Complete the stockholders' equity section from the account balances shown below:

Organization costs	$ 7,000
Retained earnings.	128,000
Paid-in capital in excess of par: preferred stock	10,000
Common stock, no-par value, 50,000 shares. .	200,000
$4 preferred stock, $100 par, 1,000 shares . .	100,000
Receivable from underwriters (from sale of stock)	$ 40,000
Plant and equipment	315,000
Accumulated depreciation	125,000
Notes payable	100,000

3 Ernst Corporation has outstanding 10,000 shares each of two classes of $100 par value stock: 5% cumulative preferred stock and common stock. The corporation reported a deficit of $20,000 at the beginning of Year 2, and preferred dividends have not been paid for one year. During Year 2 the corporation earned $180,000. How large a dividend per share did the corporation pay on the common stock if the balance in retained earnings at the end of Year 2 amounted to $25,000? Use the space below for computations.

Stockholders' equity:

$4 preferred stock, $100 par value, 1,000 shares issued and outstanding	$
Total paid-in capital	$
Total stockholders' equity	$

12

CORPORATIONS: A CLOSER LOOK

HIGHLIGHTS OF THE CHAPTER

1 To assist users of an income statement in estimating the income likely to occur in future periods, the results of unusual and nonrecurring transactions are shown in a separate section of the income statement after the income or loss from normal business activities has been determined. Current accounting practice recognizes three categories of "unusual" transactions and accords each one a different treatment in the income statement. These categories are: (1) the operating results of a segment of the business which has been discontinued during the current year, (2) extraordinary items, and (3) other nonoperating items.

2 A *segment* of a business is a component of a company whose activities represent a major line of business or class of customer. The assets and operating results of a segment of a business should be clearly identifiable from other assets and operating results of the company.

3 The operating results of a segment discontinued during the current period are reported separately in the income statement *after* developing the subtotal, *Income from Continuing Operations*. This subtotal presumably is a better indicator of the earning power of continuing operations than is the net income figure.

4 The revenue and expenses shown in the income statement for the year in which a segment of a business is eliminated include *only the revenue and expenses from continuing operations*. The net income or loss

from discontinued operations is reported separately; the total revenue from the discontinued segment is disclosed in the notes to the financial statements. Any gain or loss on the disposal of a segment should be reported with the results of the discontinued operations.

5 When an income statement includes sections for both continuing and discontinued operations, the company's income tax expense should be allocated between these sections. Only the income tax expense applicable to continuing operations should be deducted as an expense in arriving at Income from Continuing Operations. Any income tax expense (or tax savings) related to the discontinued operations should be considered along with other expenses of the discontinued segment in computing the income (or loss) from discontinued operations.

6 *Extraordinary items* are transactions and events that are *both unusual in nature and occur infrequently in the operating environment of a business*. Examples of extraordinary items include:

a Effects of major casualties, such as an earthquake.

b Expropriation (seizure) of assets by foreign governments.

c Effects of prohibition of a product under a newly enacted law or regulation.

7 When a company has an extraordinary gain or loss in its income statement, *Income before Extraordinary Items* is developed as a subtotal before presentation of the extraordinary items. The extraordinary item is then subtracted (or added) to Income before Extraordinary Items to arrive at net income.

8 Items which qualify as extraordinary losses are rare and extraordinary gains are almost nonexistent. Such things as gains and losses from disposal of plant assets and losses from strikes or lawsuits *do not qualify* as extraordinary items because they are not considered both unusual and infrequent in the environment of a business. These items may be separately identified in the income statement to focus attention on their *nonoperating* nature, but they should be included in Income *before* Extraordinary Items.

9 Income taxes relating to all income *except* the extraordinary item are an expense deducted in arriving at Income before Extraordinary Items. However, any increase or decrease in this income tax expense *which is caused by the extraordinary item* should be shown *as part of the extraordinary gain or loss*.

10 The income or loss from a discontinued segment of the business is not an extraordinary item. When discontinued operations and an extraordinary item appear in the same income statement, the income or loss from the discontinued operations is presented *before* the extraordinary item. Thus, Income before Extraordinary Items includes the operating results of any segments of the business which have been discontinued during the year.

11 Perhaps the most widely used of all accounting statistics is *earnings per share* of common stock. To compute earnings per share, the net income *available to the common stock* is divided by the *weighted-average* number of common shares outstanding during the year. Net income available to the common stock is total net income *less the current year's dividends on preferred stock*. Earnings per share is intended to show the claim of each share of common stock to the earnings of the company.

12 Convertible preferred stock and other securities convertible into common stock pose a special problem in computing earnings per share. If these securities are converted, more common stock will be outstanding and earnings per share will be *diluted* to a smaller figure. Companies with complex capital structures show two earnings per share figures: (a) *primary earnings per share*, based upon the weighted-average number of common shares *actually* outstanding, and (b) *fully diluted earnings per share*, based

on the *maximum potential* number of shares outstanding.

13 Earnings per share based upon reported net income are shown at the bottom of the income statement. If the income statement includes Income before Extraordinary Items or Income from Continuing Operations, these subtotals should also be presented on a per-share basis.

14 A *dividend* is generally understood to mean a pro rata cash distribution by a corporation to its stockholders. Dividends are declared by the board of directors after giving careful consideration to such factors as the balance in retained earnings and the company's cash position. Four dates are usually involved in the distribution of a dividend:

a Date of declaration.
b Date of record.
c Ex-dividend date.
d Date of payment.

15 Dividends are sometimes paid in a form other than cash, such as securities of other corporations or merchandise. A *liquidating dividend* usually takes place when a corporation goes out of business and distributes assets in final liquidation. A *stock dividend* is a distribution to stockholders of additional shares of the corporation's own stock.

16 A *stock dividend* causes no change in assets or in the total amount of the stockholders' equity. The only effect of a stock dividend is the transfer of a portion of the retained earnings into the Capital Stock and the Paid-in Capital from Stock Dividends accounts. A stock dividend increases the number of common shares outstanding and decreases the book value per share. Each stockholder owns a larger number of shares after the stock dividend, but his or her total equity in the corporation remains unchanged.

17 What, then, are the reasons for distributing stock dividends? The reasons usually are:

a To conserve cash. During profitable years when business is expanding, a stock dividend is distributed in lieu of a cash dividend so that all available cash can be used in the business.
b To reduce the price per share of stock. When the price of a share of stock is high, a large stock dividend will reduce the price per share to a more convenient trading range.
c To avoid income tax on stockholders. Stock dividends are not considered as taxable income to the recipients.

18 A "small" stock dividend may range from 1% of the outstanding stock to a maximum of 20 to 25%. Stock dividends of this size are recorded by a debit to Retained Earnings equal to the total *market value* of the additional shares being distributed, a credit to Stock Dividend to Be Distributed equal to the par or stated value of the additional shares, and a credit to Paid-in Capital from Stock Dividends equal to the excess of market value over par (or stated) value of the "dividend" shares. When the shares are distributed, Stock Dividend to Be Distributed is debited and Capital Stock is credited.

19 Stock dividends in excess of, say, 20 to 25% are not considered small and are subject to different accounting treatment. They should be recorded by transferring only the *par or stated value* of the dividend shares from Retained Earnings to the Capital Stock account.

20 A *stock split* is effected by reducing the par or stated value of the capital stock and issuing a larger number of shares to each stockholder. In a 5 for 1 split, for example, the par value may be reduced from $10 to $2, and a shareholder owning 100 shares before the split would own 500 shares after the split.

21 Assume that a company discovers that a material error was made in the measurement of the net income of a prior year. How should this error be corrected? Since the net income of the prior year has been closed into Retained Earnings, the error is corrected by adjusting the balance of the Retained Earnings account. Such adjustments are called *prior period adjustments*. A prior period adjustment has no effect upon the net income of the current period and does not appear in the income statement; it is shown in the statement of retained earnings.

22 The *statement of retained earnings* is a vehicle for reconciling the beginning balance in retained earnings with the ending balance. The usual format of the statement is to combine any prior period adjustments with the beginning balance as originally reported. The restated beginning balance is then increased by the net income for the current year and reduced by the amount of dividends declared in arriving at the ending balance.

23 Some companies employ a *combined statement of income and retained earnings* which shows operating results as well as a reconciliation of the beginning and ending balances in retained earnings. This form of reporting is sometimes criticized because it "buries" the important net income figure within the body of the "combined" statement.

24 Retained earnings of a corporation are either unrestricted and available for dividends or restricted (earmarked) for some specific purpose, such as to absorb possible losses or to show that retained earnings are not available for dividends because the funds generated by profitable operations are needed to finance an expansion of plant facilties.

25 Most companies disclose restrictions upon the availability of retained earnings for dividends in a note to their financial statements. A few companies, however, formally record the restriction in their accounting records by *appropriating* a portion of the balance of the Retained Earnings account. An appropriation of retained earnings is recorded by a debit to Retained Earnings and a credit to an appropriations account. The appropriation does not consist of cash or any other asset; it is simply a separate account reported within the stockholders' equity in the balance sheet. When the appropriation is no longer needed, it is returned to retained earnings by a debit to the appropriation account and a credit to Retained Earnings.

26 If a corporation acquires its own stock from stockholders, the reacquired stock is referred to as *treasury stock*. Treasury stock may be held indefinitely or may be reissued; it is not entitled to receive dividends or to vote.

27 Treasury stock is generally recorded at cost and is deducted from the total of the paid-in capital and retained earnings in the balance sheet. *Treasury stock is not an asset*. If the treasury stock is reissued, the Treasury Stock account is credited for the cost of the shares sold, and Paid-in Capital from Treasury Stock Transactions would be debited or credited for the difference between cost and resale price.

28 The purchase of treasury stock is similar to a dividend in that a distribution of cash is made to stockholders. If a corporation is to keep its paid-in capital intact, it must not pay out to its stockholders any more than it earns. Thus retained earnings equal to the cost of treasury stock purchased is restricted and is not available for cash dividends.

29 When only a single class of stock is outstanding, the *book value* per share is computed by

Retained Earning   mkt value
E/Stock Div to be dist.
gain Paid in Cap N
per value

CHAPTER 12 / CORPORATIONS: A CLOSER LOOK   **83**

dividing the total stockholders' equity by the number of shares outstanding. When both preferred and common stock are outstanding, the book value per share of common stock is computed by dividing the number of shares of common stock into the common stockholders' equity (total stockholders' equity less the redemption value of preferred stock and any dividends in arrears).

TEST YOURSELF ON CORPORATIONS

True or False

For each of the following statements, circle the T or the F to indicate whether the statement is true or false.

T F   1 The net income figure generally is considered to be a better indicator of future operating results than is the subtotal, Income before Extraordinary Items.

T F   2 The income statement of a corporation should always include the subtotal Income from Continuing Operations.

T F   3 Fully diluted earnings per share usually is a larger figure than primary earnings per share.

T F   4 Most corporations whose stock is publicly owned report the results of the current year's operations in comparison with the results of the previous year.

T F   5 When retained earnings are appropriated to cover a contingency, cash is set aside as a reserve to pay for the contingency if it occurs.

T F   6 When an appropriation of retained earnings is no longer required, the appropriation (reserve) account is closed by a debit and an extraordinary gain account is credited.

T F   7 Any cash paid by a corporation to a stockholder is properly referred to as a dividend.

T F   8 An event which is unusual and occurs only once every three or four years should be classified as an extraordinary item.

T F   9 The reason for showing Income before Extraordinary Items or Income from Continuing Operations in an income statement is that these subtotals are considered useful in forecasting future earnings.

T F   10 Stockholders must approve a dividend action taken by the board of directors.

T F   11 A policy of paying regular quarterly dividends tends to give a higher investment quality to common stock.

T F   12 Income tax effects should be ignored in computing the income or loss from a discontinued segment of the business.

T F   13 The investor who purchases shares of the X Co. on the ex-dividend date will not receive the next dividend paid by X Co.

T F   14 A 3 for 1 split places stockholders of a company in essentially the same position as a 200% stock dividend.

T F   15 A corporation's stockholders' equity accounts will be the same whether it declares a 100% stock dividend or splits its stock 2 for 1.

T F   16 It may be argued that a stock dividend is not really a dividend since the corporation distributes no assets to its stockholders as a result of such action; however, stockholders welcome stock dividends and some corporations continue to distribute them from time to time.

T F   17 Prior period adjustments include all gains or losses which are not a part of the main activities of the business.

T F   18 The reissuance of treasury stock at a price in excess of the cost of these shares is a source of paid-in capital.

T F   19 A corporation cannot acquire its own stock in the open market unless it has retained earnings at least equal to the purchase price.

T F   20 The book value of a share of common stock usually approximates the market price of the stock, particularly for growth companies such as McDonald's, Polaroid, and IBM.

Completion Statements

Fill in the necessary words or amounts to complete the following statements:

1 Large unexpected losses from inability to collect accounts receivable or from the shrinkage in the value of inventories should be taken into account in computing _Income_ before _extraordinary_ _Items_.

2 Companies with convertible preferred stock outstanding generally report both _primary_ earnings per share based upon the _weighted average_ number of common shares outstanding, and _diluted fully diluted_ earnings per share, based upon the potential number of outstanding common shares.

3 The correction of an error in the measurement of the net income of a prior year is called a _prior period adjustment_ and is reported in the _Statement retained earnings_ as an adjustment to the balance of _retained earnings_ at the _beginning_ of the current period.

4 Dividends in arrears on preferred stock are not reported as a liability in the balance sheet but should be disclosed by a _footnote_ accompanying the financial statements.

5 On January 1, the Avery Corporation had 100,000 shares of capital stock with a par value of $10, paid-in capital in excess of par of $300,000, and retained earnings of $700,000. During the year the company split its stock 2 for 1 (reducing the par value to $5 per share) and subsequently declared a 2% stock dividend (its first) when the market value of the stock was $40. It earned $200,000 during the year and paid no cash dividends. (a) At the end of the year the balance in the Capital Stock account will be $ _1,020,000_; (b) the balance in Paid-in Capital in Excess of Par will be $ _440,000_; and (c) the balance in Retained Earnings will be $ _740,000_.

6 Given below is a list of accounts which appear in a balance sheet for a corporation. The stock dividend, which has not yet been distributed, is the first in the company's history.

Appropriation for purchase of treasury stock	$ 20,000
Accumulated earnings—unappropriated	780,000
Paid-in capital in excess of par	317,400
Paid-in capital from stock dividends . .	103,400
Stock dividend to be distributed (10%)	94,000
Treasury stock, 1,000 shares at cost . .	20,000 (debit)
Capital stock, $10 par value	950,000
Paid-in capital from treasury stock transactions	14,000
Cash dividends payable	18,800
Appropriation for bond sinking fund . .	100,000

Complete the following: (a) Total of accumulated (retained) earnings, including appropriations, is $ _____; (b) the latest cash dividend per share amounted to $ _____; (c) treasury stock was acquired (before, after) _before_ the declaration of the 10% stock dividend; (d) total stockholders' equity is $ _____; (e) the market price of stock at the time the 10% stock dividend was declared was $ _____ per share.

7 The book value of a share of capital stock is $10 per share. For each of the independent events listed below, use a check mark to indicate whether the transaction or event will increase, decrease, or have no effect on the book value per share of stock.

Transaction or Event	Increase	Decrease	No Effect
a Declaration of cash dividend		✓	
b Distribution of a 20% stock dividend		✓	
c A 4 for 1 stock split		✓	
d Net income is reported for latest year	✓		
e Additional stock is sold at $8 per share		✓	
f Treasury stock is acquired at $12 per share		✓	
g Additional stock is sold at $14 per share	✓		

Multiple Choice

Choose the best answer for each of the following questions and enter the identifying letter in the space provided.

1 Which of the following is *least* important in determining the fair market value of a share of stock?

a Earnings and dividends per share.

b Book value per share.

c The available supply of the shares and the demand to purchase the shares.

d The par or stated value per share.

2 Which of the following qualifies as an extraordinary item?

a Gain on sale of unprofitable consumer goods division.

b A large, unexpected write-off of an account receivable.

c A write-off and abandonment of goods in process inventory because of a new government regulation prohibiting the use of one of the ingredients.

d Additional depreciation recorded because of reduction in useful life of assets.

3 The financial statements of Fields Corporation reported earnings of $4,000,000 from continuing operations, a $700,000 loss from a segment of the business discontinued during the year, a $300,000 decrease in retained earnings as a result of a prior period adjustment, and a $500,000 extraordinary loss. The amount appearing in the income statement as Income Before Extraordinary Items was:

a $4,000,000

b $3,300,000

c $3,000,000

d Some other amount

4 The book value per share of Company B stock on January 1, Year 4, was $31.50 per share. During Year 4, the stock was split 3 for 1, and shortly afterwards a 5% stock dividend was declared. At the end of the year, a $1 cash dividend was declared and earnings per share of $3.10 were announced. The book value per share of stock as of December 31, Year 4, amounted to:

a $10.50

b $10.70

c $12.10

d $13.10

5 The James Corporation had 100,000 shares of common stock and 5,000 shares of preferred stock outstanding at the beginning of Year 1. Each share of preferred stock was con-

vertible into 4 shares of common stock (8 shares following the 2 for 1 split in November). On April 1, 10,000 shares of common stock were sold for cash and on November 3, the common stock was split 2 for 1. The weighted-average number of shares outstanding for Year 1 in computing primary earnings per share is:

a 255,000

b 220,000

c 205,000

d 215,000

6 The distribution of a 20% stock dividend on common stock:

a Reduces the book value per share of common stock outstanding.

b Does not change the number of shares of common stock outstanding.

c Decreases total stockholders' equity.

d Increases the net assets of the corporation.

7 When a corporation declares a cash dividend on common stock, which of the following should be excluded in determining the *total amount* of the dividend?

a Shares issued in exchange for preferred stock.

b Shares held by officers and directors.

c Shares held by other corporations.

d Shares reacquired and held in treasury.

8 Revenue and expenses relating to a segment of business discontinued during the year are:

a Netted and reported as an extraordinary item.

b Included in total revenue and expenses as reported in the income statement.

c Netted and reported as a separate item following income from continuing operations.

d Netted and reported as a prior period adjustment.

9 In recording a large stock dividend, say 50 or 100%, the amount of retained earnings transferred to paid-in capital is generally measured by:

a The market value of the stock on the date of declaration.

b The book value of the stock on the date of declaration.

c The par (or stated) value of the additional shares issued.

d The amount authorized by the board of directors to be transferred from the Retained Earnings account.

10 Treasury stock is best described as:

a Unissued stock.

b Reacquired stock which was previously outstanding.

c An asset acquired by making a cash disbursement.

d Retirement of a portion of outstanding stock which increases total stockholders' equity.

Exercises

1 The Axel Company had issued 105,000 shares of capital stock, of which 5,000 shares were held in the treasury throughout the year. During the year, the company reported income from continuing operations of 5% of sales, and a loss from a segment of the business discontinued during the year of $300,000 (net of the income tax benefit). Sales from continuing operations were $4,200,000, gross profit rate on sales amounted to 30%, and income taxes were 40% of income before taxes. In the space below prepare the income statement for Axel Company, including the earnings per share figures.

AXEL COMPANY
Income Statement
for the Current Year

Sales	$4,200,000
Cost of goods sold	2,940,000
Gross profit on sales (30%)	$1,260,000
Operating expenses	
Operating income (before taxes)	$210,000
Income taxes (40% of operating income) . .	
Income from continuing operations	$
Loss from discontinued operations, net of income tax benefit	(300,000)
Net loss	$
Per share of capital stock:	
Income from continuing operations . . .	$
Loss from discontinued operations	
Net loss	$

2 The income statement of Windjammer Company shows income from continuing operations of $490,000 and income from a segment of the business discontinued near year-end of $182,000 (net of income taxes). The company had 100,000 shares of common stock and 10,000 shares of $6 convertible preferred stock outstanding throughout the year. Each share of preferred stock is convertible into four shares of common stock. Compute the following earnings per share figures for Windjammer company:

Earnings from continuing operations:	
Primary:	$_____
Fully diluted:	$_____
Net earnings:	
Primary:	$_____
Fully diluted:	$_____

3 At the beginning of Year 1, Bender Mfg. Company had 250,000 shares of $5 par value common stock outstanding. In the space provided below, prepare journal entries to record the following selected transactions during Year 1:

Mar. 1 Declared a cash dividend of 80 cents per share, payable on Mar. 21.

Mar. 21 Paid cash dividend declared on Mar. 1.

Aug. 10 Declared 5% stock dividend. The market price of the stock on this date was $40 per share.

Sept. 2 Issued 12,500 shares pursuant to 5% stock dividend declared on Aug. 10.

Dec. 21 Declared and issued a 100% stock dividend. The market price of the stock on this date was $60 per share.

Dec. 30 Acquired 1,000 shares of its own common stock on the open market at $30 per share.

	General Journal		
Year 1			
Mar. 1	Dividends		
	Declared cash dividend of $0.80 per share on 250,000 shares.		
21			
Aug. 10			
Sept. 2			
Dec. 21			
30			

13

BONDS PAYABLE, LEASES, AND OTHER LIABILITIES

HIGHLIGHTS OF THE CHAPTER

1 Bonds payable are a popular form of long-term financing. Bonds payable may be secured by specific property or may be unsecured. An unsecured bond is referred to as a *debenture bond*. Most bonds have a single maturity date (for example, 20 or 25 years from date of issue); some bond issues provide for varying maturity dates and are known as *serial bonds*.

2 Most bonds are *callable* at the option of the issuing corporation at stipulated dates and prices. Some bonds are *convertible* into common stock at the option of the bondholder. If the corporation is successful and the price of its common stock appreciates substantially, the owner of convertible bonds can share in the company's success by converting the bonds into common stock.

3 Most bonds today are *registered*, in contrast to *coupon* bonds which were popular some years ago. When bonds are registered, the issuing corporation maintains a record of the individual bondholders and mails them the periodic interest checks. When bonds have coupons attached, the bondholder receives the interest payment by depositing the appropriate interest coupon in a bank; the corporation maintains no record identifying the bondholders.

4 Bonds of large, well-established companies are readily transferable because they are generally traded on one or more securities exchanges. The quotations for bonds are usually given in terms of a percentage of the par value. Thus, a $1,000 bond sold at 97½

would bring $975 before deducting commissions or taking accrued interest into account.

5 A major advantage of raising capital by issuing bonds rather than stock is that bond interest payments are deductible in determining taxable income, while dividend payments are not. Also, if a company can earn a return higher than the fixed cost of bonds, net income and earnings per share will increase. If stock were issued, the additional shares would tend to offset the increase in earnings per share.

6 Bonds generally pay interest every six months. When bonds are issued between interest dates, the buyer is charged for the accrued interest from the last interest payment date to date of sale, and the issuing corporation credits Bond Interest Payable. This account is then debited (along with Interest Expense) at the next interest payment date.

7 The *present value* of a future cash payment is the amount that a knowledgeable investor would pay *today* for the right to receive that future payment. The present value will always be less than the future amount, because money on hand today can be invested to become equivalent to a larger amount in the future. This principle is sometimes called the *time value of money*.

8 The rate of interest which will cause a given present value to grow to a given future amount is called the *effective interest rate*. At any given time, the effective interest rate required by investors is the *going market rate* of interest. The price at which bonds will sell is the present value to investors of

the future principal and interest payments. The *higher* the going market rate of interest (effective interest rate), the *less* investors will pay for bonds with a given contract rate of interest.

9 If the contractual rate of interest that the bonds pay is lower than the "going market rate," the *bonds will sell at a discount*. If the bonds pay a rate in excess of the going market rate, the *bonds will sell at a premium*. The bond discount is deducted from the par value of the bonds and the premium is added to the par value in reporting bonds payable in the balance sheet.

10 The *carrying value* (or book value) of a bond issue is its face value plus any premium or minus any discount. At the date of issuance, the carrying value is equal to the amount for which the bonds were sold. Over the life of the bonds, the carrying value will gradually move toward the maturity value of the bonds as the discount or premium is *amortized*.

11 When bonds are sold at a discount, the corporation must repay more than it borrowed. Total interest expense over the life of the bond issue is equal to the regular cash interest payments *plus the amount of the discount*. To measure annual interest expense, the discount should be *amortized into interest expense over the life of the bonds*.

12 A discount is amortized by an entry debiting Interest Expense and crediting the contra-liability account Discount on Bonds Payable. The effects of this entry are (a) to *increase* the amount of interest expense recognized in the current period and (b) to *increase* the carrying value of the liability for bonds payable (by decreasing the balance of the contra-liability account) toward its maturity value.

13 Amortization of a discount increases interest expense but involves no additional cash payment in the current period. The additional interest expense corresponds to an increase in the long-term liability for bonds payable.

14 When bonds are sold at a premium, the corporation must repay *less* than the amount borrowed. Total interest expense over the life of the bond issue is equal to the regular cash interest payments *minus the amount of the premium*. To measure annual interest expense, the premium must be *amortized as a reduction in interest expense* over the life of the bonds.

15 A premium is amortized by an entry crediting Interest Expense and debiting the liability account Premium on Bonds payable. The effects of this entry are (a) to *reduce* the amount of interest expense recognized in the current period and (b) to *reduce* the carrying value of the liability for bonds payable toward its maturity value.

16 Amortization of the premium reduces interest expense but it does not reduce the amount of the cash interest payment for the current period. The reduction in interest expense is accompanied by a reduction in the long-term liability for bonds payable.

17 Bond discount or premium may be amortized by two methods:

a *Straight-line method* This method amortizes an equal portion of the discount or premium each period over the life of the bonds. Mechanically, straight-line amortization is similar to straight-line depreciation.

b *Effective interest method* In this method, the carrying value of the bonds at the beginning of each period is multiplied by the effective interest rate for the bond issue. The amount of discount or premium amortized is the *difference* between the interest expense computed in this manner and the contractual (cash) interest expense for the period. Since the carrying value of the liability for bonds payable moves closer to maturity value every period, this method results in a *slightly different interest expense every period*. However, the interest expense will always be a *constant percentage* of the carrying value of the liability for bonds payable.

18 The FASB requires the use of the effective interest method of amortization whenever it would produce results *materially different* from those obtained by the straight-line method. An *amortization table* can be prepared to show the effective interest expense and amount of discount or premium amortization for each period in the life of the bond issue. The periodic journal entries may then be made directly from this table.

19 A *bond sinking fund* may be accumulated in order to have sufficient cash when the bonds mature to pay off the liability. The fund is accumulated through periodic deposits with a trustee who invests the cash in the company's bonds or in other income-yielding securities. The fund represents an asset (reported as an investment) of the corporation.

20 If bonds are retired before maturity at a price above their carrying value, a loss results; if bonds are retired at a price below their carrying value, a gain is realized. Gains and losses on the early retirement of bonds should be shown in the income statement as *extraordinary items*. No gain or loss is recognized by the issuing corporation upon the conversion of bonds into common stock; the carrying value of the bonds converted is assigned to the common stock issued.

21 Companies making *long-term investments* in bonds are required by the FASB to amortize the difference between the cost of the investment and its maturity value over the life of the bonds. This amortization should follow the effective interest method, which results in a constant rate of return over the life of the investment. Investors do not use separate accounts to record the face value of the investment and any related discount or premium. Thus, amortization of the difference between cost and maturity value results in a direct adjustment of the Investment account.

22 A *lease* is a contract in which the *lessor* gives the *lessee* the right to use an asset in return for periodic rental payments. Lease contracts may be *operating leases*, in which the lessor retains the risks and returns of ownership, or *capital leases*, in which the objectives are to provide financing to the lessee for the eventual purchase of the property. Lessees should make full disclosure of the terms of all noncancelable leases in their financial statements.

23 In an operating lease, the periodic rentals are recorded as revenue by the lessor and as rental expense by the lessee. No liability is recognized by the lessee other than for any accrued monthly rentals.

24 A capital lease, which is essentially equivalent to a sale and purchase, should be recorded as a sale by the lessor and as a purchase by the lessee. The asset and related liability should be recorded by the lessee at the *present value* of the future lease payments. The lessee should depreciate the asset over its estimated useful life rather than over the life of the lease.

25 Mortgages payable generally call for monthly payments, including interest and repayment of principal. The portion of unpaid principal maturing within one year should be classified as a current liability in the balance sheet.

26 A pension plan is a contract between a company and its employees under which the company agrees to pay retirement benefits to eligible employees. In a *funded* pension plan, the employer makes regular payments to an insurance company or other agency (debit Pension Expense and credit Cash). When employees retire, their retirement benefits are paid by the insurance company.

27 The most common accrued liabilities found in the balance sheets of many businesses relate to payrolls. These include FICA Tax Payable, Liability for Income Tax Withheld, Accrued Payroll, State Unemployment Tax Payable, and Federal Unemployment Tax Payable.

28 FICA (Federal Insurance Contributions Act) taxes, or simply *social security taxes*, are withheld from the employee's pay to help pay for retirement payments and Medicare. A separate FICA tax of the same amount is levied on the *employer*. The rate of tax and the base (amount of pay to which the rate applies) have been increased many times, and more increases are scheduled for future years. For convenience in all problems in this course, we assume the rate of FICA tax to be 7% on both the employer and employee applicable to a base of $35,000 (the first $35,000 of wages and earned in each calendar year).

29 Employers also are required to withhold federal income taxes from employees' pay. The amounts withheld become a current liability of the employer and must be paid to the government within a short time period. The amount withheld from each employee varies with the level of the employee's earnings and the number of personal exemptions the employee claims. The objective is to make the amount withheld closely approximate the employee's personal income tax liability at the end of the year.

30 The following journal entry illustrates recording of a payroll and deductions from employees' pay. It does not show the payroll tax on the employer; this will be illustrated in paragraph 32.

Sales Salaries Expense	5,200	
Office Salaries Expense	4,800	
FICA Taxes Payable ($10,000 × .07)		700
Liability for Income Taxes Withheld		1,890
Accrued Payroll		7,410

To record the payroll and related deductions for period ending Jan. 31.

31 Payroll taxes levied upon the employer include social security tax (already mentioned), federal unemployment insurance tax (FUTA), and state unemployment tax (SUTA). In this course, we assume the rate of FUTA tax to be 0.7% and SUTA tax to be 2.7%, both applied to a base of $6,000 (the first $6,000 earned by each employee in a calendar year).

32 To illustrate recording the *employer's* payroll taxes, assume the same $10,000 payroll for January used in paragraph 30 above. (No merit-rating plan is involved in this example.) The journal entry would be:

Payroll Taxes Expense	1,040	
FICA Taxes Payable ($10,000 × 0.07)		700
State Unemployment Taxes Payable ($10,000 × 0.027)		270
Federal Unemployment Taxes Payable ($10,000 × 0.007)		70

To record payroll taxes on employer for period ended Jan. 31.

Since this payroll is for January, we have assumed that none of the employees has as yet reached the $6,000 level of cumulative earnings at which FUTA and SUTA taxes cease.

33 An *estimated liability* is one *known to exist* but for which the dollar amount is uncertain. An example is the liability of a manufacturer to honor any warranty on products sold. To achieve the objective of matching revenue with related expenses, the liability for future warranty repairs on products sold during the current year is estimated and recorded at the balance sheet date. The estimate generally is based upon the company's past experience.

34 A *loss contingency* is a situation involving uncertainty as to whether or not a loss has been incurred. The uncertainty will be resolved by a future event. An example of a loss contingency is a lawsuit pending against a company. Until the lawsuit is resolved, un-certainty exists as to whether or not a liability exists. Many loss contingencies may also be called *contingent liabilities*. However, the term *loss contingency* encompasses the possible impairment of assets as well as the possible existence of liabilities.

35 Loss contingencies are recorded in the accounting records only when (a) it is probable that a loss has been incurred and (b) the amount of loss can be reasonably estimated. Loss contingencies which do not meet both of these criteria should still be disclosed in notes to the financial statements.

APPENDIX A: APPLICATIONS OF PRESENT VALUE

36 As stated in paragraph 7, the *present value* of a future amount is the amount that a knowledgeable investor would pay *today* for the right to receive the future amount. The present value is always less than the future amount, because money on hand today can be invested to become equivalent to a larger amount in the future. The difference between a future amount and its present value may be regarded as interest revenue (or expense) included in the future amount.

37 The present value of a future amount depends upon (a) the estimated amount of the future cash receipt (or payment), (b) the length of time until the future amount will be received (or paid), and (c) the rate of return required by the investor. The required rate of return is called the *discount rate* and depends upon the amount of *risk* associated with the investment opportunity and upon the return available from alternative investment opportunities.

38 Computing the present value of a future cash flow is called *discounting* the future amount. The easiest method of discounting future amounts is by the use of *present value tables*. Your textbook includes present value tables which show (a) the present value of a single, lump sum amount to be received at a future date and (b) the present value of a series of equal-sized periodic cash flows, called an *annuity*.

39 We will now demonstrate the use of present value tables by finding the present value of $800 to be received annually for 10 years, discounted at an annual rate of 12%. Since we are dealing with a series of 10 equal-sized payments, we will use the annuity table on page 526 in the textbook. This table shows us that the present value of $1 received annually for 10 years, discounted at 12%, is *5.650*, meaning $5.65. Therefore, the present value of the $800 annuity is $800 × 5.650, or *$4,520.*

40 The concept of present value has many applications in accounting, including:

a *Valuation of long-term notes receivable and payable* When a long-term note does not bear a realistic stated rate of interest, a portion of the face amount of the note should be regarded as representing an interest charge. The principal amount of the note can be found by discounting the maturity value of the note and any future interest payments at a realistic interest rate.

b *Estimating the value of goodwill* Goodwill represents the present value of expected future earnings in excess of a normal return on net identifiable assets.

c *Evaluating bond prices* The market price of a bond is the present value to investors of the future principal and interest payments.

d *Valuation of capital leases* When an asset is "sold" under a capital lease agreement, the present value of the future lease payments is recorded as a receivable by the lessor and as a liability by the lessee.

TEST YOURSELF ON BONDS PAYABLE AND LEASES

True or False

For each of the following statements, circle the T or the F to indicate whether the statement is true or false.

T F 1 Total interest expense on a bond sold for less than its face value will be the cash paid as interest less the amortization of the discount.

T F 2 Unissued bonds may be reported as an asset in the balance sheet since they represent a potential source of cash.

T F 3 When the going rate of interest on the open market is 14½%, a 15% bond will sell at a premium.

T F 4 A debenture bond may be convertible, callable, and registered as to ownership.

T F 5 The time value of money concept means that the present value of a future payment is always less than the future amount.

T F 6 The lower the effective rate of interest required by investors, the lower the price at which a given bond should sell.

T F 7 In the effective interest method of amortization, bond interest expense is found by applying the effective interest rate to the carrying value of the liability at the beginning of the current period.

T F 8 When bond premium is amortized by the effective interest method, interest expense will decrease slightly from one period to the next.

T F 9 The effective interest method of amortizing bond discount or premium causes interest expense to be a uniform amount over the life of the bond issue.

T F 10 Mortgages payable usually call for equal monthly payments, consisting of interest on the unpaid balance for one month and a partial repayment on the principal.

T F 11 In accruing interest expense at the end of the period, the premium or discount on bonds payable should be amortized to the balance sheet date.

T F 12 If a company issues bonds payable at a discount, the rate of interest stated on the bond is greater than the effective rate.

T F 13 An investor who buys a bond at a premium is willing to earn a lesser rate of interest than the rate stated on the bond.

T F 14 Amortization of a discount on bonds payable increases interest expense and increases the carrying value of the liability.

T F 15 Amortization of a premium on an investment in bonds reduces interest revenue and reduces the carrying value of the investment.

T F 16 Material gains and losses on the early retirement of bonds payable are reported in the income statement as extraordinary items.

T F 17 Leases which contain provisions indicating that they are in effect equivalent to a sale and purchase of assets are called operating leases.

T F   18 When lease payments are regarded as rent expense, no liability for the present value of future lease payments appears in the lessee's balance sheet.

T F   19 When the lessee records an asset and a liability equal in amount to the present value of the future lease payments, part of each lease payment is regarded as interest expense.

T F   20 A funded pension plan does not require the recognition of pension expense in the accounting records of the employer company.

T F   21 If a worker earns $50,000 a year and the FICA tax rate is 7%, the government will receive a total of $7,000 representing the employee's and employer's FICA contribution for the year.

T F   22 Social security taxes are levied on both employee and employer.

T F   23 Federal unemployment insurance taxes are levied on both employee and employer.

T F   24 A loss contingency is an appropriation of retained earnings to provide for unexpected losses in future periods.

Completion Statements

Fill in the necessary words to complete the following statements:

1 Bonds payable reacquired by the issuing company through purchase on the open market at a price (less, greater)_____than carrying value will cause the recording of a gain, whereas bonds reacquired at a price (less, greater)_____than carrying value will cause the recording of a loss.

2 In the accounts of the issuing company, the carrying value of bonds equals the face value plus any_____or minus any _____.

3 The_____ _____ of a future payment is always (more, less)_____than the future amount because money on hand

today can be invested to become a_____ amount in the future.

4 In using the effective interest method to amortize a discount or premium, interest expense is found by _____the____ _____ _____of the investment by the_____ _____ _____. The amount of discount or premium amortized is the difference between interest expense determined in this manner and the interest based upon the_____rate of interest.

5 As the discount on bonds payable is amortized, the amount of the net bond liability (increases, decreases)_____; as the premium on bonds payable is amortized, the amount of the net bond liability (increases, decreases)_____.

6 Amortization of bond premium by an *investor* will cause a(n)_____(increase, decrease) in the amount of recorded revenue from the bond investment and will cause a(n)_____(increase, decrease) in the carrying value of the investment.

7 The lessee accounts for the monthly payments on an operating lease by debiting _____ _____. The type of lease is often called _____financing because the lessee records no_____ _____for future lease payments.

8 In accounting for a capital lease used to finance the sale of merchandise, the lessor debits_____ _____ _____ and credits_____for the_____ _____ of the future lease payments. When lease payments are received, the lessor recognizes part of each payment as_____ _____ and the remainder as a reduction in_____ _____ _____.

9 The typical deductions from an employee's gross earnings include: (a)_____ _____ ,(b)_____ _____,(c)_____ _____.

10 Payroll taxes levied on the employer usually consist of: (a)_____,

(b)_____

_____ ,

(c)_____ .

Multiple Choice

Choose the best answer for each of the following questions and enter the identifying letter in the space provided.

_____ **1** The discount on bonds payable is best described as:

a An element of interest expense on borrowed funds that will be paid by issuing corporation at maturity.

b The payment of periodic interest at less than the rate called for in the bond contract.

c An amount below par which the bondholder may be called upon to make good.

d An asset representing interest that has been paid in advance.

_____ **2** The account Premium on Bonds Payable is best classified in the balance sheet as:

a An addition to bonds payable.

b An appropriation of retained earnings.

c A deduction from bonds payable.

d An asset.

_____ **3** Bonds containing a provision for exchange into other securities of the issuing company are called:

a Callable bonds.

b Redeemable bonds.

c Convertible bonds.

d Debenture bonds.

_____ **4** Riverton Corporation has authorized an issue of 14%, 10-year bonds. At the issue date the market rate of interest for this type of bonds is 13.7%. On these facts it might be expected that:

a The company will find it difficult to sell the bonds.

b The bonds will be sold at a premium.

c The bonds will be sold at a discount.

d The bond contract will be rewritten.

_____ **5** The effective interest method of amortization results in:

a A constant amount of interest expense from one period to the next.

b An increasing amount of interest expense each period.

c A decreasing amount of interest expense each period.

d Either an increasing or a decreasing amount of interest expense each period, depending upon whether the bonds were issued at a discount or a premium.

_____ **6** Assume that a capital lease is erroneously treated as an operating lease in the accounting records of the lessee. One effect of this error will be:

a An overstatement of assets and liabilities.

b An overstatement of rent expense and understatement of interest expense and depreciation expense.

c An understatement of rent expense and an overstatement of liabilities.

d None of the above.

_____ **7** Federal unemployment taxes are levied on:

a Employees at the rate of 0.7% of the first $6,000 of wages earned.

b Employers and employees at the same rate.

c Employers only.

d None of the above.

_____ **8** The amounts withheld from an employee's gross earnings are recorded by the employer as:

a Payroll expense.

b Current assets.

c Contra-asset accounts.

d Current liabilities.

_____ **9** A tax which is levied on employers and not withheld from employees' pay is:

a FUTA tax.

b FICA tax.

c Federal income tax.

d State income tax.

_____ **10** Loss contingencies relating to pending litigation usually are:

a Disclosed in notes to the financial statements.

b Shown as current liabilities in the balance sheet.

c Shown as extraordinary items in the income statement.

d Not disclosed or recorded until the litigation has been settled.

Exercises

1 On July 1, Year 1, Caldwell Company issued $600,000 of 16%, 10-year bonds with interest payable on March 1 and September 1. The company received cash of $637,800, including the accrued interest from March 1, Year 1. Bond discount or premium is amortized at each interest payment date and at year-end using the *straight-line* method. Place the correct answer to each of the following questions in the space provided. (Use the space provided for computations.)

Computations

a What was the amount of accrued interest on July 1, Year 1? $_____ .

b What was the amount of bond discount or premium (state which) to be amortized over the period that the bonds will be outstanding, 116 months? $_____ .

c What was the amount of cash paid to bond-holders on September 1, Year 1?

$_____ .

d What amount of accrued interest payable should appear on the balance sheet on December 31, Year 1? $_____ .

e What was the amount of the unamortized discount or premium on December 31, Year 1? $_____ .

f What was the total interest expense for Year 1 relating to this bond issue? $_____ .

2 From the data in Exercise 1, prepare journal entries required on each of the following dates.

a July 1, Year 1 (issuance of bonds).

b September 1, Year 1 (payment of interest and amortization for two months).

c December 31, Year 1 (accrual of interest and amortization from Sept. 1 to Dec. 31).

		General Journal		
a	July 1			
b	Sept. 1			
c	Dec. 31			

3 Shown below is a portion of the amortization table prepared after the issuance of *$800,000* face value, 10-year bonds, with interest payable on June 30 and December 31. The bonds were issued on January 1, Year 1. Bond discount or premium is amortized by the *effective interest* method.

Computations

Six-Month Interest Period	Semiannual Interest Payment	Effective Semiannual Interest	Carrying Value of Bonds, End of Period
			$757,624
1	$52,000	$53,034	758,658
2	52,000	53,106	759,764
3	52,000	53,183	760,947
4	52,000	53,266	762,213
5	52,000	53,355	763,568

a What is the amount of the bond discount or premium (state which) to be amortized over the life of the bonds? $_____ .

b What is the amount of interest paid to bondholders *annually?* $_____ .

c What is the annual *contractual* rate of interest stated on the bonds?_____ %

d What is the *semiannual effective* rate of interest?_____ %

e What is the total amount of interest expense to be recognized during *Year 2*? $_____

f In the space below, show how the bonds would appear in the balance sheet of the issuing company at the end of Year 2.

Bonds payable . . . .$

_____ $_____ .

4 For the payroll period ended January 15, the payroll records for office salaries of Bend Company showed $20,000 of gross earnings and income tax withholding of $3,600; The payroll is subject to an FICA rate of 7% on a $35,000 base; and to state unemployment tax of 2.7% and federal unemployment tax of 0.7% on a $6,000 base.

Prepare a journal entry to record the total payroll, the deductions from employees' pay, and the payroll taxes on the employer. (Explanation may be omitted.)

General Journal

19____			
Jan. 15			

14

ACCOUNTING PRINCIPLES AND CONCEPTS; EFFECTS OF INFLATION

HIGHLIGHTS OF THE CHAPTER

1 *Generally accepted accounting principles* are the ground rules for financial reporting. The financial statements of all publicly owned corporations are prepared in conformity with these principles.

2 In order to qualify as "generally accepted," an accounting principle should be widely used and should be supported by one or more of the following groups:

a The *AICPA* (the professional association of licensed CPAs), through its research efforts and the pronouncements of the *Accounting Principles Board* (APB). (The APB has been replaced by the Financial Accounting Standards Board.)

b The *Financial Accounting Standards Board* (an organization with representatives from public accounting, industry, government, and accounting education), through publication of *Statements of Financial Accounting Standards*.

c The *Securities and Exchange Commission* (an agency of the federal government), through publication of *Accounting Series Releases*.

3 One basic accounting concept is that the information in an accounting report is compiled for a carefully defined *accounting entity*. An accounting entity is any economic unit which controls resources and engages in economic activities. An individual, a division of a corporation, or a whole business enterprise are all examples of possible accounting entities. The important thing is that the entity is clearly defined before the reports

are prepared, and then only the activities of that entity are reported.

4 Another important principle is the *going-concern assumption*. This means that we assume that a business will continue in operation for an indefinite period of time sufficient to carry out all its commitments. The going-concern principle is the reason why all assets are not valued at their liquidating value.

5 The preparation of *periodic* financial reports is another accounting principle. To be useful, financial statements must be timely and available at frequent intervals so that decision makers may observe trends and changes in the economic condition of an accounting entity. However, when the life of a business is divided into specific *fiscal periods* (accounting periods), the results can only be estimates. For instance, the portion of the cost of a building to be deducted from the revenue of the current month is based upon an estimate of how long the building will be used.

6 Another assumption underlying financial statements is the *stability of the measuring unit*. We assume that the dollar is constant and that it does not change in *purchasing power*. This means we ignore changes in the purchasing power of the dollar resulting from inflation or deflation. For example, since 1960 there has been inflation in the United States. A dollar will not buy as much today as it did in 1960. If we bought $15,000 worth of land in 1960, it might cost $50,000 or more to buy a similar piece of land today, just because of inflation. However, assets

are not written up to current dollar values in financial statements: we make the simplifying assumption that the value of the dollar is constant and does not change over time.

7 *Objectivity* is one of the most basic accounting principles. This means that the valuation of assets and liabilities is based on *objective evidence*, such as an actual *exchange price*. An objective value is one that is free from *bias* and can be verified by an independent party. Objectivity is one reason why assets are valued at historical cost (an actual exchange price) rather than at estimated current market value.

8 Even though objectivity is a major goal of accounting, some measurements must still be estimates based on judgment. Depreciation, for example, is not completely objective because it depends upon an estimate of useful life.

9 Both the balance sheet and the income statement are affected by the *cost principle*. Assets are valued at their *cost*, rather than at their current market values. Expenses represent the *cost* of goods and services used up in the effort to generate revenue. The major argument supporting the cost principle is that cost can be determined *more objectively* than can current market value.

10 The timing of revenue recognition is determined by the *realization principle*. Accountants usually do not recognize revenue until it is realized. Revenue is realized when (a) the earning process is essentially complete and (b) objective evidence exists as to the amount of revenue earned.

11 In theory it is possible to recognize revenue:
 a As production takes place.
 b When production is completed.
 c When sale or delivery of the product is made or the services are rendered.
 d As cash is collected from customers. In most cases, the accountant recognizes revenue at the time of sale of goods or the rendering of services.

12 Under special circumstances, accountants deviate from the realization principle. For example, the *percentage-of-completion* method of accounting for long-term construction projects recognizes revenue during production.

13 Companies selling goods on the installment plan sometimes use the *installment method* of reporting for income tax purposes. Under the installment method, the seller recognizes the gross profit on sales gradually over an extended period of time as the cash is actually collected from customers. The installment method is used primarily for tax purposes; it is seldom used in financial statements.

14 The timing of expense recognition is determined by the *matching principle*. Expenses may be recognized in two major ways: (a) in relation to the product sold or services rendered or (b) in relation to the time period during which revenue is earned.

15 *Consistency* is the principle which means that once an accounting method is selected, it will be constantly used and not changed from period to period. For example, if we used straight-line depreciation on our building last month, we should not switch to fixed percentage on declining balance this month. If we did, there would be a change in net income caused by the change in an accounting method rather than any real economic changes.

16 The principle of *disclosure* means that all *material* (significant) and *relevant* facts concerning financial position and the results of operations must be communicated to the users of financial statements. This disclosure may be made either in the financial statements or in *footnotes* to the financial statements.

17 The concept of *conservatism* may not be an accounting principle, but it plays an important role in financial reporting. Conservatism means that when estimates must be made, the accountant will lean toward *understatement* of asset values and net income rather than toward overstatement.

18 CPAs conduct an audit of financial statements to render their opinion on whether the statements were prepared in accordance with *generally accepted accounting principles,* and whether the statements present fairly the financial position and results of operations of the accounting entity. The CPAs *do not guarantee* the accuracy of financial statements, but their *opinion* is highly regarded by users of those statements.

19 Inflation has decreased the usefulness of cost-based financial statements. When costs and expenses are based on historical costs incurred long ago, they *understate the current value* of the resources being consumed in the

production of revenue. As a result, cost-based financial statements tend to *overstate income* and report large, but fictitious, profits during periods of sustained inflation. This is a serious problem when we consider that income tax regulations, resource allocation decisions, and wage demands are based upon the popular misconception that business profits are much larger than they really are. The need to bring financial statements into accord with economic reality is the greatest challenge facing the accounting profession.

20 Two approaches to modifying an income statement to show the effects of inflation have received much attention. These are:

a *Constant-dollar accounting*—an approach in which costs and expenses not already based on the current price level are restated for changes in the *general* price level.

b *Current-cost accounting*—an approach in which costs and expenses are based upon the current value (replacement cost) of the *specific* resources being consumed, rather than upon their historical cost.

21 By combining transactions which take place during a period of rising prices, accountants in effect ignore the "size" of the measuring unit—the dollar. The *purchasing power* (command over goods and services) of the dollar changes over time. A *general price level index* shows the relative purchasing power of the dollar at different times. For example, if the general price level index rises from 100 in Year 1 to 150 in Year 5, it takes $1.50 in Year 5 to have the equivalent purchasing power of $1 in Year 1.

22 In a conventional historical cost income statement, revenue and expenses measured in current dollars are combined with those stated in "old" dollars of greater purchasing power. Revenue and most expenses result from transactions occurring in the current year and are therefore already expressed in current dollars. Depreciation expense, however, is based on "old" dollars, spent when the depreciable asset was acquired. The cost of goods sold also includes some "old" dollars, because the beginning inventory was purchased prior to the current year.

23 In a constant-dollar income statement, costs and expenses based on "old" dollars are *restated* at the number of current dollars representing the *equivalent amount of purchasing power*. The adjustment of historical costs to the equivalent number of current dollars is made using a general price index. When all revenue and expenses are stated in units of similar purchasing power, we can see whether the amount of *purchasing power* controlled by the business is increasing or decreasing as a result of operations.

24 In addition to the increase or decrease in purchasing power resulting from revenue and expense transactions, a business may have a gain or loss in purchasing power from having monetary items during a period of changing prices. *Monetary items* are those assets and liabilities representing claims to a fixed number of dollars. If monetary assets are held while prices rise, a purchasing power *loss* results; if money is owed during a period of inflation, a purchasing power *gain* results.

25 General purchasing power accounting does not abandon historical cost as the basis of measurement, but simply *restates the historical cost* in terms of the current purchasing power of money. This is quite different from current-cost accounting, in which costs and expenses are based upon the current *replacement costs* of the specific assets being sold or used up.

26 In a *current-cost* income statement, the amounts shown for depreciation expense and for the cost of goods sold are based on the estimated replacement costs of these specific assets and are *not* computed by using a general price-level index. The replacement cost of specific kinds of assets may increase faster or slower than the general price level. In fact, some replacement costs (such as for pocket calculators) may even decline while the general price level rises.

27 An income statement expressed in current costs shows whether a company earns enough revenue to *replace* the goods and services used up in the effort to generate that revenue. The resulting net income figure represents the maximum amount that the business could distribute to its owners and *still maintain the present size and scale of its operations*.

28 The effect of inflation upon the measurement of net income is so important that the FASB now requires large corporations to include with their cost-based financial statements supplementary schedules showing:

a Net income measured in constant dollars.

b The net gain or loss in purchasing power resulting from holding monetary assets or having monetary liabilities during a period of inflation.

c Net income measured in terms of current costs.

Notice that these disclosures are *supplementary information* and do not replace the use of historical costs in the financial statements.

APPENDIX B: INVESTMENTS FOR PURPOSES OF CONTROL

29 Long-term investment in common stock made for the purpose of exercising control over the issuing company (called the *investee*) should be accounted for by the *equity method*. Ownership of 20% or more of the investee's outstanding common stock generally is considered an investment for purposes of control.

30 The accounting procedures for applying the equity method are as follows:

a The investment originally is recorded at cost.

b The investor subsequently records its proportionate share of the investee's net income by debiting the investment account and crediting Investment Income. If the investee reports a net loss, the investor debits Investment Loss and credits the investment account.

c The investor views its share of cash dividends paid by the investee as a conversion of the investment into cash. Thus, the investor debits Cash and credits the investment account when dividends are received from the investee.

No lower-of-cost-or-market adjustments are made to investments accounted for by the equity method.

31 When one corporation controls another corporation through ownership of a *majority* of its voting stock, the controlling corporation is called the *parent* company and the controlled corporation is called the *subsidiary* company. Financial statements prepared for the *affiliated* companies (the parent company and its subsidiaries) are called *consolidated financial statements*.

32 We usually think of a large organization such as IBM, General Electric, or Exxon as a single company. Actually, such organizations are really *groups* of affiliated companies. It is logical to think of an affiliated group such as IBM as a single economic entity, because all the companies in the affiliated group are under the control of one parent company.

33 Consolidated financial statements show the combined financial position and combined operating results of all the individual companies in the affiliated group *as if they were one company*. In a *consolidated balance sheet*, the assets and liabilities of the affiliated companies are combined and reported as though only a single entity existed. Similarly, in a *consolidated income statement* the revenue and expenses of the affiliated companies are combined.

34 The amounts shown in consolidated financial statements *do not come from a ledger;* they are determined on a working paper by combining the amounts of like items in the financial statements of the affiliated companies. In the combining process, certain adjustments must be made to eliminate the effects of *intercompany transactions*.

35 Intercompany transactions are transactions among affiliated companies which do not give rise to assets, liabilities, revenue, or expenses when the affiliated companies are viewed as parts of a single consolidated entity. Intercompany eliminations fall into three categories:

a Elimination of intercompany stock ownership.

b Elimination of intercompany debt.

c Elimination of intercompany revenue and expenses.

36 When a parent company invests in a subsidiary, the parent records the investment in an asset account entitled *Investment in Subsidiary*. However, in a consolidated balance sheet, we want to show the individual assets and liabilities of the subsidiary company. It would not be logical to show the assets and liabilities of the subsidiary *and also* to show the parent company's investment in those assets and liabilities. Therefore, the Investment in Subsidiary account is *eliminated* (offset) against the stockholders' equity of the subsidiary company.

37 After the parent's Investment in Subsidiary and the subsidiary's stockholders' equity have been eliminated (offset against one another), the *stockholders' equity of the parent company* is the stockholders' equity on the consolidated balance sheet. Also, the individual assets and liabilities of the subsidiary are presented *in place of* the Investment in Subsidiary account.

38 If the parent company acquires *less than 100%* of the stock issued by the subsidiary, the entry on the consolidated working papers to eliminate the Investment in Subsidiary account will not offset all of the stockholders' equity of the subsidiary. The remaining equity of the subsidiary is called a *minority interest* and is shown in the equity section of the consolidated balance sheet.

39 Often the parent company acquires the subsidiary's stock at a price above book value, indicating that either (1) certain assets are undervalued in the subsidiary's accounting records, or (2) the subsidiary possesses *unrecorded goodwill*. In the consolidated balance sheet, the subsidiary's assets should be valued at the value indicated by the parent company's purchase price, and any unrecorded goodwill purchased by the parent company should *appear as an asset* and be amortized over its useful life.

40 A consolidated income statement is prepared by combining on a working paper the revenue and expense accounts of the affiliated companies. Revenue and expenses arising from *intercompany transactions* are eliminated because they reflect transfers of assets from one affiliated company to another and do not change the net assets of the consolidated entity. Examples of intercompany revenue and expense transactions include the payment of rent or interest by one affiliated company to another.

41 If control of a subsidiary is acquired through issuance of stock and the stockholders of the subsidiary become stockholders of the parent, the consolidated statements for the two companies may be prepared on a *pooling-of-interests* basis. Consolidated statements on a *pooling* basis will differ from those on the *purchase* basis in the following respects:

a Regardless of the market value of the stock issued by the parent company, the assets of the subsidiary will appear in the consolidated balance sheet at their book values and no goodwill is recorded.

b Since no goodwill appears in the consolidated balance sheet, consolidated net income is not reduced by amortization expense relating to this asset.

c Earnings of a subsidiary for the entire year in which control was acquired are included in the consolidated income statement, even if control was achieved on the last day of the fiscal year.

42 Consolidation of a particular subsidiary may not be appropriate if the subsidiary is in a different line of business than the other companies in the affiliated group. *Unconsolidated subsidiaries* appear in the financial statements as long-term investments, accounted for by the equity method.

TEST YOURSELF ON ACCOUNTING PRINCIPLES

True or False

For each of the following statements, circle the T or the F to indicate whether the statement is true or false.

T F 1 Financial statements for companies in different industries should be prepared using the same accounting principles.

T F 2 *Generally accepted accounting principles* are well-established and not subject to change.

T F 3 If a meaningful measure of net income is to result, the same definition of accounting entity must be used in the measurement of revenue and of expenses.

T F 4 A single department or a division within a larger business organization can be viewed as a separate accounting entity.

T F 5 The going-concern principle means that a business is assumed to have an indefinite life and will continue to operate until all the firm's commitments have been satisfied.

T F 6 The assumption that the dollar is a stable measuring unit is consistent with economic reality.

T F 7 Estimates of current market values may be more relevant but less reliable than historical costs for decision-making purposes.

T F 8 If a cash offer to buy land owned by a business is received and rejected, objectivity would require that the land be revalued to the amount of the offer.

T F 9 The cost principle and realization principle are both closely related to the need for objectivity.

T F 10 The realization principle states that revenue should not be recognized until the cash has been collected.

T F 11 The percentage-of-completion method recognizes revenue during the production process.

T F 12 *Consistency* means that all companies within a given industry (such as steel or petroleum) must use similar accounting procedures in the preparation of financial statements.

T F 13 Switching in midyear from lifo to fifo as a means of valuing inventory would be a violation of the principle of consistency and would require disclosure in the financial statements.

T F 14 CPAs prepare and guarantee the financial statements of their clients.

T F 15 Gains in the value of plant assets may be recognized as earned prior to sale if the market value of such assets can be objectively determined.

T F 16 If the general price level goes up, the value of money goes down.

T F 17 Owing money during an inflationary period would be advantageous to the borrower.

T F 18 An income statement adjusted for changes in the general price level shows the amount of purchasing power flowing into or out of the business as a result of operations.

T F 19 An income statement based on current costs shows whether a business is earning sufficient revenue to replace the resources being used up in operations.

T F 20 It is possible for a company to report net income under generally accepted accounting principles but to show a net loss when its income statement is adjusted to constant dollars or current costs.

T F 21 The FASB requires large corporations to use current costs rather than historical costs in their financial statements.

T F 22 Unless inflation is severe, constant-dollar accounting and current-cost accounting will result in the same figure for net income.

T F 23 An investor using the equity method recognizes investment income whenever cash dividends are received.

T F 24 A consolidated balance sheet reports the financial condition for a group of separate legal entities.

T F 25 Most published financial statements issued by large corporations are prepared on a consolidated basis.

T F 26 Consolidated financial statements are prepared from the general ledger of the consolidated entity.

T F 27 Minority interest should be reported as an asset in the consolidated balance sheet.

T F 28 Minority interest is *increased* when the subsidiary company reports net income or when the parent company reduces the percentage of stock held in the subsidiary.

T F 29 The eliminations required on the working papers for the consolidated balance sheet to eliminate intercompany receivables and payables are not recorded in the ledger of either the parent or the subsidiary company.

T F 30 When a business combination is accounted for as a *pooling of interests*, the consolidated income statement will include the earnings of the subsidiary for the entire year, even if the combination occurred near year-end.

T F 31 As a general rule, consolidation is appropriate whenever the parent company owns 20% or more of the voting stock of a subsidiary.

T F 32 Investments in unconsolidated subsidiaries are not included in consolidated financial statements.

Completion Statements

Fill in the necessary words to complete the following statements:

1 The most influential authoritative groups that have contributed to the development of generally accepted principles are: _____

_____

_____ , _____

_____ , _____

_____ , and _____

_____ .

2 An underlying assumption that an accounting entity will continue in operation for an indefinite period of time sufficient to carry out its existing commitments is called the _____ assumption.

3 The term _____ refers to accounting measurements that are unbiased and can be verified; the term _____ assures users of financial statements that when a given accounting method is adopted, it will not be changed without adequate _____ in the financial statements.

4 The cost principle calls for assets to be valued at _____ rather than at current _____ values.

5 CPAs conduct an _____ of the accounting system of a business and render their _____ as to the _____ of the company's financial statements.

6 It would be theoretically possible to recognize the revenue of a business enterprise as realized at one of the following points in time: _____ , _____ , _____ , or _____ _____ .

7 When the general price level increases, the _____ _____ of the dollar _____ .

8 In a period of inflation, historical cost-based financial statements tend to (overstate, understate) _____ the current value of the resources used in producing revenue and (overstate, understate) _____ the profitability of the business.

9 During a period of inflation, holding monetary assets results in a purchasing power _____ and having monetary liabilities results in a purchasing power _____ .

10 In a constant-dollar income statement, costs based on "old" dollars are restated by use of a _____ _____ _____ at the number of _____ _____ representing the equivalent amount of _____ _____ . In a current-cost income statement, expenses are based on the estimated cost to _____ the specific assets being used up.

11 A company using the equity method recognizes as investment income its proportionate share of the investee's _____ _____ .

The investor regards _____ received from the investee as a conversion of the investment into _____ .

12 (a) The Investment in Subsidiary account appears in the ledger of the parent company but does not appear in the _____ balance sheet; (b) minority interest (is, is not) _____ found in the ledger of the parent company or the ledger of the subsidiary company.

13 On November 1, Year 1, P Company acquired 100% of the stock of S Company. During Year 1, P Company earned $2 million (omitting any income from S Company), and S Company earned $25,000 per month. If the business combination is accounted for as a *purchase*, consolidated net income for Year 1 will be $ _____ ; if it is viewed as a *pooling of interests*, consolidated net income will be $ _____ .

Multiple Choice

Choose the best answer for each of the following questions and enter the identifying letter in the space provided.

_____ **1** Which of the following does not represent a generally accepted accounting principle?
a Accounting information is compiled for an accounting entity.
b Consistency in the application of particular accounting methods enables the user of accounting data to interpret changes in income or in financial position from period to period.
c The going-concern assumption justifies ignoring liquidating values in presenting assets in the balance sheet.
d Constant-dollar financial statements are the primary means of financial reporting by large corporations.

_____ **2** Financial statements prepared by a business firm are most likely to be:
a Fully reliable.
b Tentative in nature.
c Relevant for all types of decisions.
d Always misleading.

_____ **3** The independent accountants' opinion on a set of financial statements:
a Consists of three parts: a description of the scope of the audit, an opinion on the fairness of the statements, and a forecast of net income for the coming year.

b Can be issued only when the accountants have performed an audit of the statements and the accounting records.

c Can be issued if the accounting records have been maintained in a consistent manner even though the company has not followed generally accepted accounting principles.

d Guarantees to users that the statements have been prepared in accordance with generally accepted accounting principles and are free from any material error.

_____ 4 Revenue is most commonly recognized at the point that:

a Cash is collected.

b The order is received from customers.

c The sale is made.

d The production of manufactured goods is complete.

_____ 5 An income statement adjusted for changes in the purchasing power of the dollar:

a Restates historical costs for changes in the general price level.

b Will show a loss from borrowing during a period of rising prices.

c Restate all monetary items (such as cash and receivables) in terms of current-year dollars.

d Will show more net income during periods of inflation than will an income statement based on historical costs.

_____ 6 During an inflationary period:

a Holding monetary assets will result in a purchasing power gain.

b The purchasing power which must be sacrificed to repay a liability of fixed amount is constantly decreasing.

c A purchasing power loss results from borrowing.

d The purchasing power of the dollar is constantly increasing.

_____ 7 Holding monetary assets of $1 million during an inflationary period results in a:

a Purchasing power gain.

b Purchasing power loss which is deductible for income tax purposes.

c Neither a purchasing power gain nor a purchasing power loss.

d Purchasing power loss, but no tax deduction.

_____ 8 Current-value financial statements:

a Restate historical costs for changes in the general price level.

b Are more objective than financial statements based upon historical cost.

c Show the current value of the costs expired during the period.

d Are required by the SEC from all large corporations.

_____ 9 One reason that a large steel company probably would show less net income on a current-cost basis than on a historical cost basis is that the current-cost income statement would include:

a Less revenue.

b A purchasing power loss from holding monetary assets.

c Greater depreciation expense.

d An adjustment of depreciation expense and of the cost of goods sold for changes in the general price index.

_____ 10 Which of the following does not appear in a consolidated balance sheet?

a Capital stock of parent company.

b Capital stock of subsidiary.

c Investment in unconsolidated companies.

d Minority interest.

_____ 11 Which of the following offers a good reason for preparing consolidated statements?

a The legal boundaries between affiliated companies are clearly presented.

b Only one set of accounting records need be kept for the affiliated companies, thus reducing operating expense.

c A financial picture of the resources and operations of an economic entity is helpful to stockholders and management of the parent company.

d Minority stockholders can ascertain the soundness of their investment.

_____ 12 Minority investment, as it appears in a consolidated balance sheet, refers to:

a Owners of less than 50% of the parent company stock.

b Parent's interest in subsidiary companies.

c Interest expense on subsidiary's bonds payable.

d Equity in the subsidiary's net assets held by stockholders other than the parent company.

_____ 13 Dividends payable on December 31, 19__, are as follows: parent company, $120,000; 100%-owned subsidiary, $30,000. The amount of dividends payable in the consolidated balance sheet is:

a $150,000

b $120,000

c $ 90,000

d $ 30,000

Exercises

1 Within the current framework of generally accepted accounting principles, show the immediate effect upon total assets, liabilities, and owners' equity that would be recorded for each of the following situations. Revenue and expenses are to be considered changes in owners' equity. Use the following code:

I = Increase, D = Decrease, NE = No effect

Situation	Assets	Liabilities	Owners' Equity
a An item with a long life and a material cost (a machine) is purchased for cash.			
b An item with a long life and an immaterial cost (a pencil sharpener) is purchased for cash.			
c An item of merchandise is acquired for cash at a price far below the price it will be sold for.			
d The item in **c** is sold for cash at a price above cost.			
e Cash is collected from a customer for a sale made last period.			
f Monetary assets are held during a period of inflation.			
g A contractor using the percentage-of-completion method of accounting for long-term contracts finds 10% of the costs have been incurred and they total less than 10% of the contract price.			
h The contractor in **g** finds 40% of the costs have been incurred and they exceed 40% of the contract price.			

2 During Year 5, Baxter Company computed the cost of product X sold (historical cost basis—fifo) as follows:

	Units	Cost
Sold from beginning inventory	50,000	$ 70,000
Sold from Year 5 purchases	90,000	153,000
Cost of product X sold during Year 5	140,000	$223,000

The beginning inventory had been acquired when the general price index stood at 140. During Year 5, the average level of the general price index was 155 and the average replacement cost of product X was $1.70 per unit. Using this information, compute the cost of goods sold for product X on:

a A constant-dollar basis.

Answer _____

b A current-cost basis.

Answer _____

3 On April 30, Year 4, Par Company purchased 100% of the stock of Sub Company for $520,000 cash. Par Company paid a purchase price in excess of book value because Sub Company possesses unrecorded goodwill. The condensed balance sheets immediately after the purchase are shown below:

	Par Co.	Sub Co.
Cash	$ 120,000	$ 70,000
Investment in Sub Co.	520,000	
Other assets	450,000	600,000
Totals	$1,090,000	$ 670,000
Liabilities	$ 400,000	$ 240,000
Capital stock.	300,000	150,000
Retained earnings.	390,000	280,000
Totals	$1,090,000	$ 670,000

In the space provided, prepare a consolidated balance sheet immediately after Par Company acquired control of Sub Company.

PAR CO. AND SUBSIDIARY
Consolidated Balance Sheet
April 30, Year 4

Assets

Cash . . . . $

Total assets . . . . $

Liabilities & Stockholders' Equity

Liabilities . . . . $

Total liabilities & stockholders' equity . . . . $

15

STATEMENT OF CHANGES IN FINANCIAL POSITION: CASH FLOWS

HIGHLIGHTS OF THE CHAPTER

1 We have seen how the income statement measures the profitability of a business. But profitability alone does not assure success; a business must also maintain adequate liquid resources to pay its maturing obligations and to take advantage of new investment opportunities. The *statement of changes in financial position* helps measure the quantity and quality of resources employed by a business. This financial statement shows the *sources and uses of working capital* and helps answer such questions as: What became of the proceeds of a bond issue? Is the company becoming more or less solvent?

2 The statement of changes in financial position is often called a *funds statement*. The word *funds* is used to mean *all working capital*, not just cash.

3 A statement of changes in financial position measures changes in working capital. If working capital continued to decrease long enough, a business would become insolvent; excessive working capital means resources are not efficiently employed. In the short run, increases and decreases in working capital may be *independent of profitability*.

4 Sources of (increases in) working capital may come from (a) operations (revenue minus expenses that require funds), (b) sale of noncurrent assets, (c) borrowing through long-term debt, and (d) issuing additional shares of capital stock.

5 Funds provided by operations are revenue minus expenses that require funds. This is the same thing as net income *plus* expenses

that *do not* require funds. Examples of expenses that do not require funds are depreciation, amortization, and depletion. These items required funds when the *asset was acquired*, not when the expense is being recognized.

6 Extraordinary and nonoperating gains and losses (if material) should be *eliminated* from net income in computing the funds generated by operations. This is because the funds generated by the disposition (or destruction) of the asset causing the extraordinary or nonoperating gain or loss will *already be included* in the statement of changes in financial position as a source of funds resulting from the disposition of a noncurrent asset.

7 Uses of working capital are (a) declaration of a cash dividend, (b) repayment of long-term debt, (c) purchase of noncurrent assets, and (d) repurchase of outstanding capital stock.

8 Transactions involving only working capital accounts (current assets and current liabilities), such as short-term borrowing or the collection of an account receivable, *do not change* the amount of working capital.

9 Transactions involving a working capital account and a nonworking capital account *must* either increase or decrease working capital. For example, the purchase of a building for cash is a *use* of working capital, and long-term borrowing is a *source* of working capital.

10 Transactions involving only nonworking capital accounts, such as the issuance of long-term debt in exchange for a building, do not change the *amount* of working capi-

tal. This is because such an *exchange transaction* consists of both a *source* of working capital (sale of bonds) and a *use* of working capital (purchase of building). Since the source and the use of funds are equal, there is no change in the amount of working capital. Instead of ignoring these transactions, a clearer picture will result if we include them in the statement of changes in financial position as *both* a source and a use of working capital.

11 Most transactions involving only nonworking capital accounts are exchange transactions. Two exceptions are stock dividends and stock splits. Stock dividends and stock splits do not involve an exchange and do not affect the financial position of the business. Thus, they are not shown in a statement of changes in financial position.

12 It is not necessary to have a list of all transactions occurring during a period to prepare a statement of changes in financial position. In practice, the statement is usually prepared on a working paper from analysis of changes in *noncurrent accounts* as presented in a *comparative balance sheet*.

13 Working papers for analysis of the changes in noncurrent accounts are prepared by listing the amount of working capital and the balances of the noncurrent accounts at the beginning of the period in the left-hand column, and the balances at the end of the period in the right-hand column. In the middle columns, the total change which has occurred in each account during the period is entered as a debit or a credit, and the resulting effect on working capital is listed below as a source or use of working capital. Each change in a noncurrent account generally results in a change in working capital.

14 After all the changes in noncurrent accounts have been recorded as changes in working capital, a total *increase or decrease* in working capital for the period is computed by *subtracting the uses of working capital from the sources of working capital*. This total increase or decrease in working capital should be the difference between the beginning and ending amounts of working capital listed in the working papers. (Carefully study the working papers for the Allison Corporation shown in your text.)

15 A formal statement of changes in financial position is prepared from the working papers once the total change in working capital has been confirmed. The statement of changes in financial position should be followed by a schedule showing the *changes in the composition of working capital*. This schedule shows the change occurring during the year in each current asset and current liability account.

16 A statement of changes in financial position shows the inflow and outflow of liquid resources (working capital) during a period. However a company may have adequate working capital and still not be able to pay its debts if the working capital is primarily tied up in inventory and receivables. Management may therefore prepare a *cash flow statement* which shows the cash position of a business.

17 A cash flow statement shows (in summary form) all cash payments, all cash receipts, and the increase or decrease in cash during the period.

18 Much of a company's cash flow is generated by operations. We may prepare a report of cash flow from operations from an income statement by converting from the accrual to the cash basis of accounting.

19 Net sales can be converted to cash receipts from customers by *adding any decrease* (or subtracting any increase) *in accounts receivable*. The cost of goods sold can be converted to cash payments for merchandise by *adding any increase* (subtracting any decrease) in inventory to find the total merchandise purchases, and *adding any decrease* (subtracting any increase) in accounts payable.

20 Expenses can be converted to the cash basis by two steps. From the listed expenses, (a) subtract any increase (or add any decrease) in accrued liabilities and (b) add any increase (subtract any decrease) in short-term prepayments.

21 Some expenses, such as depreciation and amortization of bond discount, correspond to changes in the carrying value of a noncurrent asset or liability. Such expenses do not involve cash outflows in the current period.

22 When an income statement is restated on the cash basis, the net income figure will be converted to *cash flow from operations*. In the short run, cash flow may be independent of profitability.

TEST YOURSELF ON FUNDS FLOW ANALYSIS

True or False

For each of the following statements, circle the T or the F to indicate whether the statement is true or false.

T F 1 The primary purpose of a statement of changes in financial position is to measure short-run profitability.

T F 2 The statement of changes in financial position is sometimes referred to as a funds statement.

T F 3 A statement of changes in financial position shows the sources and uses of working capital during an accounting period.

T F 4 In accounting terminology, the word *funds* is used to refer only to cash.

T F 5 Short-term borrowing may be a source of cash, but it is not a source of working capital.

T F 6 Selling a noncurrent asset is a source of working capital, even if the asset is sold at a loss.

T F 7 If the income statement shows a net loss for the period, there cannot have been any funds provided by operations.

T F 8 A company which is profitable cannot have decreasing working capital.

T F 9 A company with decreasing working capital cannot be profitable.

T F 10 If a long-term liability is incurred for the purchase price of a noncurrent asset, there will be no change in the amount of working capital, but the event will appear in the statement of changes in financial position as both a source and a use of working capital.

T F 11 A transaction that affects only current assets and current liabilities cannot cause a change in working capital.

T F 12 The payment of a cash dividend, not the declaration of the dividend, is a use of working capital.

T F 13 Transactions which affect a current asset or current liability account and a noncurrent account will cause a change in working capital.

T F 14 Depreciation expense is not a use of funds in the current period and should be added back to net income to determine working capital provided by operations.

T F 15 Extraordinary gains or losses are sources or uses of working capital and should be included in the working capital provided by operations figure.

T F 16 A cash flow statement shows only receipts and payments of cash and does not show other changes in working capital.

T F 17 Net sales may be converted to cash received from customers by adding any decrease (subtracting any increase) in receivables from customers.

T F 18 The delivered cost of net purchases may be converted to cash paid for merchandise by adding any increase (subtracting any decrease) in accounts payable to suppliers.

T F 19 Short-term prepayments increased during the year by more than the increase in accrued liabilities. This means that more cash was paid for expenses than is shown in the accrual basis income statement.

Completion Statement

Fill in the necessary words to complet the following statements:

1 The statement of changes in _income_ _statement_ shows _source_ and _uses_ of _work_ _capital_.

2 A statement prepared by management to analyze the sources and uses of cash is called a _cash_ _flow_ statement.

3 The _payment_ of a cash dividend is a _use_ of working capital. The sale of a noncurrent asset at a loss is a _source_ of working capital. Repurchase of outstanding capital stock, at a price below the original issue price, is a _use_ of working capital.

4 Depreciation expense should be _added_ to _net_ _income_ to determine working capital _provided_ _by_ _operations_, because depreciation expense does not decrease working capital.

5 It is possible to prepare a statement of changes in financial position by analyzing the changes in _non-current_ accounts.

6 A transaction which changes only ___current___ accounts is neither a source nor a use of working capital.

7 The cash flow from operations may be determined by converting an income statement from the ___accrual___ basis to the ___cash___ basis of accounting.

8 To convert net sales to cash receipts from customers, you should add any ___decrease___ in receivables from customers. Expenses may be converted to the cash basis by adding any ___increase___ in short-term prepayments and subtracting any ___increase___ in accrued liabilities.

Multiple Choice

Choose the best answer to the following questions and enter the identifying letter in the space provided.

___a___ 1 Which of the following is not a use of working capital?
a Repayment of long-term debt.
b Acquisition of treasury stock.
c Cash dividend declared but not paid.
d Payment of an account payable.

___b___ 2 Net income may be adjusted to show the working capital provided by operations by:
a Adding expenses not requiring working capital, adding nonoperating gains, and subtracting nonoperating losses.
b Adding expenses not requiring working capital, subtracting nonoperating gains, and adding nonoperating losses.
c Subtracting depreciation and amortization expenses.
d Adding any decreases in receivables and subtracting any increases in accounts payable and notes payable.

___c___ 3 Purchases amounted to $10,000; inventories increased by $4,000; accounts payable decreased by $1,500. The cash paid to creditors was:
a $ 8,500
b $10,000
c $11,500
d $15,500

___b___ 4 The purpose of a statement of cash flow is to:
a Compute cash earnings per share.

b Explain increases or decreases in the cash balance from one date to another.
c Explain the reasons for changes in working capital.
d Restate net income on a cash basis.

___a___ 5 Which of the following events would appear on a statement of changes in financial position?
a Issuing long-term bonds in exchange for land.
b Purchasing inventory on credit.
c Repayment of a short-term loan.
d None of the above.

_____ 6 Bondholders in Bluebell Corporation converted $2 million of long-term convertible bonds payable into 80,000 shares of common stock. In Bluebell Corporation's statement of changes in financial position, this transaction should be shown as:
a Neither a source nor a use of funds, because working capital was not affected.
b Only a $2 million source of funds from the issuance of common stock.
c Only a $2 million use of funds for the retirement of long-term debt.
d Both a $2 million source and a $2 million use of funds.

___c___ 7 The composition of working capital at the beginning and end of a period:
a Appears in the working paper for the statement of changes in financial position.
b Appears in comparative balance sheets and therefore should not be included in the statement of changes in financial position.
c Appears in the lower part of a statement of changes in financial position.
d Has little or no significance for users of financial statements.

Exercises

1 Indicate the immediate effect upon working capital of each transaction listed below. Use the following code:
S = A source of working capital
U = A use of working capital
SU = Both a source *and* a use of working capital
N = Neither a source nor a use of working capital

___U___ Paid semiannual interest on bonds payable.
___N___ Recognized depreciation expense.
___U___ Made monthly payment on operating lease.
___N___ Paid six months' rent in advance.

Declared cash dividend for payment in the next accounting period.

Declared a stock dividend for distribution in the next accounting period.

Outstanding convertible preferred stock is converted into common stock.

Sold treasury stock at a price below cost.

Sold marketable securities (a current asset) at a price below carrying value.

Issued common stock in exchange for the net assets of another corporation.

2 From the following information, prepare a statement of changes in financial position (without showing the composition of working capital) for Year 2 for Patriotic Fireworks Corporation:

a Net income for Year 2 was $112,000.

b Depreciation expense for Year 2 was $25,000.

c During Year 2, land which had cost $40,000 was sold for $60,000, net of the tax on the gain.

d A six-month bank loan of $50,000 made in Year 1 was repaid in Year 2.

e Additional equipment was acquired during Year 2 at a cost of $84,000.

f An earthquake caused $30,000 of damage to plant assets.

g A cash dividend of $50,000 was declared at the end of Year 2 to be paid in January of Year 3.

PATRIOTIC FIREWORKS CORPORATION
Statement of Changes in Financial Position
For Year Ended December 31, Year 2

Sources of working capital:
  Operations:
    Income before nonoperating gain and
      loss . . . . $

    Add:

                        $

    Total sources of working capital . . . . . $
Uses of working capital:
                        $

    Total uses of working capital . . . .
Increase in working capital . . . . $

3 The net income for the Baker Corporation in Year 1 amounted to $100,000 and included the following items:

Interest revenue	$ 2,000
Depreciation expense	40,000
Accrued salaries and wages	4,000
Amortization of patents	5,000
Gain on sale of plant assets (net of taxes) . . .	20,000
Amortization of premium on bonds payable .	2,500
Income tax expense	80,500

In the space provided below, compute the working capital provided by regular operations:

Net income	$100,000
Add:	
Subtotal . . . . $	
Less:	
	$
Working capital provided	
by operations	$

4 The financial statements of Stacy Corporation provide the following information:

	Year 5	Year 4
Accounts receivable	$ 29,000	$25,000
Inventory	35,000	28,000
Prepaid expenses	500	1,500
Accounts payable (for merchandise) . . .	17,000	14,000
Accrued liabilities	2,000	750
Net sales	320,000	
Cost of goods sold	200,000	
Operating expenses (including depreciation of $8,000)	90,000	
Net income	30,000	

Using the given data, compute for Year 5:

a Cash collected from customers.

b Cash paid for merchandise.

c Cash paid for operating expenses.

d Cash provided by operations.

16

ANALYSIS AND INTERPRETATION OF FINANCIAL STATEMENTS

HIGHLIGHTS OF THE CHAPTER

1 *Financial statements* represent a report on managerial performance. In order to interpret the information contained in financial statements, the user should understand the workings of the accounting system. Financial statements are of interest to many groups, each with a different set of needs.

2 The published financial statements of corporations have been audited by CPA firms and reviewed in detail by governmental agencies such as the Securities and Exchange Commission. Consequently, users of these financial statements may have confidence that the information in the statements is reasonably reliable and is presented in accordance with generally accepted accounting principles.

3 Some sources of financial data available to users other than management include:

a Annual reports of corporation.

b Data filed with the Securities and Exchange Commission.

c Investment advisory services and stock brokerage firms.

d Organizations such as Moody's Investors Service, Standard & Poor's Corporation, and Dun & Bradstreet, Inc.

4 A given figure contained in financial statements is seldom significant to the reader; the *relationship* of figures, or the *change* over time, is generally much more useful.

5 Critics of business often blame "excessive" corporate profits for rising prices and other economic problems. In evaluating the reasonableness of corporate profits, we must relate the dollar amount of net income to the volume of sales and the value of the economic resources necessary to produce that profit. Also, we must consider the need for profits as a means of financing expansion, creating jobs, and increasing the supply of goods and services.

6 It is also important to remember that during periods of inflation, financial statements based upon historical cost tend to overstate the profitability of a business by failing to recognize the current value of the resources consumed in the production of revenue. The SEC requires large corporations to disclose the replacement cost of their inventories, cost of goods sold, plant assets, and depreciation expense. This information should be used to help answer such questions as: Are the company's earnings sufficient to keep "physical capital" intact *given the rising cost of replacing inventories and plant assets?*

7 Three techniques commonly used in the analysis of financial statements are:

a Dollar and percentage changes.

b Component percentages.

c Ratios.

8 *Dollar and percentage changes* are taken from *comparative* financial statements and give valuable clues to growth and other important trends affecting the business. The percentage of relationship between any figure appearing in financial statements and the total which includes this figure (total assets on a balance sheet, and net sales on an income statement) is known as a *component percentage.* It can be used to measure the importance (or possible imbalance) of the item in question. A *ratio* measures the rela-

tionship of one financial item to another and calls attention to a significant relationship which may suggest further investigation.

9 In interpreting the significance of percentage changes, component percentages, and ratios, some *standards of comparison* should be used. Two widely used *standards* are:

a The past performance of the company.

b The performance of other companies in the same industry or the performance of the industry as a whole.

10 Comparison of data over time gives some idea of the company's performance compared with its past record and may be helpful in forecasting future performance.

11 Comparison of a company's performance with that of other companies similarly situated or with the aggregate results for an industry offers valuable clues relating to a company's ability to compete and perhaps to surpass the industry's performance.

12 The key objectives of financial analysis are to determine a company's *future earnings performance* and the *soundness of its financial position*. To evaluate earnings performance and financial soundness, we are interested not only in the *amount* of earnings and assets, but also in the *quality of earnings*, the *quality of assets*, and the *amount of debt*.

13 The quality of earnings depends upon the *source* and *stability* of those earnings. The quality of earnings helps us to evaluate how likely it is that earnings will continue to grow or whether future earnings are likely to fluctuate widely. An analysis of the accounting principles and methods used by a company is helpful in evaluating the quality of earnings reported by the company.

14 A company may become insolvent even though it is profitable. The health and even the survival of a company may therefore be dependent not only on earnings, but also on the *quality of assets* and the *amount of liabilities* outstanding. A firm with inadequate cash position, slow-moving inventories, past-due receivables, and large amounts of short-term liabilities may be facing serious financial difficulties.

15 The concept of return on investment (called *ROI*) is a measure of management's efficiency in using the resources under its control. The ROI concept is used in many situations, such as evaluating the performance of a branch, product line, total business, or par-

ticular investment. ROI is computed several different ways, depending upon the circumstances; two common measures of ROI are *return on assets* and *return on stockholders' equity*. A summary of these and other ratios is contained at the end of the chapter in your textbook.

16 *Stockholders and potential investors* in the common stock of a company are primarily interested in the following:

a Earnings per share.

b Price-earnings ratio (the earnings rate).

c Dividends paid and the yield based on the market value of the stock.

d Book value per share.

e Revenue and expense analysis (the increase or decrease in specific revenue and expense items).

f The rate of return on the total assets used in the business, and the asset turnover rate.

g The rate of return on common stockholders' equity.

h Equity ratio (the proportion of total assets financed by stockholders).

17 Financing a business with fixed-return securities (bonds and notes payable and preferred stock) is known as using *leverage* or *trading on the equity*. If the rate earned on total assets is *greater* than the rate paid on the fixed-return securities (the cost of borrowing), the common stockholders will gain from the use of leverage. Common stockholders will gain because the capital provided by the fixed-return securities is being invested to earn more than the amount which must be paid to the providers of that capital. The excess of the earnings generated by that capital over the fixed return paid out belongs to the common stockholders.

18 If the return earned by invested capital (return on assets) is *less* than the fixed return paid to the providers of that capital, the common stockholder will *lose* by trading on the equity.

19 The *debt ratio* (total liabilities ÷ total assets) measured the degree to which a company is trading on the equity. A high debt ratio means that a high percentage of the total assets is financed by creditors and that the company is making extensive use of leverage.

20 The *equity ratio* (stockholders' equity ÷ total assets) shows the percentage of total assets financed by stockholders. The equity ratio plus the debt ratio must always equal 1,

so a low equity ratio means a high debt ratio. A low equity ratio may be profitable to common stockholders in periods of prosperity (when return on assets is greater than cost of borrowing) but can lead to serious trouble in a period of low earnings (if return on assets falls *below* the cost of borrowing).

21 *Long-term creditors* are primarily interested in the following measurements:

a The rate of return on investment, known as the *yield* on investment in bonds.

b The firm's ability to meet periodic interest requirements.

c The firm's ability to repay the principal of the debt at maturity.

22 The *yield* on bonds is the *effective interest rate* (after amortization of any discount or premium) that an investor will earn by buying the bonds at their current market price and holding them to maturity. The yield varies *inversely* with changes in the market price of a bond. The safety of an investment in bonds depends on the ability of a firm to meet the interest and principal payments. An indication of the ability to pay interest is the *number of times* that the interest requirement was earned. This is computed by dividing the income from operations by the annual interest expense. The safety of principal is, to some extent, measured by the *debt ratio*. The lower the debt ratio, the safer the position of creditors.

23 *Preferred stockholders* are primarily interested in the yield on their investment and the number of times that preferred dividends were earned. The *yield* is computed by dividing the annual dividend received on a share of preferred stock by the market value of a share of stock. The *times preferred dividends were earned* is computed by dividing net income by the annual dividends paid on the preferred stock.

24 *Short-term creditors* are primarily concerned with the relationship of *liquid assets* to current liabilities and the *turnover* of accounts receivable and inventories. These are usually analyzed by computing the following:

a Working capital, the excess of current assets over current liabilities.

b Current ratio, current assets divided by current liabilities.

c Quick ratio, quick assets (cash, marketable securities, and receivables) divided by current liabilities.

d Inventory turnover, cost of goods sold for the year divided by the average inventory during the year.

e Turnover of accounts receivable, credit sales for the year divided by the average receivables for the year.

25 The inventory turnover and accounts receivable turnover may be expressed in *days* by dividing 365 (days in a year) by the number of times the average inventory or receivables have turned over in one year. The result is the number of days necessary to turn inventory into receivables and receivables into cash.

26 Adding the days required to turn over inventory to the days required to turn over receivables gives the days necessary to convert inventory into cash. This is the *operating cycle* for a merchandising business (for firms that manufacture their inventory, this would be only part of the operating cycle). An operating cycle which lengthens from one period to the next may indicate that the firm is having trouble selling its inventory or collecting its accounts receivable.

TEST YOURSELF ON ANALYSIS OF FINANCIAL STATEMENTS

True or False

For each of the following statements, circle the T or the F to indicate whether the statement is true or false.

T F **1** The dollar amount of a change during a period in a certain item appearing in financial statements is probably less significant than the change measured as a percentage.

T F **2** Percentage changes are usually computed by using the latest figure as a base.

T F **3** It is possible that a decrease in gross profit rate may be more than offset by a decrease in expenses, thus resulting in an increase in net income.

T F **4** In a common size income statement each item is expressed as a percentage of net sales.

T F **5** Industry standards tend to place the performance of a company in a more meaningful perspective.

T F   6 Two earnings per share figures frequently appear in an income statement: earnings per share before taxes and earnings per share after taxes.

T F   7 Dividing the market price of a share of common stock by the dividends per share gives the price-earnings ratio.

T F   8 If some expenses are fixed (do not fluctuate in proportion to change in sales volume), net income should increase by a greater percentage than the increase in sales volume.

T F   9 Dividing net sales by average inventory gives the inventory turnover rate, which is a measure of how quickly inventory is selling.

T F   10 If the rate of return on assets is substantially higher than the cost of borrowing, the common stockholder should want the company to have a high equity ratio.

T F   11 If a company gets into financial difficulty, both the debt ratio and the equity ratio might decline at the same time.

T F   12 The common stockholder will lose from trading on the equity when the cost of borrowing exceeds the return on assets.

T F   13 The number of times preferred dividend requirements were earned is computed by dividing income *before* taxes by the amount of the annual dividend requirement of the preferred stock.

T F   14 A high current ratio may indicate that capital is not productively used and that inventories and receivables may be excessive.

T F   15 It is possible to "doctor up" many balance sheet ratios by completing certain transactions just before the close of the fiscal period.

T F   16 Certain account balances at the end of the accounting period may not be representative for the entire year, and as a result the ratios (or turnover figures) may be misleading.

Completion Statements

Fill in the necessary words or amounts to complete the following statements:

1 The three most widely used analytical techniques are _____ and _____ change, _____ _____ , and _____ .

2 The four groups that supply capital to a corporation are _____ _____ , _____ _____ , _____ _____ , and _____ .

3 The market price of common stock divided by earnings per share is known as the _____ _____ .

4 The debt ratio may be found by deducting the _____ _____ from 100%.

5 The current ratio is 3 to 1; working capital amounts to $100,000; and the quick ratio is 1.5 to 1. Compute the following: (a) current assets, $_____; (b) current liabilities, $_____; (c) total investment in inventories and short-term prepayments, $_____.

6 The number of times interest is earned is primarily important to _____ _____ , and may be found by dividing _____ _____ _____ by the annual _____ _____ .

7 When the _____ _____ _____ is less than the cost of borrowing, common stockholders should prefer a _____ debt ratio.

8 Cost of goods sold during a year divided by the average cost of _____ gives the _____ _____ for the year.

9 The _____ turnover plus the _____ _____ turnover, expressed in days, measures the length of the _____ _____ of a merchandising business.

Multiple Choice

Choose the best answer for each of the following questions and enter the identifying letter in the space provided.

_____ 1 An income statement showing only component percentages is known as a:
a Common dollar statement.

b Condensed income statement.

c Common size income statement.

d Comparative income statement.

_____ **2** Which of the following *is not* a valuable standard of comparison in analyzing financial statements of a company engaged in the manufacture of mobile homes?

a Past performance of the company.

b Performance of another company engaged in the manufacture of mobile homes.

c Performance of all companies engaged in manufacture of mobile homes.

d Performance of companies engaged in construction of apartment buildings.

_____ **3** Common stockholders would be *least concerned* with which of the following?

a Earnings per share of stock.

b Revenue and expense analysis.

c Book value per share.

d Number of times interest earned.

_____ **4** A company has a current ratio of 2 to 1 at the end of Year 1. Which one of the following transactions will *increase* this ratio?

a Sale of bonds payable at a discount.

b Declaration of a 50% stock dividend.

c Collection of a large account receivable.

d Borrowed cash from bank, issuing a six-month note.

_____ **5** Bondholders would be *most* interested in which of the following?

a Quick ratio.

b Inventory turnover.

c Times interest earned.

d Operating cycle.

_____ **6** If we added the average number of days required to turn the inventory over and the average age of receivables (in number of days), we would have an estimate of:

a The company's fiscal period.

b The sales volume of the business.

c The company's operating cycle.

d Nothing meaningful.

_____ **7** In projecting the future profitability of a merchandising company, investors will be least concerned with changes in:

a The gross profit rate.

b The rate earned on total assets.

c The quick ratio.

d Sales volume.

_____ **8** If sales increase by 10% from Year 1 to Year 2 and cost of goods sold increases only 6%, the gross profit on sales will increase by:

a 4%

b 10%

c 6%

d Some other percentage

Exercises

1 There are 10 transactions or events listed below. Opposite each item is listed a particular ratio used in financial analysis. Indicate the effect of each transaction or event on the ratio listed opposite it. Use the following symbols: Increase = *I*; Decrease = *D*; No Effect = *NE*. (Assume that the current ratio and the quick ratio are higher than 1 to 1.)

	Transaction or Event	Ratio	Effect
a	Purchased inventory on open account.	Quick ratio	
b	A larger physical volume of goods was sold at reduced prices.	Gross profit percentage	
c	Declared a cash dividend of $1 per share.	Current ratio	
d	An uncollectible account receivable was written off against the allowance account.	Current ratio	
e	Issued additional shares of common stock and used proceeds to retire long-term debt.	Rate earned on total assets (before interest and income taxes)	
f	Distributed a 20% stock dividend on common stock.	Earnings per share of common stock	
g	Operating income increased 25%; interest expense increased 10%.	Times interest charges earned	
h	During period of rising prices, company changed from fifo to lifo method of inventory pricing.	Inventory turnover	
i	Paid previously declared cash dividend.	Debt ratio	
j	Issued shares of common stock in exchange for plant assets.	Equity ratio	

2 The balance sheets of the Olympia Corporation at the beginning and end of Year 1 and the income statement for Year 1 are presented below:

OLYMPIA CORPORATION
Comparative Balance Sheet

Assets	Dec. 31, Year 1	Jan. 1, Year 1
Cash	$ 60,000	$ 45,000
Marketable securities	30,000	40,000
Accounts receivable (net)	50,000	70,000
Inventory	140,000	130,000
Plant and equipment (net of accumulated depreciation)	420,000	330,000
Total assets	$700,000	$615,000

Liabilities & Stockholders' Equity

	Dec. 31, Year 1	Jan. 1, Year 1
Accounts payable	$ 95,000	$ 30,000
Accrued liabilities	10,000	15,000
7% bonds payable	80,000	100,000
Capital stock, $5 par	300,000	300,000
Retained earnings*	215,000	170,000
Total liabilities & Stockholders' equity	$700,000	$615,000

*Dividends paid amounted to $0.65 per share.

OLYMPIA CORPORATION
Income Statement
For Year Ended December 31, Year 1

Net sales (all on credit)		$800,000
Cost of goods sold:		
Inventory, Jan. 1, Year 1	$130,000	
Purchases	500,000	
Goods available for sale	$630,000	
Inventory, Dec. 31, Year 1	140,000	490,000
Gross profit on sales		$310,000
Operating expenses (includes depreciation of $25,000)		160,000
Income from operations		$150,000
Other expense: Bond interest expense		7,000
Income before income taxes		$143,000
Income taxes		59,000
Net income		$ 84,000
Earnings per share		$ 1.40

On the basis of the information in the Olympia Corporation financial statements, fill in the blanks below with the appropriate amounts (do not compute the ratios):

a The *current ratio* at the end of Year 1 would be computed by dividing $_____ by $_____.

b The *acid test* (or *quick ratio*) at the end of Year 1 would be computed by dividing $_____ by $_____.

c The *average turnover of receivables* during the year would be computed by dividing $_____ by $_____.

d The *average turnover of inventories* during the year would be computed by dividing $_____ by $_____.

e The number of times bond interest charges were earned during Year 1 (before income taxes) would be determined by dividing $_____ by $_____.

f The *rate earned on average investment in assets* would be determined by dividing $_____ by $_____.

g The *equity ratio* at the end of Year 1 would be determined by dividing $_____ by $_____.

h The *rate of return on the average stockholders' equity* would be determined by dividing $_____ by $_____.

i The *earnings per share* of capital stock would be determined by dividing $_____ by _____ shares outstanding.

j If the capital stock had a market value at the end of the year of $42 per share, the *price-earnings ratio* would be determined by dividing $_____ by $_____.

k The *yield* on the stock, assuming a market value of $42, is computed by dividing $_____ by $_____.

l The book value per share of capital stock at the end of Year 1 would be computed by dividing $_____ by _____ shares outstanding.

m The *gross profit percentage* would be computed by dividing $_____ by $_____.

n The *operating expense ratio* would be computed by dividing $_____ by $_____.

3 From the following comparative balance sheet for the Gulfstream Company, compute the dollar and percentage changes from Year 1 to Year 2:

GULFSTREAM COMPANY
Comparative Balance Sheet
Year 1 and Year 2

Assets	Year 2	Year 1	Increase (or Decrease) Amount	Percentage
Current assets	$150,000	$120,000	$	
Investments	160,000	80,000		
Plant and equipment (net).	360,000	300,000		
Intangibles.	80,000	100,000		
Total assets	$750,000	$600,000	$	

Liabilities & Stockholders' Equity

	Year 2	Year 1	Amount	Percentage
Current liabilities	$ 76,000	$ 80,000	$	
Long-term debt	116,000	100,000		
Capital stock, $5 par	250,000	200,000		
Retained earnings	308,000	220,000		
Total liabilities & stockholders' equity	$750,000	$600,000	$	

17

INCOME TAXES
AND BUSINESS DECISIONS

HIGHLIGHTS OF THE CHAPTER

1 As the role of government in our society increases, so does the level of taxes. Taxes, which were almost insignificant in the early part of this century, now represent a major expense of doing business.

2 Because taxes have become such a significant expenditure, careful *tax planning* is essential to operating a business efficiently. Tax planning refers to determining in advance the income tax effect of every proposed business action, and so the burden of taxes may be considered in the business decision.

3 In terms of revenue produced (to government), the four most important taxes are *income taxes, sales taxes, property taxes,* and *excise taxes.* Income taxes probably exceed all others and are most important in business decisions.

4 There are four classes of taxpayers: *individuals, corporations, estates,* and *trusts.* A *partnership* does not pay any income tax, but it must file an *information* return. Partners must include their share of the partnership net income in their *personal* income tax returns, regardless of the amount they withdraw from the business.

5 The earnings of corporations are subject to *double taxation.* Corporate earnings are subject to corporate income tax when earned by the corporation and then are subject to personal income tax when distributed as dividends to stockholders.

6 Almost all individual tax returns are prepared on the *cash basis* of measuring income. In-

dividuals may use the accrual basis if they choose, but the cash basis is simpler, requires less record keeping, and permits tax savings by allowing the taxpayer to shift the timing of revenue and expenses from one year to another.

7 Taxes may be *proportional* (constant percentage of the base), *progressive* (increasing percentage of the base as the base increases), or *regressive* (decreasing percentage of the base as the base increases). Income tax rates on individuals are *highly progressive,* ranging in recent years from 12 to 50% of taxable income.

8 Because of the progressive nature of income taxes, an individual whose income fluctuates from year to year would have to pay more taxes than an individual who earned the same total amount at a more even annual rate. Therefore, individuals whose income fluctuates widely are permitted to average out their income and pay income taxes as if the income had been earned at an even rate over the last five years.

9 Income taxes are increased each year *as a result of inflation* even though the schedule of tax rates remains unchanged. Inflation moves people into higher tax brackets even though their higher salaries represent no increase in purchasing power. This problem may end in 1985 when *indexing* is scheduled to begin. Indexing refers to adjusting the tax brackets each year to reflect changes in the Consumer Price Index.

10 In analyzing the tax effect of a transaction, the *marginal* tax rate, not the average tax rate, should be used.

11 The income tax formula for individuals is as follows: Total income minus exclusions equals gross income. Gross income minus deductions equals adjusted gross income. Adjusted gross income minus excess itemized deductions minus personal exemptions equals taxable income. The tax on the taxable income minus any tax credits equals the tax payable to the government.

12 Gross income of individuals includes *all items of income not specifically excluded by law*. Among the items *excluded* are:

a Interest on state and municipal bonds.

b Gifts and inheritances received.

c Life insurance proceeds resulting from death of insured.

d Workmen's compensation and sick pay.

e Social security benefits, military bonuses, and pensions to veterans.

f Compensation for personal damages.

g Certain income earned outside the United States.

h First $100 of dividends from domestic corporations ($200 on a joint return).

13 Deductions *to arrive at* adjusted gross income are:

a Business expenses.

b Employees' expenses.

c Expenses attributable to rents and royalties.

d Losses from the sale of property used in a trade or business.

e Net capital losses up to $3,000 in any one year.

f Sixty percent of the excess of net long-term capital gains over net short-term capital losses.

g Net operating loss carry-overs from preceding years.

h Contributions to retirement plans (IRAs and Keoghs).

i The "two-earner married couple" deduction, which is 10% of the income of the lower earning spouse, with the deduction limited to $3,000.

14 Deductions from adjusted gross income are limited to excess itemized deductions and personal exemptions. *Excess itemized deductions* consist of such items as charitable contributions, interest paid on home mortgage and other borrowings, and taxes paid to state, cities, or counties. The term *excess* means that these items are deductible only to the extent that they exceed the zero bracket amount (presently $3,400 for married taxpayers filing a joint return and $2,300 for single taxpayers).

15 The *zero bracket amount* is a specified amount of income which is subject to a tax rate of 0%. The zero bracket amount is built into the tax tables to assure that a given amount of the income earned by every taxpayer is not subject to income taxes. In effect, the zero bracket amount represents an "automatic" deduction from adjusted gross income in determining the amount of income actually subject to income tax. As stated in paragraph 14, taxable income can be reduced further if the taxpayer can itemize deductions in *excess* of the zero bracket amount.

16 *Personal exemptions* (presently $1,000 each) may be deducted for the taxpayer, spouse, and each dependent. A taxpayer and spouse may each claim an additional exemption if he or she is blind, and another exemption if he or she has reached the age of 65.

17 The preceding steps lead us to the taxable income of the individual, the amount to which the appropriate tax rates are applied.

18 *Gains and losses from the sale or exchange of capital assets* are granted special treatment for income tax purposes. A gain or loss on the sale or exchange of capital assets held more than one year is a *long-term* gain or loss; the sale or exchange of capital assets held for less than one year results in a *short-term* gain or loss.

19 The amount of capital gain or loss included in the tax return for individuals is determined as follows:

a Long-term gains and losses are combined to produce a *net long-term gain or loss*. Short-term gains and losses are similarly combined into a *net short-term gain or loss*.

b If there is a net long-term gain and a net short-term gain, only 40% of the net long-term gain is included in taxable income, but 100% of the net short-term gain is included. Similar rates are applied when the net gain (of either type) exceeds the net loss (of either type).

c If there is a net short-term loss and a net long-term loss, the short-term loss is combined with 50% of the long-term loss, and up to $3,000 of this total may be deducted to arrive at adjusted gross income. If the total exceeds $3,000, the excess may be carried to future tax years.

20 Many people believe that investors benefit

from losing money because of "tax losses." This is simply not true. Except for the allowable $3,000 deduction for capital losses, capital losses are deductible only against capital gains. Thus, an investor who loses $50,000 and has no capital gains may take only a $3,000 tax deduction in the current year. Even if this investor is in the maximum 50% tax bracket, a $3,000 deduction saves only $1,500 in taxes. Although the excess may be carried forward to future years, the investor will *never* come out ahead for having lost money.

21 The ratio of capital investment to gross national product in the United States has fallen below that of many other countries. Capital investment is, of course, vital to high employment, high productivity, and a high standard of living. To encourage investment, some countries have *no* tax on capital gains. In the United States, gains are taxed heavily while large capital losses are deductible only against capital gains. This policy may be inconsistent with the national policy of encouraging private investment.

22 *Tax credits* differ from deductions. A deduction, such as a charitable contribution, reduces the *income subject to tax*, but a tax credit is subtracted *directly from the tax owed*. Major types of tax credits include the investment tax credit, new jobs credit, credit for the elderly, and foreign tax credit.

23 The investment credit exists as an incentive to investment. When a business buys certain types of long-lived productive assets, it can take a credit of from 4 to 10% of the cost of the property as a deduction from its income taxes.

24 Individuals who compute their income on the calendar-year basis must file an income tax return by April 15 of each year. Corporations must file a return 2½ months after the end of their fiscal year.

25 Quarterly payments of estimated tax are required for self-employed persons and for others having income not subject to withholding. An example of such income is rent received from tenants.

26 A *corporation* is a separate taxable entity. Income tax expense therefore appears on the income statement of a corporation and income taxes payable appear as a current liability on the balance sheet.

27 Tax rates for corporations are in a graduated

five-step structure. The rates in effect at the time of publication are:

	Tax Rate, %
First $25,000 of taxable income	15
Second $25,000 of taxable income	18
Third $25,000 of taxable income	30
Fourth $25,000 of taxable income	40
All taxable income over $100,000	46

A short-cut method of computing the tax for a corporation with taxable income above $100,000 is to multiply the *entire amount* of taxable income by 46% and then subtract $20,250 from the resulting figure.

28 Corporations cannot deduct a net capital loss. However, a corporation can offset the net capital loss of one year against any capital gains in the three preceding years or in the following five years. The concepts of excess itemized deductions and personal exemptions are not applicable to corporations.

29 Corporations are not entitled to the dividend exclusion of $100 allowed to individuals; corporations are, however, allowed to deduct 85% of the dividends they receive from other domestic corporations. Corporations are subject to a maximum tax rate of 28% on net long-term capital gains.

30 *Accounting income* often differs from *taxable income* because each is computed with different purposes in mind. Furthermore, taxable income is computed by reference to specific laws, and laws generally do not govern the computation of accounting income.

31 A taxpayer usually can elect to use either the *cash* or the *accrual* basis of determining taxable income. When merchandise is a significant factor in a business, the accrual method is required. If the cash basis is used, depreciation must be computed in the same way as under the accrual basis, and income *constructively* received must be included in income even though cash has not been physically received.

32 The three major sources of differences between *accounting income* and *taxable income* are:
 a *Special tax treatment* of revenue and expenses. (For example, municipal bond interest and 85% of intercompany dividends are excluded from taxable income, whereas

political contributions and amortization of goodwill are not deductible.)

b *Differences in timing* of revenue and expenses. (For example, income received in advance is taxed in the year of receipt, while certain expenses are not deductible for tax purposes until they are actually paid.)

c *Alternative accounting methods* for tax purposes and financial reporting (for such items as inventories, depreciation, and installment sales). Business executives will generally select an accounting method for tax purposes that will minimize their current tax liabilities.

33 Significant differences between accounting income and taxable income may be caused by differences in timing of revenue and expenses or by using alternative accounting methods. *Interperiod income tax allocation* should be used to avoid the distortion of net income computed for financial reporting purposes. The objective of interperiod tax allocation is to *accrue income taxes in relation to accounting income* whenever differences between accounting and taxable income are caused by *differences in timing* of revenues and expenses (including those differences resulting from the use of alternative accounting methods).

34 Income tax considerations may be of great importance in making certain business decisions. Some of these decisions are:
a Choice of the form of business organization.
b Choice of accounting methods for inventories, depreciation of plant and equipment, long-term construction contracts, etc.
c Timing and manner in which property is sold.
d Allocation of values to assets when a business is acquired or sold.
e Types of securities to be issued in raising capital to finance a business.

35 *Tax shelters* are investments which produce a loss for tax purposes in the near term but hopefully will prove profitable in the long run. For example, investments in real estate may show a short-term loss because of deductions for interest, property taxes, and depreciation but may prove profitable in the long run because of rising market values. Many tax shelters lose money, however, and the tax savings *never offset the full amount of the loss.*

TEST YOURSELF ON INCOME TAXES

True or False

For each of the following statements, circle the T or the F to indicate whether the statement is true or false.

T F   1 Planning a business transaction in advance to minimize the amount of tax that will become due is termed *tax avoidance* and is usually illegal.

T F   2 Individuals with large incomes pay a lower percentage of their incomes as income taxes than do individuals with low incomes.

T F   3 Individuals, corporations, and partnerships must all pay taxes on business income.

T F   4 Interest on municipal bonds, life insurance proceeds, social security benefits, and the first $100 of dividends from domestic corporations are examples of items which may be excluded from gross income for tax purposes by an unmarried taxpayer.

T F   5 The highest tax rate applied to a corporation is higher than the highest tax rate applied to individuals.

T F   6 Income averaging is designed to benefit individuals whose income fluctuates widely from year to year.

T F   7 A taxpayer with a net long-term capital gain of $8,000 and a net short-term capital loss of $14,000 may deduct $6,000 as a net short-term capital loss.

T F   8 A taxpayer with a net long-term capital loss of $1,800, and no net short-term gain or loss, has a $900 deduction to arrive at adjusted gross income.

T F   9 The federal income tax is designed to serve a number of purposes other than obtaining revenue for the government.

T F 10 Any action by a high-bracket taxpayer which reduces taxable income tends to reduce income taxes; therefore, any investment which results in a loss will be advantageous to such a taxpayer.

T F 11 From the viewpoint of tax planning, a corporation will usually find it advantageous to finance expansion through the issuance of preferred stock rather than bonds payable.

T F 12 Full-time students earning $2,500 per year can qualify as dependents for their parents.

T F 13 Corporations are not entitled to a $100 dividend exclusion but may deduct 85% of dividends received from other domestic corporations.

T F 14 If a taxpayer used the accrual basis in preparing a tax return, income for tax purposes would have to be the same as income for accounting purposes.

T F 15 The cash basis of determining taxable income is more commonly used by individuals than the accrual basis.

T F 16 Any business, whether incorporated or not, can elect to use a different method of depreciation on its income tax return from that used in its financial statements.

T F 17 The objective of interperiod income tax allocation is to accrue income taxes in relation to accounting income whenever differences between accounting and taxable income are caused by differences in the timing of revenue or expenses.

T F 18 The cash basis is often more beneficial to the taxpayer than the accrual basis because it often permits postponing the recognition of taxable income by controlling the timing of expenses and collections.

Completion Statements

Fill in the necessary words to complete the following statements:

1 If income tax rates remain constant during a period of inflation, most people will pay a _____ _____ of their earnings as income taxes merely as a result of inflation.

2 The four classes of taxpayers are _____, _____ , _____ , and _____ .

3 The four types of taxes which raise the most revenue for government are _____ taxes, _____ taxes, _____ taxes, and _____ taxes.

4 A partnership does not pay any tax but must file an _____ return.

5 Interest credited by a bank to a savings account is taxable to the depositor even though not withdrawn, because it is _____ _____ _____ .

6 The major categories of itemized deductions on the tax returns of individuals are _____ , _____ , _____ , _____ , _____ (in excess of 3% of adjusted gross income), _____ _____ and expenses related to the _____ of _____ .

7 A procedure designed to accrue income tax expense in relation to pretax accounting income is called _____ _____ _____ _____ . This procedure is used when differences in accounting income and _____ income are caused by differences in the _____ of revenue or expenses.

Multiple Choice

Choose the best answer for each of the following questions and enter the identifying letter in the space provided.

_____ 1 The expression *tax planning* is usually taken to mean:
a The analysis of the tax consequences of alternative business decisions and the means of minimizing the tax burden on the taxable entity.
b Preparing the various tax returns and making sure that cash is available to make the payments.
c The classification of various types of taxes in the accounts and the presentation in financial statements.
d Preparation and filing of a declaration of estimated tax.

_____ 2 The income tax rules affecting corporations:
a Treat all corporations alike regardless of size.
b Deliberately favor small corporations.
c Deliberately favor large corporations.
d Specify a wider range of tax rates than do the tax rules affecting individuals.

_____ **3** The investment tax credit is:

a Deductible from adjusted gross income to the extent it exceeds the zero bracket amount.

b Computed as a percentage of dividend income and deducted from adjusted gross income.

c Computed as a percentage of the cost of depreciable business property acquired during the year and deducted from the tax owed.

d Used in place of the zero bracket amount.

_____ **4** John has ordinary income of $18,600, a long-term capital gain of $1,600, and a short-term capital loss of $5,600. Based on these facts, John should report adjusted gross income for federal income tax purposes of:

a $15,600

b $14,600

c $13,000

d Some other amount

_____ **5** Susan has short-term capital gains of $2,000 and short-term capital losses of $3,000. She also has long-term gains of $6,000 and long-term losses of $1,000. The net amount of capital gains that she would include in taxable income is:

a $4,500

b $1,600

c $2,000

d Some other amount

_____ **6** The taxable income for an individual is determined as follows:

a Gross income less personal exemptions.

b Adjusted gross income less exclusions.

c Total income less exclusions less adjusted gross income.

d Adjusted gross income less excess itemized deductions less personal exemptions.

_____ **7** John and Judy Lee have an adjusted gross income of $25,000 on their joint tax return. They have paid property tax of $500, state income tax of $400, and interest of $2,200. The zero bracket amount is $3,400, and each personal exemption is $1,000. The Lees have two small children. The taxable income the Lees should report is:

a $14,500

b $17,600

c $21,000

d Some other amount

_____ **8** In determining whether the corporate or noncorporate form of business organization is preferable from an income tax standpoint for a small enterprise, which of the following factors would _favor incorporation?_

a The major stockholder is the active manager of the business.

b The major stockholder is single and withdraws most of the earnings of the business to meet personal living expenses.

c The sole stockholder has substantial income from holdings of municipal bonds.

d The owner-manager has substantial income from dividends on blue-chip stocks and prefers that earnings of the business be used to finance its expansion.

_____ **9** The cash basis of accounting:

a Cannot be used in filing income tax returns.

b Is widely used by manufacturing corporations.

c Should be used whenever possible since it enables the taxpayer to postpone the payment of income tax.

d Is permissible but usually results in a larger amount of tax than does the accrual method.

_____ **10** Which of the following would _not_ be a source of difference between accounting income and taxable income?

a Straight-line amortization of a patent over its useful life.

b Depreciation computed by different methods in tax return and accounting records.

c Inventory valuation by different methods in tax return and accounting records.

d Rental income received several years in advance.

Exercises

1 The Miller Corporation reports income before taxes of $100,000, which includes, among other items, the following:

Dividends from other corporations	$ 20,000
Net long-term capital loss	8,000
Amortization of goodwill	5,000
Interest received on municipal bonds.	4,500

Compute the income that would be taxable to the Miller Corporation.

Income before taxes		$100,000
Add:	$	
Subtotal		
Less:	$	
Taxable income		$

2 Robert and Betty Hill have six dependent children. In preparing their income tax return you obtain the following information:

Gross income:

Salaries (before deductions)

Robert Hill.	22,000
Betty Hill	22,000
Dividends from domestic corporations (assume joint ownership).	580
Proceeds on life insurance policy upon death of father	5,000
Interest on City of Medford bonds	2,100
Interest on savings account.	1,320
Gain on stock held over one year	8,200
Loss on stock held two months	(4,200)
Inheritance from father's estate	12,500
Christmas gift from family friend	50

Personal expenses:

Living expenses: food, clothes, etc.	5,800
Sales taxes	400
State income taxes paid.	2,300
Contribution to church and other allowable organizations.	800
Property taxes on residence	1,650
Federal excise taxes.	150
Interest on mortgage and personal loan.	6,520
Medical expenses	1,800
Subscription to investment advisory service	200
Federal income tax withheld by employer.	4,840
Social security taxes withheld by employer.	3,080

Instructions Assuming that the zero bracket amount is $3,400 and each personal exemption is $1,000, compute the taxable income that Robert and Betty Hill should report on a joint return.

ROBERT AND BETTY HILL
Computation of Taxable Income for 19___

Gross income: $

                                      _____ $

Deduction to arrive at
adjusted gross income:

                                      _____

Adjusted gross income . . . . . $
Deductions from adjusted
gross income:
Itemized deductions:
                                      $

                                      _____
                                                   $
Less: Zero bracket
amount. . . . .   _____
Excess itemized deduc-
tions . . . . $
Personal exemptions
(___ × $1,000). . . . .   _____ _____
Taxable income . . . . $

**ANSWERS TO
QUESTIONS AND
SOLUTIONS TO
EXERCISES**

CHAPTER 1

True or False

1 T	5 T	9 T	13 T	17 T
2 T	6 F	10 F	14 F	
3 F	7 T	11 F	15 F	
4 F	8 T	12 F	16 T	

Completion Statements

1 Income statement, balance sheet. 2(a) Recording, (b) classifying, (c) summarizing. 3 Generally accepted accounting principles. 4 Audit. 5 Securities and Exchange Commission. 6 Financial Accounting Standards Board. 7(a) Profit, (b) solvent. 8 Internal control. 9(a) Single proprietorships, (b) partnerships, (c) corporations. 10(a) Name of the company, (b) name of the statement, (c) date. 11 Going-concern, objectivity, replacement, historical. 12 Creditors, owners, residual. 13 Assets, liabilities, owners' equity. 14 Assets, $80,000. 15 Understated, understated, correct. 16(a) Investment, (b) profits. 17 Increase. 18 Dividends, stockholders.

Multiple Choice

1 b	3 c	5 a	7 d
2 a	4 c	6 b	

Solutions to Exercises

1

TITAN CORPORATION
Balance Sheet
December 31, 19___

Assets		Liabilities & Stockholders' Equity		
Cash	$ 14,000	Liabilities:		
Accounts receivable	37,000	Accounts payable		$ 28,000
Land	35,000	Income taxes payable		12,000
Buildings	60,000	Total liabilities		$ 40,000
Office equipment	16,000	Stockholders' equity:		
Automobiles	8,000	Capital stock	$100,000	
		Retained earnings	30,000	130,000
Total assets	$170,000	Total liabilities & stockholders' equity		$170,000

2

UNITREX CORPORATION
Balance Sheet
December 31, 19___

Assets		Liabilities & Stockholders' Equity		
Cash	$ 42,000	Liabilities:		
Accounts receivable.	144,000[b]	Notes payable		$ 10,000[d]
Land	90,000	Accounts payable		62,000 [c]
Building	260,000	Income taxes payable.		40,000
Office equipment	56,000	Total liabilities		$112,000
		Stockholders' equity:		
		Capital stock.	$400,000[g]	
		Retained earnings	80,000[f]	480,000[e]
	$592,000[a]			$592,000

[a]Total assets must be $592,000 to agree with the total of liabilities and stockholders' equity.

[b]Accounts receivable must be $144,000 to achieve a total asset figure of $592,000.

[c]Cash, $42,000, plus accounts receivable, $144,000, equals $186,000. Accounts payable are stated to be one-third of the combined total of cash and accounts receivable; that is, $186,000 ÷ 3 = $62,000.

[d]Total liabilities are given as $112,000 and consist of three items. One item, income taxes payable, is given as $40,000, and we have determined a second item, accounts payable, to be $62,000 (see footnote c). Therefore, notes payable must be $10,000; that is, $112,000 − $40,000 − $62,000 = $10,000.

[e]Total liabilities and stockholders' equity is given as $592,000, and total liabilities as $112,000, therefore, the difference must be stockholders' equity of $480,000.

[f]Earnings are stated to be $100,000 and dividends $20,000; so retained earnings must be $80,000.

[g]Capital stock equals stockholders' equity of $480,000 minus retained earnings of $80,000.

3

	Assets					=	Liabilities		+	Owners' Equity
	Cash	Accounts Receivable	Land	Building	Pool Tables		Notes Payable	Accounts Payable		Capital Stock
July 1	+$20,000									+$20,000
3	−$10,000		+$21,000	+$30,000			+$41,000			
Balances	$10,000		$21,000	$30,000			$41,000			$20,000
10	−$ 6,000				+$10,000			+$4,000		
Balances	$ 4,000		$21,000	$30,000	$10,000		$41,000	$4,000		$20,000
14	+$ 500	+$ 500			−$ 1,000					
Balances	$ 4,500	$ 500	$21,000	$30,000	$ 9,000		$41,000	$4,000		$20,000
20	−$ 2,000							−$2,000		
Balances	+$ 2,500	$ 500	$21,000	$30,000	$ 9,000		$41,000	$2,000		$20,000
24	+$ 200	−$ 200								
Balances	$ 2,700	$ 300	$21,000	$30,000	$ 9,000		$41,000	$2,000		$20,000
30	−$ 600				+$ 600					
Balances	$ 2,100	$ 300	$21,000	$30,000	$ 9,600		$41,000	$2,000		$20,000

CHAPTER 2

True or False

1	F	5	T	9	F	13	F	17	T
2	T	6	F	10	F	14	T	18	F
3	T	7	F	11	T	15	F	19	T
4	T	8	T	12	T	16	T	20	F

credits, debits. **5** Left, debit, right, credit. **6** Cash, Notes Payable, debit, credit. **7** Debit. **8(a)** Date, **(b)** account, debited, **(c)** account, credited, **(d)** explanation. **9** L/P (ledger page), posted, numbers, cross-reference. **10** Trial balance, debit balances, credit balances. **11** Book of original entry. **12** e, b, a, d, c.

Completion Statements

1 Left, ledger account, right. **2** Transaction, account. **3(a)** Title, **(b)** debit side, **(c)** credit side. **4** Debits,

Multiple Choice

1	a	3	b	5	c	7	c
2	c	4	d	6	b	8	a

Solutions to Exercises

1	Journal Entry	Dr	Cr	Assets	=	Liabilities	+	Owners' Equity
Example:								
	Office Equipment	600		+ 600				
	Cash		150	− 150				
	Accounts Payable		450			+ 450		
	Effect of transaction			+ 450	=	+ 450	+	
a	Accounts Receivable	230		+ 230				
	Cash		230	− 230				
	Effect of transaction			-0-	=	-0-	+	-0-
b	Cash	5,000		+5,000				
	Capital Stock		5,000					+5,000
	Effect of transaction			+5,000	=		+	+5,000
c	Cash	800		+ 800				
	Notes Payable		800			+ 800		
	Effect of transaction			+ 800	=	+ 800	+	
d	Accounts Payable	350				− 350		
	Cash		350	− 350				
	Effect of transaction			− 350	=	− 350	+	
e	Land	8,000		+8,000				
	Cash		2,000	−2,000				
	Notes Payable		6,000			+6,000		
	Effect of transaction			+6,000	=	+6,000	+	

2

Cash			
(1)	70,000	(3)	40,000
(2)	12,000	(7)	3,000

Notes Payable		
	(2)	12,000
	(3)	50,000

Land	
(3)	30,000

Accounts Payable			
(6)	600	(4)	6,000
(7)	3,000	(5)	5,000

Building	
(3)	60,000
(5)	5,000

Capital Stock		
	(1)	70,000

Office Equipment			
(4)	6,000	(6)	600

RIVIERA CORPORATION
Trial Balance
September 30, 19____

	Debit	Credit
Cash	$ 39,000	
Land	30,000	
Building	65,000	
Office equipment	5,400	
Notes payable		$ 62,000
Accounts payable		7,400
Capital stock		70,000
	$139,400	$139,400

CHAPTER 3

True or False

1 T	5 F	9 T	13 T	17 F
2 T	6 T	10 T	14 T	18 F
3 F	7 F	11 T	15 F	
4 T	8 T	12 F	16 F	

Completion Statements

1 Profits, losses, investment. **2** Revenue, expense. **3** Cost, depreciation. **4** $49,000; $68,000; $57,000. **5** Producing revenue, decrease, stockholders' equity. **6** Net income, increase. **7** Retained Earnings, credits. **8** Closing entries. **9** Dividends, Dividends Payable, Dividends Payable, Cash.

Multiple Choice

1 c	3 b	5 d	7 a
2 a	4 c	6 c	8 b

Solutions to Exercises

1a

MISSION AUTO REPAIR, INC.
Income Statement
For the Month Ended May 31, 19____

Repair revenue		$24,000
Expenses:		
Rent	$ 2,000	
Wages.	11,350	
Advertising.	1,400	
Utilities.	300	
Depreciation.	350	
Total expenses.		15,400
Net income		$ 8,600

1b

MISSION AUTO REPAIR, INC.
Statement of Retained Earnings
For the Month Ended May 31, 19____

Retained earnings, Apr. 30, 19____.	$40,000
Net income	8,600
Subtotal	$48,600
Dividends	8,000
Retained earnings, May 31, 19____.	$40,600

1c

MISSION AUTO REPAIR, INC.
Balance Sheet
May 31, 19____

Assets

Cash		$18,600
Notes receivable.		4,000
Accounts receivable.		42,000
Garage equipment.	$33,600	
Less: Accumulated depreciation	9,100	24,500
Total assets		$89,100

Liabilities & Stockholders' Equity

Liabilities:		
Notes payable		$ 8,200
Accounts payable		10,300
Total liabilities		$18,500
Stockholders' equity:		
Capital stock.	$30,000	
Retained earnings	40,600	70,600
Total liabilities & stockholders' equity		$89,100

2

Error	Total Revenue	Total Expense	Net Income	Total Assets	Total Liabilities	Total Owners' Equity
1	NE	U	O	O	NE	O
2	O	NE	O	O	NE	O
3	NE	U	O	O	NE	O
4	NE	NE	NE	NE	U	O
5	NE	U	O	O	NE	O
6	NE	NE	NE	NE	NE	NE

CHAPTER 4
True or False

1 F	5 F	9 T	13 F	17 F
2 T	6 T	10 T	14 T	18 F
3 T	7 F	11 T	15 T	19 T
4 F	8 F	12 F	16 T	

Completion Statements

1 Recorded costs, unrecorded expenses, recorded revenue, unrecorded revenue. 2(a) Allocates, expense, (b) asset, Unexpired Insurance. 3 Revenue, expense. 4 Debit, expense credit, asset. 5 Debit, asset, credit, liability. 6 Debit, expense, credit, liability. 7 Debit, expense, credit, asset, liability. 8 Debit, asset, asset, liability. 9 Debit, credit, debits, credits, credit. 10 Management Fees Receivable, Management Fees Earned, Cash, Management Fees Receivable, $200, Management Fees Earned, $200. 11 Salaries Payable, Salaries Expense, January 1, Year 5.

Multiple Choice

1 b	3 c	5 c	7 d	9 b
2 a	4 c	6 a	8 d	10 c

Solutions to Exercises

1

	Trial Balance		Adjustments		Adjusted Trial Balance		Income Statement		Balance Sheet	
	Debit	Credit	Debit	Credit	Debit	Credit	Debit	Credit	Debit	Credit
Cash	5,100				5,100				5,100	
Accounts receivable	17,300				17,300				17,300	
Unexpired insurance	360			a 60	300				300	
Office supplies	900			b 650	250				250	
Office equipment	4,800				4,800				4,800	
Accumulated depreciation: office equipment		560		c 40		600				600
Notes payable		8,000				8,000				8,000
Accounts payable		1,800				1,800				1,800
Unearned commissions		1,500	e 800			700				700
Capital stock		9,000				9,000				9,000
Retained earnings, June 1, 19__		7,000				7,000				7,000
Dividends	2,000				2,000				2,000	
Commissions earned		16,000		e 800		16,800		16,800		
Rent expense	2,400				2,400		2,400			
Salaries expense	11,000		f 200		11,200		11,200			
	43,860	43,860								
Insurance expense			a 60		60		60			
Office supplies expense			b 650		650		650			
Depreciation expense: office equipment			c 40		40		40			
Interest expense			d 50		50		50			
Interest payable				d 50		50				50
Salaries payable				f 200		200				200
			1,800	1,800	44,150	44,150	14,400	16,800		
Net income							2,400			2,400
							16,800	16,800	29,750	29,750

2

19___	**General Journal** **Adjusting Entries**		
	a		
June 30	Insurance Expense	60	
	Unexpired Insurance		60
	To record insurance expired during June.		
	b		
30	Office Supplies Expense	650	
	Office Supplies		650
	To record consumption of office supplies during		
	June.		
	c		
30	Depreciation Expense: Office Equipment	40	
	Accumulated Depreciation: Office Equipment		40
	Depreciation expense for June ($4,800 ÷ 120 months).		
	d		
30	Interest Expense	50	
	Interest Payable		50
	To record interest expense for June.		
	e		
30	Unearned Commissions	800	
	Commissions Earned		800
	To record commissions earned during June.		
	f		
30	Salaries Expense	200	
	Salaries Payable		200
	To record salary expense and related liability at		
	June 30.		
	Closing Entries		
30	Commissions Earned	16,800	
	Income Summary		16,800
	To close the revenue account.		
30	Income Summary	14,400	
	Rent Expense		2,400
	Salaries Expense		11,200
	Insurance Expense		60
	Office Supplies Expense		650
	Depreciation Expense: Office Equipment		40
	Interest Expense		50
	To close the expense accounts.		
30	Income Summary	2,400	
	Retained Earnings		2,400
	To close the Income Summary account.		
30	Retained Earnings	2,000	
	Dividends		2,000
	To close the Dividends account.		

CHAPTER 5

True or False

1 F	7 T	13 F	19 T	25 F
2 T	8 T	14 F	20 F	26 T
3 F	9 T	15 F	21 F	27 T
4 T	10 T	16 F	22 T	28 T
5 T	11 F	17 F	23 F	
6 F	12 T	18 T	24 F	

Completion Statements

1 Perpetual, physical count, periodic. 2 Gross profit.
3 Credit, debit, Income Summary, Inventory, Income
Summary. 4(a) Liability, (b) Sales, Sales Tax Payable. 5(a) Current assets, (b) plant and equipment,
(c) other assets. 6 Working capital, current ratio, solvency. 7 Administrative, accounting. 8 Subdivision,
organization, serially numbered, internal audit. 9 Purchase order, receiving report. 10 Sales, purchase,
purchase order. 11 Debit memorandum, credit memorandum. 12 $4,900, debit, Purchase Discounts Lost,
$100, $5,000.

Multiple Choice

1 d	3 c	5 c	7 d	9 a	11 b
2 b	4 b	6 d	8 a	10 b	

Solutions to Exercises

Sales			$161,000
Sales returns & allowances		$ 4,500	
Sales discounts		1,500	6,000
Net sales			$155,000
Cost of goods sold:			
Inventory, Jan. 1		$ 22,000	
Purchases	$ 98,500		
Transportation-in	3,600		
Delivered cost of purchases	$102,100		
Purchase returns & allowances	$3,100		
Purchase discounts	2,000	5,100	
Net purchases		97,000	
Cost of goods available for sale		$119,000	
Inventory, Dec. 31		26,000	
Cost of goods sold			93,000
Gross profit on sales			$ 62,000
Operating expenses			46,500
Net income			$ 15,500

Invoice Number	Invoice Date	List Price	Trade Discount	Purchase Price	Credit Terms	Date Paid	Amount Paid
2071	July 17	$1,000	40%	$ 600	2/10, n/30	Aug. 16	$ 600
42	July 24	500	20%	400	2/10, n/30	Aug. 3	392
4286	Aug. 5	1,600	25%	1,200	5/20, n/60	Aug. 25	1,140
0093	Aug. 12	640	None	640	10 eom	Sept. 10	640
1249	Aug. 23	2,000	50%	1,000	2/10, n/30	Sept. 2	980
8163	Sept. 3	240	25%	180	10 eom	Oct. 10	180

CHAPTER 6

True or False

1 F	5 T	9 F	13 T	17 F
2 F	6 T	10 T	14 F	18 F
3 F	7 F	11 T	15 F	19 T
4 T	8 T	12 F	16 T	

Completion Statements

1 Posting. 2 Purchases, general, debit. 3 Debit, Accounts Receivable, credit, Sales. 4 Sales invoices, invoices, general, controlling. 5 Input, program. 6 Not be posted. 7 Occurs frequently. 8 Control total, limit test.

Multiple Choice

1 d	3 c	5 c	7 b
2 a	4 a	6 b	8 c

Solutions to Exercises

1

a	S
b	CP
c	CP
d	CR
e	J
f	J
g	J
h	CP
i	J
j	CR
k	P
l	J
m	J
n	J

	Debit	Credit
a	P, CP	J
b	J	J, CR
c	J	CP
d	J	S, CR
e	J, CP	J
f	CR	J
g	J, CP	P, J
h	S	CR, J
i	CR	CP
j	J	J

CHAPTER 7

True or False

1 T	6 T	11 T	16 T	21 T
2 F	7 T	12 T	17 F	
3 T	8 T	13 F	18 T	
4 T	9 T	14 F	19 T	
5 F	10 F	15 F	20 T	

Completion Statements

1 Maintenance of accounting records. 2 Deposited intact. 3 Collusion of two or more persons. 4 Outstanding checks, deposits in transit. 5 Not sufficient funds, Accounts Receivable. 6 Deducted from, bank statement, added to, bank statement, deducted from, depositor's records, added to, depositor's records. 7(a) Voucher register, Telephone Expense, Vouchers Payable; (b) check register, Vouchers Payable, Cash. 8 Accounting, finance, payee, perforated, accounting. 9 92½. 10 Accrued Bond Interest Receivable. 11 Return, risk, diversification, risk.

Multiple Choice

1 d	3 a	5 b	7 b	9 d
2 c	4 c	6 a	8 d	10 b

Solutions to Exercises

1	Sept. 11	Petty Cash	300	
		Cash		300
	Sept. 30	Postage Expense.	48	
		Travel Expense	26	
		Miscellaneous Expense	55	
		Cash		129

2

HUNTER CORPORATION
Bank Reconciliation
July 31, 19____

Balance per depositor's records, July 31, 19____. . . .			$11,364
Add: Note receivable collected for us by bank			1,800
			$13,164
Deduct: Service charge	$ 6		
NSF check of Jay Kline	264		
Error on check no. 295.	108		378
Adjusted balance			$12,786
Balance per bank statement, July 31, 19____.			$17,018
Add: Deposit on July 31.			1,950
			$18,968
Deduct: Outstanding checks:			
No. 301	$2,500		
No. 303	600		
No. 304	1,800		
No. 306	1,282	6,182	
Adjusted balance (as above)			$12,786

3 | **General Journal**

Year 5			
Sept. 1	Accrued Bond Interest Receivable	1,000	
	Investment in Bonds	88,250	
	Cash		89,250
	Purchased $100,000 par value of World Airlines 12% bonds		
	at 87¾ and accrued interest, plus commission of $1,000.		
Dec. 31	Accrued Bond Interest Receivable	4,000	
	Bond Interest Earned		4,000
	To accrue bond interest earned to Dec. 31 ($100,000 $\times$ 12% $\times$ $^4/_{12}$).		
Year 6			
Feb. 1	Cash	6,000	
	Accrued Bond Interest Receivable		5,000
	Bond Interest Earned		1,000
	Received semiannual bond interest on World Airlines bonds ($100,000		
	$\times$ 12% $\times$ ½).		
Apr. 1	Accrued Bond Interest Receivable	2,000	
	Bond Interest Earned		2,000
	To accrue interest to date of sale of investment in World Airlines		
	bonds ($100,000 $\times$ 12% $\times$ $^2/_{12}$).		
Apr. 1	Cash	92,500	
	Investment in Bonds		88,250
	Accrued Bond Interest Receivable		2,000
	Gain on Sale of Investments		2,250
	To record sale of $100,000 par value of World Airlines 12% bonds		
	at 91 plus accrued interest of $2,000 and minus commission of		
	$500.		

4	General Journal		
Year 1			
Dec. 31	Unrealized Loss on Marketable Securities	24,000	
	Valuation Allowance for Marketable Securities		24,000
	To establish valuation allowance for decline in market		
	value of marketable securities as current assets.		
	($325,000 − $301,000 = $24,000)		
Year 2			
Dec. 31	Valuation Allowance for Marketable Securities	9,000	
	Unrealized Gain on Marketable Securities		9,000
	To reduce valuation allowance as a result of partial recovery of		
	market value of securities in current portfolio.		
	($270,000 − $255,000 = $15,000 required amount of allowance.)		
Year 3			
Dec. 31	Valuation Allowance for Marketable Securities	15,000	
	Unrealized Gain on Marketable Securities		15,000
	To eliminate valuation allowance as a result of recovery of market		
	value of marketable securities.		
Year 4			
Jan. 2	Cash	52,000	
	Gain on Sale of Marketable Securities		7,000
	Marketable Securities		45,000
	To record sale of marketable securities at a realized gain.		

CHAPTER 8

True or False

1 T	6 T	11 T	16 T	21 T
2 T	7 T	12 F	17 T	22 T
3 F	8 F	13 F	18 T	23 F
4 T	9 T	14 F	19 F	24 T
5 F	10 T	15 F	20 T	

Completion Statements

1 Matching costs and revenue, net income.   2 Overstated, overstated, overstated.   3 Uncollectible accounts expense, allowance for doubtful accounts.
4 $15,940, debit, Interest Expense, $60, $16,000.
5 15%.   6 Accrued Interest Receivable, Interest Revenue, Interest Revenue.   7 $4,032, debit, Credit Card Discount Expense, $168, credit, Accounts Receivable — Global Express, $4,200.   8 Contra-liability, deducted, interest expense.   9 Contra-asset, deducted, notes receivable, interest revenue.   10 $10,075, $10,075, $10,150, $10,150.

Multiple Choice

1 d	3 d	5 b	7 d
2 a	4 d	6 c	8 d

Solution to Exercises

1

	Accounts	
	Debited	**Credited**
	A,C	X
1	D	C
2	A	E
3	A,J	C
4	A,I	B
5	C	D
6	I	G
7	A,F	E
8	A	C
9	E,G,I	A
10	I	F

2

a $280
b $315
c $120
d $375
e $975

CHAPTER 9

True or False

1 T	6 T	11 T	16 T	21 T
2 T	7 F	12 F	17 T	
3 T	8 F	13 F	18 T	
4 F	9 F	14 F	19 F	
5 T	10 T	15 F	20 F	

Completion Statements

1 Title, seller, buyer. 2 $5,000; $37,000; $18,000.
2 Specific identification, average cost, first-in, first-out, last-in, first-out. 4 Replacement, replacement, historical, overstating. 5 Replacement cost, reinvested, inventory, fifo. 6 Decrease, replacement, increase, replacement. 7 Lifo. 8 Retail, cost, ratio (or percentage). 9 Inventory, (a) Sales, sales, (b) Cost of Goods Sold, Inventory, cost.

Multiple Choice

1 c	3 b	5 b	7 b
2 b	4 a	6 c	

Solutions to Exercises

1

	Revenues	Costs and/or Expenses	Net Income	Assets	Liabilities	Owners' Equity
a	NE	NE	NE	U	U	NE
b	NE	U	O	O	NE	O
c	NE	O	U	U	NE	U
d	NE	O	U	U	NE	U

2

	Inventory	Cost of Goods Sold
a	$ 6,300	$ 16,600
b	$ 6,250	$ 16,650
c	$ 5,000	$ 17,900
d	$ 5,725	$ 17,175

3

Physical inventory, July 10, 19 _	$30,000
Less: Net purchases for period July 1-July 10 ($17,500 − $550)	16,950
	$13,050
Add: Cost of goods sold for period July 1-July 10: $15,200 − $400 = $14,800 net sales; $14,800 × 77.5% (cost percentage)	11,470
Approximate inventory, June 30, 19 _	$24,520

CHAPTER 10

True or False

1 T	6 T	11 F	16 T	21 F
2 T	7 T	12 F	17 T	22 T
3 F	8 F	13 T	18 T	23 T
4 T	9 F	14 F	19 F	24 F
5 T	10 T	15 T	20 F	25 T

Completion Statements

1(a) Physical deterioration, (b) obsolescence.
2 Capital revenue, understated. 3 $40,000; $35,000; $37,000. 4 1981, income tax, not acceptable. 5 Current value, historical, overstate.
6 Original cost, Accumulated Depreciation.
7 Book value, additional amount. 8 Amortized, straight-line, 40.

Multiple Choice

1 c	3 b	5 d	7 d	9 c
2 a	4 c	6 c	8 c	

Solutions to Exercises

1

		Year 1	Year 2
a	($11,000 − $1,000) × $\frac{1}{4}$ × $\frac{9}{12}$ . .	$1,875	
	$10,000 × $\frac{1}{4}$		$2,500
b	20,000 × 10 cents	$2,000	
	40,000 × 10 cents		$4,000
c	$10,000 × $\frac{4}{10}$ × $\frac{9}{12}$	$3,000	
	$10,000 × $\frac{4}{10}$ × $\frac{3}{12}$ + ($10,000 × $\frac{3}{10}$ × $\frac{9}{12}$)		$3,250
d	$11,000 × 50% × $\frac{9}{12}$	$4,125	
	($11,000 − $4,125) × 50% . . .		$3,437.50

2   **General Journal**

a	Cash	4,000	
	Accumulated Depreciation	1,800	
	Loss on Disposal of Equipment	200	
	Equipment		6,000
b	Cash	3,500	
	Accumulated Depreciation	2,700	
	Gain of Disposal of Equipment		200
	Equipment		6,000
c	Equipment	7,300	
	Accumulated Depreciation	3,600	
	Equipment		6,000
	Cash		4,900

3 Normal earnings ($8,000,000 × .20) $1,600,000
Excess earnings ($2,080,000 − $1,600,000) $ 480,000
Goodwill ($480,000 ÷ .25) $1,920,000
Price offered ($8,000,000 + $1,920,000) . . $9,920,000

CHAPTER 11

True or False

1 T	5 F	9 T	13 F	17 F
2 F	6 F	10 T	14 F	18 F
3 T	7 T	11 T	15 T	19 T
4 F	8 F	12 F	16 T	20 T

Completion Statements

1 Drawing, cost. 2 Corporation, single proprietorship, partnership. 3 $(4,000) loss; $16,000. 4 $29,000. 5(a) Heavy taxation; (b) greater regulation. 6 The amount of their investment. 7 Par value, credited, Common Stock, credited, Paid-in Capital in Excess of Par. 8 Legal capital. 9 Preferred Stock, Common Stock, Paid-in Capital in Excess of Par. 10 $400,000; $80,000; $118,000.

Multiple Choice

1 d	3 c	5 b	7 c	9 a
2 c	4 b	6 b	8 b	10 c

Solutions to Exercises

			A's Share	B's Share
1	First situation:	a	$48,000	$ 72,000
		b	82,200	37,800
		c	65,400	54,600
	Second situation:	a	$ (8,000)	$ (8,000)
		b	2,400	(18,400)

2 a Income Summary 25,000
      K, Capital 15,000
      L, Capital 10,000
K, Capital 11,000
      K, Drawing 11,000
L, Capital 16,000
      L, Capital 16,000

b
K&L
Statement of Partners' Capitals
For Year 1

	K	L	Total
Balance, beginning of year . . .	$18,400	$17,750	$36,150
Add: Net income for year . . .	15,000	10,000	25,000
Subtotal	$33,400	$27,750	$61,150
Less: Withdrawals.	11,000	16,000	27,000
Balance, end of year	$22,400	$11,750	$34,150

3 Net income for Year 2 . . . . $180,000
Less: Deficit at beginning of Year 2 20,000
Retained earning available for dividends $160,000
Less: Dividends on preferred stock for 2 years
(10,000 × $10) 100,000
Available for common stock . . . . $ 60,000
Less: Balance in retained earnings at end of Year
2 25,000
Dividends paid on common stock . . . . $ 35,000
Dividends per share: $35,000 ÷ 10,000 . . . . . . $3.50

4 Stockholders' equity:

$4 preferred stock, $100 par, 1,000 shares issued and outstanding	$100,000
Common stock, no-par value, 50,000 shares issued and outstanding	200,000
Paid-in capital in excess of par: preferred stock	10,000
Total paid-in capital	$310,000
Retained earnings	128,000
Total stockholders' equity	$438,000

CHAPTER 12

True or False

1 F	5 F	9 T	13 T	17 F
2 F	6 F	10 F	14 T	18 T
3 F	7 F	11 T	15 F	19 T
4 T	8 F	12 F	16 T	20 F

Completion Statements

1 Income, extraordinary items. **2** Primary, weighted average, fully diluted. **3** Prior period adjustment, statement of retained earnings, retained earnings, beginning. **4** Footnote. **5(a)** $1,020,000; **(b)** $440,000; **(c)** $740,000. **6(a)** $900,000; **(b)** $0.20; **(c)** before; **(d)** $2,358,800; **(e)** $21 [($103,400 + $94,000) ÷ 9,400 shares].

7

Transaction or Event	Increase	Decrease	No Effect
a Declaration of cash dividend		✓	
b Distribution of a 20% stock dividend		✓	
c A 4 for 1 stock split		✓	
d Net income is reported for latest year	✓		
e Additional stock is sold at $8 per share		✓	
f Treasury stock is acquired at $12 per share		✓	
g Additional stock is sold at $14 per share	✓		

Multiple Choice

1 d	3 b	5 d	7 d	9 c
2 c	4 c	6 a	8 c	10 b

Solutions to Exercises

1

AXEL COMPANY
Income Statement
For the Current Year

Sales	$4,200,000
Cost of goods sold (70%)	2,940,000
Gross profit on sales (30%)	$1,260,000
Operating expenses [$1,260,000 − ($210,000 ÷ .6)]	910,000
Operating income before taxes ($210,000 ÷ .6) . .	$ 350,000
Income taxes ($350,000 × .4)	140,000
Income from continuing operations ($4,200,000 × .05)	$ 210,000
Loss from discontinued operations, net of income tax benefit	(300,000)
Net loss	$ (90,000)
Per share of capital stock:	
Income from continuing operations	$ 2.10
Loss from discontinued operations	(3.00)
Net loss	$ (.90)

2 Earnings from continuing operations:

Primary: ($490,000 − $60,000) ÷ 100,000 shares	$4.30
Fully diluted: $490,000 ÷ 140,000 shares	$3.50

Net earnings:

Primary: ($672,000 − $60,000) ÷ 100,000 shares	$6.12
Fully diluted: $672,000 ÷ 140,000 shares	$4.80

3	General Journal		
Year 1			
Mar. 1	Dividends	200,000	
	Dividends Payable		200,000
	Declared cash dividend of $0.80 per share on 250,000 shares.		
21	Dividends Payable	200,000	
	Cash		200,000
	Paid dividend declared Mar. 1.		
Aug. 10	Retained Earnings	500,000	
	Stock Dividend to Be Distributed		62,500
	Paid-in Capital from Stock Dividends		437,500
	Declared 5% stock dividend on 250,000 shares of $5 par value		
	stock.		
Sept. 2	Stock Dividend to Be Distributed	62,500	
	Common Stock		62,500
	Distributed 12,500 share stock dividend.		
Dec. 21	Retained Earnings	1,312,500	
	Common Stock		1,312,500
	Declared and issued 100% stock dividend on 262,500 shares of		
	$5 par stock.		
30	Treasury Stock	30,000	
	Cash		30,000
	Purchased 1,000 common shares for treasury.		

CHAPTER 13

True or False

1 F	6 F	11 T	16 T	21 F
2 F	7 T	12 F	17 F	22 T
3 T	8 T	13 T	18 T	23 F
4 T	9 F	14 T	19 T	24 F
5 T	10 T	15 T	20 F	

Completion Statements

1 Less, greater. 2 Premium, discount. 3 Present value, less, larger. 4 Multiplying, carrying value, effective interest rate, contractual. 5 Increases, decreases. 6 Decrease, decrease. 7 Rental Expense, off-balance-sheet, liability. 8 Lease Payments Receivable, Sales, present value, interest revenue, Lease Payments Receivable. 9(a) Social security taxes, (b) federal and state income taxes withheld, (c) other deductions such as union dues, insurance premiums, etc. 10(a) Social security taxes, (b) federal unemployment insurance taxes, (c) state unemployment insurance taxes.

Multiple Choice

1 a	3 c	5 d	7 c	9 a
2 a	4 b	6 b	8 d	10 a

Solutions to Exercises

1 a $32,000 ($600,000 $\times$ 16% $\times \frac{4}{12}$)

 b The premium amounted to $5,800 ($637,800 − $600,000 − $32,000)

 c $48,000 ($600,000 $\times$ 16% $\times \frac{6}{12}$)

 d $32,000 ($600,000 $\times$ 16% $\times \frac{4}{12}$)

2   **ROBERT AND BETTY HILL**
         Computation of Taxable Income for 19___

Gross income:

Salaries.	$44,000	
Dividends ($580 — $200)	380	
Interest on savings account	1,320	
Net long-term capital gain		
($8,200 — $4,200)	4,000	$49,700

Deduction to arrive at adjusted gross income:

Long-term capital gain deduction		
(60% of $4,000 reported in gross		
income)	$ 2,400	
Two-earner married couple		
deduction ($22,000 × 10%)	2,200	4,600

Adjusted gross income $45,100

Deduction from adjusted gross income:

Itemized deductions:

Sales taxes	$ 400	
State income taxes		
paid.	2,300	
Contributions	800	
Property taxes on		
residence.	1,650	
Interest on mortgage		
and personal loan	6,520	
Medical expenses,		
$1,800 less $1,353		
(3% of $45,100).	447	
Subscription to invest-		
ment advisory service. . .	200	$12,317

Less: Zero bracket amount	3,400	
Excess itemized deductions	$ 8,917	
Personal exemptions (8 × $1,000) . . .	8,000	16,917

Taxable income $28,183